MY AFRICA

MY AFRICAN STORY

FRANCIS O'HARE

W9-CHB-058

outskirtspress
DENVER, COLORADO

The opinions expressed in this manuscript are solely the opinions of the author and do not represent the opinions or thoughts of the publisher. The author has represented and warranted full ownership and/or legal right to publish all the materials in this book.

My Africa
My African Story
All Rights Reserved.
Copyright © 2015 Francis O'Hare
v2.0

Cover Photo © 2015 thinkstockphotos.com. All rights reserved - used with permission.

This book may not be reproduced, transmitted, or stored in whole or in part by any means, including graphic, electronic, or mechanical without the express written consent of the publisher except in the case of brief quotations embodied in critical articles and reviews.

Outskirts Press, Inc.
http://www.outskirtspress.com

ISBN: 978-1-4787-5872-3

Outskirts Press and the "OP" logo are trademarks belonging to Outskirts Press, Inc.

PRINTED IN THE UNITED STATES OF AMERICA

This true story is dedicated to the delightful memory of Anna Louise Cunningham O'Hare, my wife and my friend. She stood beside me as a staunch ally and wife through all the trials, tribulations and joys of our rugged, many times daunting life, in the most remote parts of Africa. Most of the time our only friends being the wild life, that used to abound in those areas. All the well known wild animals: elephant, lion, rhinos and a huge abundance of deer and antelope known to us by the South African description of buck. We pitched our tents and established a big camp central to the area in which we were operating. Louise was a born American and did not come from this background or environment yet she made it her life.

The more detailed description of this life comes to the fore in the various chapters within the book but Louis's magnificent part in it is worth a mention here in this dedication to her work there and in my memory of our 49 years marriage.

Another mention I want to make is to Pamela Millicent Rowe, The Assistant Librarian at Harvard University. We corresponded and she was impressed by some of my experiences to the extent she said, you must write a book. I had no idea I was to be a writer but Pam just didn't give up. She was closely involved looking at my work and gave me all the generous benefit of her experience and knowledge in this area of work.

Finally, I want to thank Aida Rosa Dorante, my dear friend in Venezuela for encouraging me to keep going when I sometimes just wanted to forget about my writing a book. I will always remember she said, You are better than this Frank, you know how to write a story I have read some of it, now just finish it, and I did. Thank you Aida!

Table of Contents

1
My Story

The Years 1935 - 1940

I could go back into some of my past writing work of the time which covered this period, however, that work is still fresh in my mind and I want a second run at it. My tendency, in writing is to be very concise and to the point and yet descriptive. This is due to my years of technical and progress report writing that are striven in this direction but this is a book, the reader has to be entertained as well as informed and must therefore experience it in a different sense. This period, this first paragraph is to give the reader some information on the writer: where I come from, who I am and what formed me and how I became what I am by the time you finish the story

Before embarking on this written account of my life experiences, I consulted some of my written journals of the time, and found that the most significant experiences and events still remain fresh in my mind. In recording these reminiscences, I have endeavored to reflect anew on my experiences and to bring fresh insights and unique perspectives to the events that shaped my life.

We, the O'Hare's, come from the Irish families who moved across from Ireland at the turn of the 19th Century seeking work. I have not researched it but the potato famine and shortage of work drove many families out of Ireland to come to England as the industrial revolution was in its infancy and work was becoming available in areas such as Cumberland (Cumbria) immediately straight across the Irish Sea.

I have been reluctant to get this story told because in many ways I am embarrassed by it. Most of my life I have hidden it and pretended I came from something different, better, it was like a stigma for me and I was afraid someone would uncover the truth and dislike me more than I thought they did already. I just did not fit into society in all of my life and don't even to this time. I have analyzed this to the best of my psychiatric ability but can only come up with this, I must have thought I was better than what I was and as soon as I got away from home I wanted to be someone else and from some place different to what I considered my miserable poor start in life so, I adopted the people of a small farm I worked for up in the Lake District area as my own, they had already adopted me.

Francis O'Hare

(Early School Years 1935 - 1940)

I came in to this life, into existence, as a sick, weak and undernourished child and the consequences of that deficient beginning in life dogged me all through my lifetime until now. I have always had to fight against a lack of sound health and strength so I developed grit and staying power in a sense to overcome these, my deficiencies. But, robust health and strength was never mine as a right to life like it is with most children in America and England today. Those who are born today in this age of nourished, fine toned moms who are fed on a balanced diet through their infant growth years, and have a completely different start in life. For many, there are follow-up supplemental school-feeding programs, giving them that healthy ongoing essential feeding in the formative years of their lives. In the past we prepared balanced feeding and vitamins for sheep and cattle but completely ignored the working class, the underprivileged whose families barely survived those early days. Of course, there were no fast-food restaurants and mothers had to prepare meals from the cheapest source, vegetables being grown locally and a natural source of vitamins, calcium and other desirable minerals and although she fed us well with fresh garden vegetables mine evidently were not assimilated properly. Meat was also comparatively cheap as there were many small local slaughter houses requiring little or no control to process their animals and sell them wholesale to the again, small local butchers shops. Our town then, had maybe three automobiles, but deliveries were being done by horse and cart until after WWII.

I was born in the north-west of England of Irish origin, families who came across the Irish Sea in the mid nineteenth century looking for work in the widening industrial phenomenon of that period as it opened in many areas in England. This particular beautiful English Western Lakes area had a new pig-iron blast furnace (pig-iron is an essential ingredient of steel making) located next to the iron ore mines there on the

Cumberland Coast, also an integral part of iron and steel manufacturing. Cheap labor was moving in from Ireland, the wages were below family life sustenance levels and the work was incredibly hard which only the strongest were capable of surviving. Many of these hard working laborers frequented the drinking taverns, public houses known as pubs and money, which was desperately needed for their families, went over the swilling counter-tops to benefit the tavern owners and breweries. In retrospect it was a terrible existence which we can hardly comprehend today with all of our rights and amenities but those tough men worked 10 and 12 hour days, all kinds of shifts and 6 and 7 days a week loading small ships that came into the estuary and tied up against a pier. Also, the women, who had nothing to alleviate their poorest of existence other than large families and babies born at home, often under hygienically poor conditions resulting in several fatalities, many of them had alcoholic drunken husbands to contend with from which they had to try and get a couple of shillings to buy food to put on the table for their starving children. (Kids running raggedly naked and half wild in the streets) I think back now with a better understanding of how it must have been and I shiver with fear to believe what it must have been like for them all, me included. I was often sick and suffering from rotten teeth and diarrhea as well as being born with a herniated abdomen in the groin area which was never corrected until I was 10 years of age — life was nothing like what we know and consider as a right like it is nowadays. I do not wish to belabor the hard life of that period but for my story it is necessary that I give a limited account of my earlier years that had an effect on me in later life

Shortly after the operation on the hernia I developed a huge lump in my neck gland, which was eventually diagnosed as tuberculosis, following years of emulsion, cod liver oil and ultra violet ray treatments. My poor mom took me for these treatments to the neighboring town of Whitehaven by train to receive the ultra violet ray sessions from a huge hanging bucket-like container which sputtered and spluttered as we miserable thin kids stood worshiping it in a circle. The train fare was 3 shillings and 4 pence for the two of us which was always a struggle to come up with. I doubt the ultra violet treatment had any value because we got more sun in season than kids are allowed to have in a lifetime today. The thing that hurt me the most was the rejection of my presence in school by my peers and eventually their moms. When it was decided I had to go into a sanitarium for the stricken and afflicted it was a big relief for me finally after getting settled in there. Consumption as it was then known, because it usually consumed the individual, was feared in a way like Aids was when it first emerged today. In fact, Aids patients are protected and treated with all rights in school and the work place. Aids sufferers have more rights than any normal individual not so for those with TB at that time, we were pariahs in society. I simply write about it now because it is a fact worthy of note. Here again is yet one more item in my list of rejections which was also the cause of much loss of schooling and, it was only when I started to write about my life that I discovered that painful period. However, it was the beginning of a life I found suitable for me living on the fringe of society so to speak because I had very low esteem as a result of being rejected during my school years and again afterwards once it was discovered I was a TB sufferer I liked the aloneness of working on a small farm and later in life Africa became my home where I was a surveyor in the remote areas and that was how I liked it.

These times, the 1930's were very bad for all and a young newly wedded couple soon after marriage very quickly went down into the depths of despair and common hatred for one another simply because life was so awful. Women wished that they had never married such a drunken slob and men wanted more than a hovel and ugly women. These are terrible descriptions and awful words but they ring true for many of the children who are still left from that bygone era. There was one or two only who accepted their circumstances, did their best to rear the children and hope for them a better future than was available to their own generation. There was no way out and those that accepted it, the men working and providing and the women keeping a clean home, children with a full tummy and a clean house had a better life than the disappointed and dissenters.

Education was minimal, we were taught barely the basics of Mathematics, English and a lot of poetry and religion. Discipline was the strictest and being whacked and knuckled was daily fare. In fact, those who were not punished were considered sissies and wimps. Being Irish we were also Catholic and for the many that came over from Ireland there was a Catholic School and a Catholic Church to ensure we did not take up the English Protestant ways and end up in hell. Our teachers were women who had been turned out by the Nuns and the Parish Priest, who was an all powerful dominant tyrant. I was an Altar Boy and lived in fear of not knowing the Church Latin or even how to pronounce it correctly. However, I remained as a Catholic through life until we came to America to work and I discovered the biblical truth direct – another story maybe.

So much has been written about those poverty stricken days prior to WWII which had not come about by any political extreme, it was simply the way it was back then, wealth was only available to the privileged few because the origin of wealth was not fully understood. There are convicted socialists who claim that it was unnecessary suffering and as a direct result of the nobility and capitalism (what about Russia this last century) some of those beliefs may have merit but not all that much. Life was evolving, as it always is, and will do until Christ returns to this earth to once again show us how to live but this time in His own powerful authority. I tend towards capitalism surprisingly having gone through so much early life poverty and hard labor. I do not like the way socialism holds back the best brains so as to make us all equal in reward and I do not hold with powerful unions who stunt individualism. Yes, we are all born equal, maybe but, it is only an equal right to go forth and make your own way in life – (life liberty and the pursuit of happiness). Some work hard and others don't care to work much at all and still others just don't work they prefer to live off the state, indulge in laziness, alcohol and drugs, the tax payer should not have to encourage or support these people. The western world began to evolve and the individual to obtain a certain wealthy status following WWII which had no bearing on the coming about of raising the standards for all in fact, it may have held it back. It was in the 60's things started to change in a big way, one half of the youth society gave in to immorality and drugs the other half saw opportunities which had never before presented itself. A college education was made available to everyone who qualified and those that partook of it moved on in life to a better standard of living. There is much more could be written here about what all came about in this period but this is not my story. Plastics were starting-up, early computers were about to become part of life and many more things of this nature requiring an educated work force.

My education was sadly lacking directly related to my illnesses and the inadequacy of the educational system. I went into the tuberculosis sanitarium about the time I would have been going into secondary school, had I qualified, which I didn't due my bad school attending record as a result of sickness. The sanitarium had no teaching affiliation nor was it set up to teach and one of the nurses simply did the best she knew how to in a room set aside for those who were able to go there. She had an affiliation to a religious school and that was what most of our education was grounded in. I had no complaints then and in retrospect very little now in regard to how it all unfolded and turned out. Today, it would not be permissible to put away children for a year or more and not educate them. Laws like that were not in effect then, especially for kids who were pretty much considered terminal. Most of us survived, only the ones who had bad lung infections didn't make it. There was no treatment other than to be removed from society and be exposed to the open air of the cold north east climate as much as possible. It was believed by some doctors that the cold would control the disease if not cure it, amazing! And, we almost froze to death as well as suffering from the TB

We were dying from exposure to the weather more than from the disease. It was believed that the fresh air would kill off the bacterial infection that is if the British medical authorities ever knew in those days that it was a bacterial infection, I have to assume they did but there wasn't anything available yet to fight diseases like this. I met my very first girl here in the sanitarium and fell deeply in love, as only teenage boys can with first loves. I don't believe girls experience young love in the same mad way that boys do but I loved her and she sent me little notes with the help of one of the nurses. She had TB of the spine and spent two years in a half cast lying mostly on her stomach – it just didn't make a lot of sense, she survived regardless of he cruel and unusual treatment. When I left there she was still a patient but not long afterwards her mother took her home in defiance of the medical advice, to Newcastle, an over populated area in the north east on the River Tyne. Doris survived and was soon free of TB How? Why? No one knows, we never married, she found a professional soccer player and lived happily ever after, I am so glad.

Following my discharge which was in disgrace because, I ran away with another patient from Newcastle. Neither of us was allowed to return as we were considered a bad example to the other poor in-terns. I was not even upset or home sick, I was reasonably content and knew I would be out within six months but allowed myself to be influenced by a bad boy. We were only gone a weekend before they got us but it was Good-bye sanitarium. I was popular with the young nurses because I was a good help to them working almost as hard as they did. Making beds began early in the morning and a host of other duties throughout the daytime. I learned a lot from the nurse who took school, mostly biblical scripture which I knew so little about being a Catholic. She was just a wonderful person and I admired her and loved her and we sang and studied the bible. There were other more worldly type young nurses there too and they were quite happy to flirt with us budding young men. However, I believe they were angels in disguise, only in their teens and early twenties themselves and working tirelessly and devotedly amongst a section of society that was supposedly not fit to be out there in it. The rejection of ones peers was the hardest thing to take. The fear of TB was great, many died from it among the undernourished and poor families causing mother's to tell their young not to get anywhere near the afflicted. Regardless of why it was done it was very hard to suffer for a youngster and I was relieved finally to go into the institute where we were all alike and the nurses showed love and caring without cringing away from us. A few of them did contract the disease and had to go into an adult place themselves for a period of treatment but mostly they were healthy young beautiful girls who cared for us suffering types. I didn't have much physical pain other than the pain of self-consciousness hurting from the ugly big lump in my neck. It was finally removed by aspirating the abscess on the gland something that should have been done at the very beginning of its emergence. As for my education and my schooling it was over as I was still not acceptable in class, it was too late the damage had been done.

(Later School Years 1940 1944)

My mother wanted me to continue my schooling but I would have had to go down at least two classes and I doubt it was permissible to do so. My schooling was sadly lacking I had a natural talent for mathematics and had been reading avidly from about the age of four years so I had the basics but no continuing education when it was so urgently needed. Unfortunately, however, it had to be shelved and I went out into the world with only the basic knowledge to survive and much yet to learn. Again, my mom wanted to protect me from life and got me a job through a contact as a learner in the laboratory in a tannery (curing animal skins). I hated it and felt like I was imprisoned. I went to work daily on my bicycle as the plant was about three miles from my home, the jobs I was given by *the girls* – the lab was managed and run mostly by rugged tough women – were menial, very crude and I had really nothing to do with lab type work, They knew I was in there by favoritism and did not approve or like it. They enjoyed humiliating me and laughed at my plight. In later years, as I matured and understood how life works, I realized they wanted to get rid of me and they succeeded. One Friday after I received my few shillings pay I told the one in charge I was given them my weeks notice to quit, she replied, there is no notice here you are finished and that was it. I cycled home knowing there would be a scene with my mom and, of course she made a huge one. Told me how she had suffered and struggled, had to save pennies to take me around for doctor appointments and treatments and this is how I repaid it after she used her influence to procure this desired lab position where I could have been *something*. Well, that's debatable but that something was not for me, I had to move in another direction and this period at home was unsettling and painful for me and for my mother who certainly did have her trials and tribulations. Quarrels broke out constantly and she kept repeating, nobody will give you a job now, look what you have done, and now what are you going to do. You won't go back to school and you are too sick to do laboring work in the local iron-ore mines, where local school level boys found work, or the housing contractor's who were starting up in the burgeoning post World War II housing estate boom. It wasn't that I couldn't go along and maybe get a start in one of these industries, I just didn't want it and this indecisiveness of mine and my mom's fear I would not get a suitable clerical type job because of my poor health caused tension in the home for them too. All this indecision caused unrest and quarrels in the home. My mom never let up with her lamenting and finally my dad, who had kept out of it until now said, we can't afford to feed and clothe you so find yourself a job, and that did it for me. I had always been interested in farming and we lived in a farming community area so I thought about starting that for a living and. It only was a living kind of like an indentured servant, food and basic lodging for twelve hours a day hard work.

I dedicated myself to this life up in the foothills of The English Lake District for four years and what a blessing it all turned out to be. I found a new family and that took away the stress of life in my own family. I was wanted in the business and quickly started to value myself as a useful member. We worked twelve-hour days and six and one half day s a week but I enjoyed it. I filled out and grew to look like a man and became strong and healthy.

I was now healthy and had forgotten all about Tuberculosis and I was strong and beginning to think about a different way of life. My education was lacking so I decided to volunteer for the army. My interests were mechanical other than animal and crop husbandry so I was going into an army transportation company. After I left home and went into farming my brother and I drifted apart but we kept in touch. I was home one weekend and he was finishing college. All the animosity was now gone, and he said, why don't you go to army school of engineering and be an engineering surveyor? I said, I will never qualify but, he responded you will never know if you don't try. To qualify to be a "Royal" Engineer means having the minimum education to enroll. I was not confidant I could make it with my poor educational record nevertheless I applied and went for the initial medical and education interview and lo and behold a couple of weeks later I received a large manila envelope accepting me into the regiment and to report at Engineering Park Camp in Warminster

..And Now a Royal Engineer 1948

After we had finished our basic training we were sent to what was called a distribution camp. Guys had decided what units they wanted to get into and we were just hanging out waiting to be moved to our new postings. My army four friends were all well schooled and well educated, two of the Scotsmen where the educational system was superior to what it was in England. We were all going to try for the engineering school and see what was available afterwards. I reminded them that I was a way behind in math's and most subjects because of childhood sickness. They had a hard time believing me on the sickness because I was so strong and muscular due to farm work. However, they said, Frank you are intelligent and we are going to get you through and our evening classes began, night after night until I wanted to quit but they would not let me out of it. For some reason I was able to absorb and learn like I had not been able to do in school, the atmosphere was totally different. We needed geometry, trigonometry and other math's so, for me it was an awful lot to take in at once. All the other guys were out on farewell parties and there were many as different twos and threes moved out to their new companies. All within the Royal Engineers but it had a very wide scope of jobs. I apologized for being such a drag and wet blanket but they said, we got lots of time, we're here for five years so don't sweat it Frank you have to get through and stay with us. I never forgot their generosity, we were kids 18 years of age and they had this great attitude and all from a poor working class background like me.

We were the last to move out because the positions we had applied for were not the usual run of the mill and to spend a long period in an international engineering school a lot of pre qualification was needed and our applications were being scrutinized carefully. I was very apprehensive and not confident of getting into the school at all with what I had, nothing! Finally, we had to report to a place called, Longleat Park Camp, the army had taken it over for special commando training during the war and it was still used for special training purposes. It had been a private home of one of the aristocracy, a Lord in the upper house. He had dedicated it to the army when the war started and that was his way of saving England. We had to do a two week aptitude course to see how we stacked up for our engineering and land surveying, they were not going to allow anyone to do this schooling if they didn't have a bent towards it. I was genuinely astonished when I, along with the other three who were sure things passed the aptitude test. It was not just a routine thing like so many army courses are, we had to have the aptitude and attitude to qualify for the time and money that the British Army was now going to spend on the likes of us. Longleat Park was in the county of Warminster a very pleasant place in the south of England west of London. We were given a 72 hour pass and I had relations in Kent, my Grandmother's sister so I hopped a train and went over there to stay for two nights, I was treated like a prince. Aunty Ethel and her daughter Alice, Aunt Alice, who was an aide to a Kings Solicitor lived in a nice home in a house built after the war and it was all very grand for me who had only lived in old houses more than one hundred years of age. The time passed royally and pleasantly then it was time to return to Longleat. Alice took me to the railway station making sure I had the right train and Aunty Ethel gave me the names, addresses and phone numbers of other relations around where I was stationed and told me to get in touch with them, they will welcome you and do what they can to make your time there pleasant.

The following week we reported to the school also in the park (beautiful rolling grass park lands). We noted that the intake had a number of foreigners, some Indians and similar from countries in the Far East and also, a few black men obviously from Africa. We were maybe a bit puzzled by this but it added. We discovered as the weeks rolled past that most of these "foreigners" as we became acquainted were officers in their regiments bur were not permitted to display any rank badge during schooling, there was to be no authority other than the instructors and lecturers. I have gone in to this army education of mine because it is where I passed from being a nonentity, so to speak, and became someone I might have been had I not been ill. It was helping me to move away from my lower self, my unworthiness. I did not in any way despise my previous life and I was a farmer at heart but I need a bit of elevation and I was starting to get it and also getting respect for myself and achievement which maybe should have been directed to my Buddies, they did it for me. The courses, classes and schooling were demanding and needed all of our attention and application we certainly could not waste time partying because we had homework. It was not delegated as such but without reviewing and studying our notes and paperwork we might as well have gone back to my first choice of transportation but even those guys had schooling to do.

The main thing for me is I developed some respect for myself and was able to hold up my head around others which I mentally had not done before. The engineering other than surveying was not too stressful for me as it was designed more on the fieldwork side even though we were in class but I had no difficulty with the calculation related to our learning in that field but, surveying, especially astronomy was a challenge initially, a long initial period, it was hard to grasp and I learned that this is where the army intended to deploy us. Once again I needed the help of my friends who grasped it quicker than I did but they were happy to help because teaching me helped them. We had one or two little parties by now but we realized this was something we needed to put on the back burner until we had our certificates of success. We met up with many of our Empire compatriots and it was most interesting for us and them. They were mostly from wealthy families and were insistent that we were welcome to come to their country and home for a visit after we all qualified. I said, you may be sorry you made this invitation when we all sew on our rank badges again but they said, no. It was a wonderful year for me and I really blossomed mentally in more ways than one, I was very fortunate indeed.

The time came and results were posted up on the bulletin boards and you can believe this or not, the top guys were our little group of four lowly engineers. We had worked so hard putting all we had into it and I learned that hard work pays off. There was a big party that night, everyone was permitted to wear their rank as tomorrow we would all break up and go our ways and many of these officers of the Empire were very high ranking, but this engineering school was most desirable, and any officer who could show he had graduated from the school of survey was a man to count on. For once I drank like a gentlemen and it was a wonderful evening one I will cherish to the end of my life, my graduating *and making it*. My army book was stamped as engineer 3rd class and surveyor II Once again we were on stand by for a posting to our final unit and destination, within a couple of days I was sent to a stand-by camp in Winchester further south and separated from my friends who had made this opportunity for me but that is army life. I went to see the school command and asked why I couldn't stay with my buddies but was told it had nothing to do with them the appointments were made by a group of officers that no one really knew. So, we had our farewell party and I could barely keep back the tears especially as they were all going to be together at another camp where they might be doing more class work and I was beginning to like that as well. I knew I was going overseas simply from where I was reporting to, it was an overseas dispatch place. What I learned there was not much more but I was honored to some extent in that the army had assembled a new aerial survey unit to operate in Africa attached to the RAF and I deduced that this would be a good posting away from the stamping and marching of typical big army regimental type camps. I was kitted out for Africa and told that I would be sailing out of Southampton and would get my shipping orders when I returned meanwhile I had seven days leave and a ticket up to Cumberland.

2

A Young Soldier Departs England En Route Mombassa, Kenya – April 1950

I spent my seven day leave time at home in Cumberland and also visited my old adopted farming family in Kendal, Westmorland. The Hayton's, old Arthur didn't think much about going off to Africa, he snorted about it and said it would be better had I stayed with them and maybe married Doris, the eldest daughter, and could have been running the farm now, she didn't know which way to look for relief. He had let off (leased) most of the land just keeping the orchard and the home field with the house on it; he was now a very old man now. Next, I visited with another farming family I had lived with and become very friendly, the Lawrence's in Grange over Sands, on the coast and they were my age and I had lots of good memories of my time there with them. I came back to them following my army years in Africa in1954 and following agricultural college at Newton Rigg where I got my certificate. I enjoyed working with them again, however, Rita Lawrence said, Frank you have studied hard and successfully and I know you like

this life now when you are young but you must do something different now even if you go back to Africa as a civilian and practice you're
surveying career. A good friend, and a smart girl, we were passively
more than, just friends

Soon time was up for my leave period and I had kept close to my
mom other than the two brief visits with old friends. We didn't have
a car and even had I rented one we didn't have any place to go especially, so we stayed home and she cooked and baked until I thought I
was going to blow up. I think my brother was still away in college in
Manchester studying to be an architect and was only able to be there
for a brief visit. I thanked him for encouraging me to persevere with
my education with the military and it had all turned out better than
I could have expected because I was so deficient in formal education. Nevertheless, my time ran out and I had to report once again to
another mustering camp at Winchester to be ready to board the ship
when it sailed in a few days time out of Southampton. We boarded
the ship the night before it sailed and although we were stacked and
packed in an area that had once been a sort of hold so far it did not
seem too awful as troop ships are known to be. This Empire Medway
had once been a ship that sailed back and forth to India in the glory
days bringing British Raj (Colonialists) people home for their vacations.
We headed out into the English Channel then south by the coast of
France and past Portugal and Spain into the Straits of Gibraltar to sail
into the Mediterranean Sea. The trip, so far was exciting and uneventful, especially for a young soldier going foreign for the first time in life.
We stopped again off Tunis and then Tripoli to unload small units to
leave off at military camps we acquired during the war time period
here in North Africa and had not yet handed them back over to their
governments. We tied up for two days in Port Said at the huge Nile
delta in Egypt. It was amazing to me how these ships found their way
through this delta it is so massive and spread out. We were able to go

ashore and see those local sights of Egypt. I was totally unimpressed, it was crowded and we were unable to move very far because of being accosted by people begging for Pounds Sterling and children simply begging. Unfortunately this was mostly organized and managed and I really saw nothing of any consequence and was pleased to get back on board ship. Meanwhile bum boats had pulled alongside, some vendors were allowed to come on board and set up their stalls while others operated from their boats. Comparing this activity to the shore visit it was preferable and more fun to watch here onboard ship. We were going out so why would we be interested in buying anything but it was kind of fun for a day. After leaving Port Said in Egypt we entered the Suez Canal and the heat began to be unbearable at nights down in those inadequately ventilated holds because they had never been planned as such dense living quarters, it was terrible and the stench of too many bodies in a poorly ventilated area was not good, putting it mildly. Some of us began not going down to our bunks at night at all but then the military red caps cleared the decks and chased us down below but, we came back up and if we were not too many and kept out of the way under the boat slips they ignored us knowing what we were enduring.

By now we were having boat drills every morning and some of us with rank had to bring our sections to order when the officer came around to check the turn-out which was virtually impossible. We were supposed to be responsible for hold # so and so and bunks #'s such and such but it didn't work out that well. We were not concerned and realized it was better left more casual than having it all in an uproar and we told the sergeant who had elected himself to command our section, all present! I had linked up with some Engineers I knew from base camp who were going out but not to the same rendezvous, I met three who were headed to my same unit and had known them briefly before I went to the military school of engineering. They had been surveyors for a couple of years already and had originally been what was known as boy soldiers. They were allowed to join up (enlist) at 16 years of age and became regular soldiers at 171/2 years old. Mostly, their dads were army officers and they had enlisted them in Boy's Military Academy. They were hard and real tough guys but good to have around. The self appointed Sgt in command of our quarter became somewhat unbearable yelling, threatening, and barking orders. We were a technical unit and believe it or not known as gentlemen. Finally, "Squeers" (as he was known) Barker, one of the ex Boys School said to me, I've had enough of this idiot I'm going to toss him overboard, no one will ever know where he went, they may not miss him or even be glad he hasn't showed up again. I said you are being the idiot; we just need to let him rant until we get to Mombassa but Squeers wasn't having any of it or him. Next day when he started his yelling again, Squeers and one other guy got him and had him half over the side before I got there and stopped it. Squeers said damn you, you have now put us in jeopardy I said, I don't think so, that man is very afraid and I don't even think that he is a sergeant, he didn't show up next morning and we never saw him again. I went down as a chicken in Barker's book. As far as life drills and muster stations all was good for the remainder of our voyage and I was pleased over that.

On down through the Red Sea and the days were more bearable due to the breezes on deck caused by the increase in knots of the moving ship. The canteens opened about 10 a.m. after boat stations with very tepid canned beer, we had never drunk American beer and we considered it to be swill. We stopped again in the Port of Aden but there was not much to see, just busy port activity and we put ashore another small unit replacement troops for a camp somewhere in there – very hot! Putting out to sea again early morning and out into the Indian Ocean and with steam up we got a cooling breeze again but for some of us we never slept below for the remainder of the voyage. After getting around

The Horn of Africa (Somalia) and heading into the Indian Ocean we only had about one week before sailing into Mombassa and what a pretty picture it was after being at sea. In reality there is not a lot to say about Mombassa but as we crept in to port the palm tree lined coast looked good and mysterious to our young inexperienced eyes. By the time we disembarked we had changed our minds as we rattled along the dirt roads through the outskirts of the town which we never did see. We got down at an old camp about 12 miles west of Mombassa and hung around trying to keep cool and hoping that a canteen would open soon. It was devastatingly hot, no breeze just hot and dusty with that terrible sun blazing down I thought, what in god's name have I done now. Later some very brown well turned out army lads came and led us to a sleeping place on cots made of bamboo and skins. They told us to find the canteen which was about to open and there was a mess where we would get a meal later, I was not happy. Reveille blew before dawn and we were up getting ready to depart by train within a couple of hours for Nairobi as we thought.

By Rail Up to Nairobi with a Strange Delay

Every inch of a soldier's life is orchestrated, like lining up beside the rail road tracks, there was no platform, and boarding the train was by the numbers. It finally chugged in from somewhere near as it barely had enough steam to limp into the "station" I did not sign up for this, I wanted to use my mind and brains like I had been doing in my farming life and at the school of engineering but, we were in the army now. Finally, we were told to board filling the cars from the back forward taking whatever position fell to you. After boarding we sat for another hour in the morning sun inside those ovens waiting for enough steam to roll out of the camp. So far, after 3 hours of steaming along with enough black smoke to change the face of Kenya we were only do-ing little better than had we gone up cavalry fashion. The heat had now become unbearable in these closed in carriages, down in this low veldt country assigned mostly to the wild game. We pushed down what windows we could and allowed in the hot air with all the soot and smoke to choke along with and after about 10 hours hopefully, we were half way. We had entered Tsavo, one of the famous wild game reserves, but no game was visible in this devastating heat and the visibility was limited because of it. (There is a book called "The Man Eaters of Tsavo" my wife bought it for me before we were married in 1957. It tells the story of two lions that went psycho and constantly raided the railroad trains carrying off humans out of the windows as they slept in a siding). Supposedly, we were here in Africa for 3 years and if it was going to be anything like this I had made a huge mistake. We chug-chugged into another camp in this god forsaken place and discovered we had another night on the road to endure. I think we were somewhere close to Kilimanjaro and hoped to get a glimpse of it tomorrow when we headed out for the high veldt land of Nairobi. From what I had read up on about Nairobi it is a gentle climate and a big city at an elevation of 5,000 AMSL, roll on Nairobi.

Once again we got off by the numbers, lined up and marched into the camp proper. It was very neat with all the tents militarily laid out in lines with the flaps folded and tied back. We were taken to an old temporary area and allocated to our tents. A sergeant of that hell regiment told (yelled) us in army fashion how we were to arise, clean up our tent and area and have it open for inspection before going on a run prior to breakfast – a run in this heat, why would anyone volunteer for this. We found the mess that evening and managed to get what they called food, I had an idea we were sucking the hind tit and no one really wanted us, suited me right down to the ground but, a major disaster was looming ahead.

The next day when we thought we would be headed out for Nairobi there was no such action on the part of the military authority to have us be ready to move on. Later, following breakfast we were lined up, just we few surveyors, and greeted by the camp commandant Colonel James. He said he had the authority to detain us for important military activities; we were mystified not to mention being terrified thinking we were going to be surveying out in this territory. He warned us not to be rebellious or the consequences would be detention and he was not going to explain himself or tell us how long we would be there, just do our job as directed he said, you are soldiers not a survey company. I detected some irony and envy in his remarks, he had become very sarcastic. He said one of his lieutenants would meet with us later and explain what he wanted to be done in his camp — In his camp? We were mystified and could only await some explanation. We were not infantry not foot sloggers; we were engineers, surveyors. Later that morning the 2nd Lieutenant showed up with a roll of blank paper in his possession and began to ramble on in a mystifying way about some mapping of this ridiculous camp. We tried to explain to him the bare necessities we required if it was a camp plan they wanted. We needed a couple of plane table boards, a level and a theodolite (transit) and steel tapes, a compass and pencils etc. Now he looked mystified and returned to his boss with this information and then back he came saying this was preposterous. We asked him, with all due respect, not to be a mouthpiece for the Colonel over something they knew little about. And we begged his indulgence while we first reiterated what it was we believed they wanted and how these things are carried out with the barest of equipment, in this case no equipment. Then, what do you want us to do? Off he went again and this time came back with the disgruntled colonel who began again telling us what could happen to us, we were spoiled, not really soldiers in fact and by god he was going to change that. We said nothing simply stood there until he said, NOW DO IT! Permission to speak sir! Do it with what? (This time he had the Lieutenant take us to an old ragged dusty tent where we rooted around in and came up with two staves, half a dozen range poles, an old broken transit and what might be made into a plane table. Here we were, costly and highly trained and educated engineers stuck in this hell-hole playing games because the camp commander was envious of us our abilities and going on up to Nairobi, he had neither. We discovered this as we got to know our Lieutenant who was a conscript doing his two years which meant he only did about 12 months here in this camp and he couldn't wait to get out of it. Meanwhile we were not going to lie down and take this although we knew our boss, Major Hellings would be doing something about it but we wanted that something as quickly as possible.

However, to stay out of detention we fixed up the rubbish so called equipment as best we could and made it appear we were doing something around the sandy, dusty camp grounds. There was no vehicle allocated to us and it was a very long way around the perimeter. We decided not to go far out of the main area hoping and praying Hellings would come through. This young Lieutenant, when he discovered he could trust us and that we were a different kind of soldier told us that the Col. Had made many attempts to get a transfer up to the regiment in Nairobi but they didn't want him and he just couldn't live with that and was using us as a tool and punishing us because of where we were going. One of our guys, Barker again, wrote a letter to our destination address and sneaked off one evening and managed to give it to someone going through on the train, the letter did get to its destination but it was unnecessary as by this time Maj. Hellings had sent someone down on the train to rescue us, a Sergeant Loak with a formal and official letter for our release and immediate dispatch. The Col would never have told us until the very last minute but our now friend, the Lieutenant, told us we were out of here tomorrow. He said give me your work this evening and I will put it all away, the whole thing was meaningless.

We pulled out in the afternoon of the next day with Sgt. Loak who became our friend. Army life for us was a lot different to what the usual British army is like, more akin to the American army but in this instance we were attached to the RAF, Royal Air Force because of the predominant aerial survey aspect of the task. We were singing and happy most of the remainder of the way up to the railroad station in Nairobi when we pulled in early the following morning. One may wonder here why Hellings simply didn't phone through to the camp. Well, in those days in Africa the telephone system was extremely unreliable and he had not been able to get through and one wonders about that Col whether he had his line connected. I can't say enough here about the huge relief this was to escape that camp and the Commander; it was a hell-hole of his making and disappointments. Our destination was not with the East Africa Command Regiments in Nairobi, we were on the outskirts in what was known as Nairobi West. Nairobi West which was the airport prior to the "new" airport which was built sometime after WWII, however, International traffic was using Nairobi West when we were stationed there doing our work. Some of these airlines were barely up and running following the war and were using old used wartime aircraft. Air France had acquired British Wellington Bombers which they had converted into passenger planes, how or why I don't know because the fuselage was extremely limiting and they only seated about 25 passengers but everyone was excited and full of the future of flying and wanted to claim their part and route in it. These Wellingtons were bad even in their good days and were designed to fly across the English Channel with a load of heavy bombs. They had one very bad defect which dogged them forever; they blew tires virtually every time they landed. The French air hostesses were brave and beautiful and we got to know many of them and of course, entertained them in our club which we set up in a very short time to capture these beauties. Air France brought out a big supply of tires for this ugly machine and boy did they need them. The air line that got out of the blocks the quickest and some how had some American passenger planes was the Dutch Airlines, all the other European airlines at that time following the war had to use converted bomber aircraft until new passenger planes were available. It was an exciting and crazy time for us, this new job which was just getting under way and our now friendship with the new airlines Pilots and hostesses. They much preferred our club at the airstrip on a routine basis to going on into downtown Nairobi. It was a great club and became very popular in a short period of time, so much so we had to stop managing it ourselves and got an East Indian group in to do it for us. They were mostly gentlemen crooks but not much seemed to bother us in those times.

3

My Military Years WA

On the Other Coast (West Africa)
Same Period 1950 – 1953

Africa also has seasons, and the rain (in the non desert arid climates) comes in deluges and can last up to four months and then requires time to dry up the trails for jeep travel, river and temporary lake crossings and, in our case, for aerial photography the clouds to disperse again. This can mean five months out of field action and can be a financial loss even to a government if one had to sit and wait. However, the west side of the continent is the adverse of the east side and we had territories over there in dire need of maps so off we would go west young man. In the first wet East African the 1951 Season we opened up in Kano, Nigeria and Takoradi, Gold Coast as it was known then (now Ghana).

The old Lancaster Bombers would load up with all of their requirements and their crews and go direct to the area with their long range capability. If we pongo's, the RAF jargon for army guys, were lucky we might just get a ride straight across, if they liked you. The rest of the motley crew got to fly in the British army's old Viking Valetta's (much like a Dakota 3) only not as reliable and compared to present times were only very short ranged without refueling. The British Southern Army Command sent out 8 of these unreliable planes from out of moth-balls where they should have remained, only seven made it to Nairobi and it took 3 days to get there. We had the RAF boys check them out but typically they never sent any spares. Three were stranded on the trip over through the Sudan in El Genina and El Fasha. The RAF guys revitalized one and somehow flew it to Kano in Nigeria, the army fliers had already given up on them, they just couldn't trust flying in them, and can you blame them. Army regulations forbade cannibalizing parts from one aircraft to another but the RAF Mechanics worked around this and fixed up the remainder so as to do another run then Major Hellings sent them back to Blighty. The pilots and crew wanted to remain with us on the Gold Coast but their planes had to go back into mothballs, the only place for them.

We got set up in an abandoned American Air Base in Takoradi which had been used for ferrying planes over into England. I am not sure why they had this base here but there it was a huge area of concrete and massive hangers. I found an old Dodge big pick up, got our RAF Mechs to get it in running order for me and I was like the proverbial pig in clover. We did it up (down) to appear non military as best we could so as to use it for all purposes. Americans always did things on a grand scale and it was no less that scale here. Down near the beach I found some excellent bungalows boarded up, we opened them up replaced the damaged fly screening and got a local plumber in to do the rest, we had heavenly housing virtually on the beach. It was a godsend as the climate was into the 90F+ and high humidity. These bungalows were bug screened and had wooden latticed shutters, no glass in them at all. We were in our seventh-heaven here the other cloud 9 was yet to come.

The air base itself was a huge layout of workshops and hangers, monstrous hangers where planes had been housed on what they called ferried stop-over. The big Lancaster Bombers were not housed in these hangers due to there size, daily use and the tractors to pull them around were missing. In the event a Lancaster required extended mechanical work done it was pushed into a hanger to give the mechanics sun protection. Obviously there was lots of hanger space and the "*Banana Girls*" had a claim on a base or two in one hanger remembering their earlier good old days when the Americans were there. Consequently they were rewarded with half a hanger space and it filled up with beautiful girls carrying huge bundles of bananas on their heads and massive baskets of other local tropical fruit balanced on their lovely heads. As a result these young girls walked so regally they literally took our breaths away as they were light brown skinned beauties, And as a twenty year old young soldier far from home these girls were incredibly desirable under any circumstances but being a soldier we mostly lived for the moment and these were special girls and very special moments. I believe they were from the Tarkwa Tribe on the edge of the Ashanti Plain where the gold mines were discovered The Gold Coast, like most of Africa is made up of many tribes speaking a variety of different languages which impeded development regionally. However, we were fortunate here as most tribes spoke English, as a first language since the arrival of the British administrators in the 19th century. The British Administrative and District Officers set up schools teaching English only and as it turned out it was a blessing in disguise for all.

When the gold was discovered or, re discovered. All the coastal area was already a hive of industry; with many ports all along this coast for inter trading. This heavily populated coastal belt was thriving and if you think that we Americans are the proverbial entrepreneurs you better think again. The whole west coastal strip of Africa, regardless of the name of the country, has had inter trade since the Portuguese ventured down there in the 16th century and got involved in this very lucrative trading themselves. The Portuguese traded along that area for over half a century before they ventured down to what we now call Cape Town, South Africa and along around into the Pacific Ocean. From Latitude 10 through Angola all on down to Lat.30 plus was in those days derelict uninhabited country. Now back to Takoradi, our port of call. Once we told the Banana *Moms* they could come in and sell bananas they literally took over and *moved in*. Never had business been so good for them, our guys bought bananas and didn't know what to do with them, and there was lots of giggling and selling of bananas. The older women, the mama's, were smart enough to have these Nubians up front at the massive stalls while they watched carefully from behind managing it all.

Fraternizing on base with these hawkers was not allowed, of course, and I think that added to the lure of these brown skinned beauties always managing to have one perky breast appear from their clever folds of cloth. Their attire was imported colorful cotton cloths of many colors and made up into an intricate wrap around affair somewhat like a Sari but not quite, and it was constantly readjusted and hitched up. The big attraction of the banana girls prompted the RAF equivalent of an army sergeant-major to get everyone on parade as soon as we were all there and gave a typical talk and warning as to what would happen to anyone who interfered with these girls, our guests. He then went on to tell in detail the health problems one could contract and suffer from, for life. There were no antibiotics available to the British Military at that time and contracting an STD was a military crime. Several guys were sent back to England for treatment which for syphilis was painful and unreliable but I doubt they got it from these girls, the port sides were full of tantalizing creatures. However, we loved these banana girls, as we called them, and purchased bananas by the dozens.

We worked hard too but because of that climate we finished at 1 p.m. (working 7a.m. thru 1 p.m., no air conditioning and no breaks). We purchased our bananas from the girls as we went through into another hanger now converted into a huge photo plotting room, and again on the way out as we went down to the bungalows on the beach. We got to know the girls and their moms in typical casual British fashion and the moms blossomed out and came to the fore mingling with their younger attractions and we got to know them all by name, it was all great fun and etched into my psyche for life.

We had a kind of dining section and a couple of good local chefs who had previously worked for the Americans. Once they discovered how we ate they served us well and devotedly. After lunch we would go straight out into the hot sun on the beach area. The Seas, the Atlantic Ocean, was very rough along that coast and dangerous unless one was a strong swimmer – we loved it! We also discovered another group of happy girls to harass; we called them the **sand girls** because they loaded head pans with sand dug out at the back of the beach sand which was too salty for concrete making. It was not uncommon practice in those days, In Africa, for local builders to use sand selected from the back beach areas for concrete and plaster sand. (It still has a high salt content crumbles and washes away unlike the non salty hard clean sand aggregates. Plaster sand is a pit-sand softer and finer than other sand aggregates which are more suitable to concrete mixes). The girls head-pans were typical saucer shaped and made from alloy and were about 22" diameter. They keep pieces of coiled cloth carefully shaped and readjusted for every head-load to protect their skulls and to fit comfortably under the head-pan. Too much cloth and the head-pan would totter; too little cloth and one would have an awful sore head. There was a *ganger* man in charge down with the girls in the sand pit area but this ganger did not do any digging, he simply showed the girls where to excavate with their hands or pans and was a kind of tyrant overseer until we came along. Each girl knew how much she could carry and presented that amount in the head pan to the ganger who thereafter, he knew if they were cheating on their loads and periodically all hell would break out if he accused one of lighting their loads – it was a hard job and they were fighters. He kept their loads tallied by dropping little white shells in hollowed out cup size holes in the sand, one for each girl. It took two girls to hoist one pan load up on to one of them and the other would stand there until the one with the load signaled with her eyes or hand she was ready to go. These loads were carried in that beautiful regal pose up these diagonal somewhat easier trails up the headland which was about 500 yards up to the flat bodied *Lories* at the top of the bank. This was extremely hard work and the girls were anywhere between 16 and 22 years of age. (I know this because one girl told me she was 22 years of age and the eldest and had become a regular dance girl at the Seaman's Mission weekend nights) They wore the usual sari like flimsy wraps with only one turn around the body for this work and often not covering the breasts. When loading was done for the day they would all troop down to the waters edge and splash around getting washed off. If any guy tried to go near them at this time the rest of the guys on the beach would set up a warning shout and the girls were guarded and given their privacy

Again, they regally walked off with approximately 40 pounds of sand on their heads up to the Lorries higher up on the headland. I guess they were chided to get on with the work but they also enjoyed all the attention they were getting from us and sometimes a little fun fight in the sand pits with one of the military guys until Maj. Hellings, our intrepid leader, called me in and asked me to see what I could do about the sand girl interaction. He said, I know you are away from home for a 3 year stint, but we need to keep our noses clean and other things clean so, we got it in check except for Malcolm one of our Engineers, our aristocrat lad. He was too far gone on his little light skinned-brown skinned girl and they were one as bad as the other but I just let them go on, I hope he compensated her for lost head-pan loads. He would get too close evidently, and she would scream and yell and tear off along the beach sands, no covers with Malcolm in hot pursuit; and not a care in the world running along the sands in this hot beach country where we drank gallons of beer in the torrid sun. None of the guys gave a hoot except for hoots of laughter as these two crazy *in-love* couple ran around naked most days. The guys sat around in groups drinking and swimming in this mighty surf, just like we were on vacation and, in a sense we were. We simply loved that place and many of us loved these girls and protected them and our ganger friend and the Lorry guys knew that too and managed with more cajoling in place of meanness..

Not being able to flirt madly with the sand girls we went off down the beach coast to a large fishing village – no white people ever in this area at all. The surf here was ferocious and yet they went out in sea canoes fishing. These canoes did not have outriggers and were 30 and 40 feet long. The fishermen paddled through that surf to get into the calmer waters on the other side to let in their lines. We were impudent and confident enough to jump one into each canoe and pick up a paddle without asking their consent, youth and military prerogative I suppose. These people were strong and cared nothing about our military might or status but they were tolerant and let us stay. My first trip, the whole canoe was upended on a mighty wave and we had to regroup and start again When we got through the actual fishing was about 4 hours duration and I just didn't have it in me to sit there and I jumped out and swam back to shore, easy. Most of us guys who took up the canoeing also took up fishing and we all became friends. We never took offers of fish from our new fishing friends, our mess was too big and the chefs went to market and got all that anyway. We did contribute extra to the mess for specials over the budget but we lived well there better than most places we were ever billeted.

Weekends became another drama as Takoradi was a main port for the ocean going merchant ships picking up bananas, cocoa nuts and other export goodies as well as gold from the upland mines. The Gold Coast, as it was called then, because of the inland gold mining companies who mined and processed the ore up country and railed it down to be exported to England. You cam imagine the guards and safety regulations to ship it down and out but we never heard of any heists while we were there — Exploitation! (We had some Gold Miners from there in my home town in the north of England but they died young from malaria, mostly of the alcoholic kind), evidently they didn't know the sand girls. Near the port about 5 miles away from our bungalow was the Seaman's Mission, a big place with only one little chapel the rest of the facility was all devoted to R&R kind of thing including a large dance floor type of room which soon became a night club with the girls who had to know the rules and be approved I'm not sure by whom. The rules were, to dance with anyone who asked and no close fraternizing on the premises.

These missions were set up all along the West African coast in all the regular *Ports of Call*. (I believe also in many other parts of the world) They are organized and funded by the Seaman's Institute a kind of union group the merchant seaman pay into for looking after their affairs and they provide and set up these much appreciated missions. Some reserve and respect for self and the institute is expected of the users, we were allowed in by the mission because of being in the military and we really appreciated the facility and conducted ourselves in a manner worthy to the mission. It was fun and interesting to discover a number of the banana girls and a few sand girls became regular dance girls just because we were there. They told us that there were other places "nightclubs" but they were of bad renown – don't go there! The girls told us. They also said that the merchant sailors went to these other places for their girls and many times drunken fights with no restrictions. I had my regular banana girl, she had to dance if anyone asked but she always came back to sit close to me at our regular table where we gathered on weekend nights (all night) and I took her home when it was time to close up, I was captivated by her allure and beauty. It is not a good idea to fall in love with a local girl under certain circumstances such as mine. Number one, the army then wont condone it and number two, the emotional stress when it came time to leave was so painful especially if you weren't the kind to love 'em and leave 'em – and I wasn't, it tore me up some.

Being a long standing seaport there was a mixture of skins of all shades, take your pick but the popular Saturday night club shuffle song was "Brown Skin Gal Stay Home and Mind Baby" Oh how we loved that ditty and every brand of beer and liquor for the asking. We naturally became weekend regulars and were mighty popular with the girls because we were naïve and generous unlike the seamen. Sometimes there would be a drunken riot break out even here in the mission and the RAF Military Police and local Police would arrive with Billy Clubs. We were never in these brawls and we were never picked up or clubbed but sometimes, we needed to disappear quickly. Our status was so high with the girls they ran us in to their own private quarters nearby until the riot was quashed and the culprits hauled off. The big fights were mostly the merchant seamen going wild, Norwegians, Swedes, Danes and so many others. Strangely enough these particular nations had a long standing history of occupation on the Gold Coast dating back to the 15th Century but I guess these descendants didn't know it. There were other nearby night clubs but this was the prize place and safest for the milder people. We were about four and one half months in Takoradi on that occasion and I never wanted to leave, it was one of the great times in my youth and life I was enjoying all of it. Our dear chief, Maj. Hellings, couldn't show his face in a club like that and he missed a lot, I told him so but he said, he had had his day at that game. WOW! What a time and what a memory.

NOTE:

The Gold Coast, as it was when I was there in 1952 and later was called Ghana was originally made up of big wealthy kingdoms dating back many years. They were all wealthy as traders and the purveyors of ivory, gold, cacao and other valuable resources. They traded with the Ivory Coast to the West, Togoland on the East and the Sudan countries to the north. However, the conglomeration and tribal mixes came about around the coastal areas as the Gold Coast peoples were great traders and came to the coastal areas and ports to trade and protect their merchandise. They were great intelligent people long before being invaded by the Portuguese in the 14th Centaury.

Now, my girl was of the Tarkwa's, Ashanti, one of the greatest central empires. That empire was still in them. They were so beautiful and carried themselves with dignity and stateliness, I fell in love with all of them but was fortunate in having a "girlfriend" from this magnificent group of people and I wanted to be with her forever, that is my nature I suppose.

4

Back to England 1953

Germany - England Again - Agric College - West Africa Again

Our three year African stint eventually came to a close and the Post WWII Africa Development Fund was closing all accounts. This meant no more aerial photography and mapping to be done in Africa by the RAF army was getting smaller by the day and African countries that were once Protectorates were now commencing some kind of independence. We had flown and photographed many thousands of square miles, more than the mapping machines had yet plotted so they could run on with it in England finishing the series of this very useful map coverage of thousands of square miles of Africa. Flown with the old Lancaster Bombers mostly over countries that were once protectorates, and this small unit known as "rassles" (RASLS) Radar Air Survey Liaison Section was located in everyone of those countries to do ground work establishing beacons for the Lancaster's to fly on and know their whereabouts. All these beacons were ground fixed from known stars values executing a spherical trigonometric triangle resolution to know our particular whereabouts on the earth's surface in the middle of nowhere. These young men did a superb job of bush whacking mostly in remote game park territory often with no trails to establish a beacon. Unfortunately, it came to an end and we all dispersed in different directions and for most it was the end of their army service

There was a huge demand in Africa for these 1:30,000 scale maps obviously the mission was a huge success and they were still being plotted and produced for many of these countries which we had covered many years later. I know because I used them in those countries covered years later when I returned to Africa. The more conventional map scale is, of course, 1:50,000 but our old Lancaster's were now, after many hundreds of hours of weary wartime flying, unable to get up to the height necessary to produce this desired and more conventional user scale. The best aerial photographical camera immediately after the war was the Kodak (K17) and it had a fixed focal length that always gave the scale of twice the flying height Unfortunately, when taking into account the mean height of topography in Africa (height above ground level) which is 3,000 Ft. AMSL the Lancaster's had to fly at 25,000 Ft AMSL to produce a 50,000 scale map, apply the ground level and it was way outside of the height range of these old birds. It was now way outside the limit of those magnificent Rolls Royce Merlin Engines which had done magnificent service with thousands of hours on them and could no longer fight the rarified atmosphere.

My Brief Time in Germany

Leaving Africa for me was a sad occasion. I had grown to love it and it was my home now and I knew I was going to feel strange and lost back in England, especially up in the North West sparsely populated country as it was then where I came from. As it turned out I was told to catch a ride in one of the returning Lancaster Bombers which brought me to RAF Benson and I was informed I would be going to Germany to head up the only mapping depot in Germany at Bad Oyenhausen (sp). Germany was still operating under a war time condition with no one seeming to know anything where I landed up and the towns and cities were still mostly razed to the ground. I found what I assumed was an Engineering Regiment, I don't know what they did but they made it clear they didn't want me. I had no movement papers and no one in particular to report to I was lost with nowhere to go. So, being still under wartime conditions and having war substantive rank I proceeded to commandeer a house on the Mittel Strasser and be damned with the consequences; I was an old African hand who knew how to exist comfortably under duress. It was good, when any military police (Red Cap) asked what camp I was from I simply told them I was given a house in town, it worked. I was still a British Army of the Rhine soldier but was sort of on loan to the American Command who had no survey company and yet wanted to change the status quo which was, oddly, the Germans had a very ancient and poor mapping cover of their country. It was a patch work of many different systems with no common origin. The American grand command in the USGS wanted it all to be commonly connected on one Longitudinal Origin and all these local systems, according to USGS, must be transposed onto a central system. The ranking officer who told me to do this didn't know a map from a sketch plan, he had no idea what was involved in transposing coordinates form the existing many systems onto one all inclusive mapping control projection of common coordinates. He theoretically knew those coordinates now had to refer to a new origin but I doubt he was able to think even that through. Some British General had told him, we have the boys who can do this for you and that's how it goes. Then they too started to look around to see how they could fulfill this ridiculous offer and could only find my small group whose job was not doing what some computer office somewhere should be handling. Nevertheless, I was told I would be working for the "Yanks", what a croc. I told our guys we weren't set up for this and the answer

I got was, you are the expert we sent out to Africa at great expense to get you now get on with it. I was going to fight it but then realized I could not educate military mapping ignoramuses about projections, grids and graticule as a sergeant telling senior officers that they are a bunch of idiots so I just let it go and would deal with it when the time came, and come it did.

For a honeymoon short period I collected 3 army engineering surveyors and established an office in town. The army transferred over to me two very useful Bad Heidelberg graduates (collaborators) whom they didn't know what to do with, Herr's Kulicke and Schwartz. These guys just wanted to be occupied, do something and make a Dollar, they were paid a pittance as "collaborators" I didn't like that word and forbad its use in regard to these two experienced, knowledgeable and intelligent and most likeable guys. We were not established as a regional office very long when a high ranking American Officer paid us a visit. Tromped in without as much as an introduction of him or the need to know who we were, we could have been spies for all he knew. He had evidently contacted the Brits who quickly referred him to an active Engineering group that knew nothing but did know we now had a survey office in Bad Oyenhausen and there he was, as large as life all stars and stripes and gongs. He declared this was top secret and not to be viewed by, and he glanced at Herr Kulicke with much disdain sitting next to me with his own desk, who is he, demanded this stalwart American. A qualified professional and translator I replied, but it seemed not to be to his liking. He suggested they go away and he muttered something about wanting an American common origin for all areas of mapping. I decided to humiliate him and began asking technical questions about projections and origins et al, he had no idea what I was talking about, all he had was some information from Geological Surveys about Common Origins, I doubt he had even looked at a German Map which in itself was tricky because you couldn't extend one against another because of many different scales and local origins of all kinds often not recorded. I was trying to explain this to him when he said, just do your job Sergeant we are in dire need of this coverage we had already gone ahead and selected one uneven line of longitude as the new origin. Meridians naturally are odd and even numbers, 1...2...3 and onwards. However, the further from the line of origin on a sphere the more distortion comes in, he wanted the whole theater of operations on one meridian. I told him this would be unusual and would mean left and right reference plus and minus values difficult for calculations but he said again that is your business sergeant and I hope you know it and can do it, I looked at him putting all into that look saying, what an idiot. I had tried everyone for an approval of my Meridian selection and belt distance including the Colonel but he backed off at that saying it's your job to know these things and do it; others didn't understand or didn't want to. I am afraid there was no one who understood what was being done so I simply went ahead with what we had selected. However, you just cannot take coordinates based on some local grid (German Map) and change them into geographical coordinate references with a few simple strokes of a calculator; a lot of transformation calculation is involved. One first has to find the old map origin usually arbitrary and then give it the new value now there is one common point from this all other map references have to be recalculated in relation to this new point involving trigonometric signs and natural signs to the eighth place to be calculated on an old carriage machine for each point to be transformed (I have tried to explain it simply just to give an idea for the uninitiated) I tried to telling this to the mighty man but he simply looked away and said, We are at war Sergeant and this information is needed and he would be back to pick up the new coordinates within the week....What!. He assumed he had straightened me out. What a clown, the war had been over a couple of years now but we were on a certain footing and he wanted to sound important He didn't want to discuss it because he had no idea what he was asking for nor how to talk about it, he had simply said he would get it done and straighten out those dumb Brits. He should have come and explained as far as he knew how what was needed and asked if this was adequate if not he would relate our questions and get more information; he was too insecure and arrogant to do it that way.

I knew what was involved but in those days, with the only hand cranked German Brunsvega calculators we had, it would be laborious and time consuming with logs and sine's etc. I was stewing over this when Kulicker suggested I go down to the shop (his wife had a lingerie shop where we sold American liquor and cigarettes under the counter which were in big demand) and take his wife out to lunch. Some little lunch places were opening and it was real good to go out, most of it was black market stuff but presented in a German fashion. We took our time, went back to the shop and spent more time finally going back to the office. One bundle was already in the out box still tied with a red "secret" ribbon – how ridiculous can one get. The second bundle was completed the next day while I was out again so as not to see a *collaborator* doing my secret work god forbid, somebody might finally find out where Germany is. It was a real eye opener to me and maybe others eventually that the Germans worked from these unconnected maps. I guess they assumed that they would never have to be concerned with locating anything accurately on German homeland, a big mistake. Putting all these independent map references on one longitudinal system was the obvious idea and that is what we were progressing with but there was no one to discuss it with. The Brits now said we were on loan and an American unit and the Americans didn't have anyone in the country who understood mapping. This brilliant American colonel who blew in out of nowhere had talked with someone back home on a bad phone and rather than show his ignorance he resorted to the old slogan, just do it! (That'll show them!)

In the military, all "cushy" set-ups come to an end and as did my comfortable Bad Oyenhausen one. A direction from HQ was hand delivered to my lovely home on the Mittel Strasser telling me to skinny down and gets my two-bit unit over to Munchen Gladbach. Meet with another American Officer who has an important job that has to be done in Holland and they need an engineering group to control this planned work. As it turned out I later discovered this guy and his Buddy had time on their hands and had heard about the German short range Stuka Bombers that created so much havoc in non essential towns around Southern England. Why had they concentrated in spreading fear around in this manner? They read up the facts on this aircraft and discovered it was deadly but critically limited because of its short range flying and the crossing the English Channel took up much of its range. Then they found out from the Dutch that these Stuka's had short bases dotted along the flat coastal lands but were somehow no longer visible. You guessed it, Sergeant, find these bases it is of the utmost importance, we were back in the war again.

I had to set up a tent unit (the tents were useless) in that constant rain and established my own operational base under canvass. The said colonels paid an initial visit but didn't like the dampness and the rain. We were unable to mark up our progress on the maps we acquired because they were either too damp or wet. This was insanity, of course, and was done so that some two bit colonel could say look what I did in Germany. We found most of the strips simply by talking to the Dutch people. The Germans when the fled as the Allies came in cut down Pine Tree breaks allowing the sands to blow and cover the short concrete strips that these Stuka's needed for take off, only half returned the Spitfires shot down the others in England or over the Channel on their return flight, they were no match for Spitfires..

I had several bad sessions with the colonel in charge and told him a few home truths that he didn't like. He said he was returning me to the Brits; I laughed and said, I like that idea so he backed off that threat, as he hadn't finished his little game yet. He needed someone to manage the dozers and plant equipment that was going to open up these strips.. I told him it was insanity now as everywhere was a swamp and a marsh he replied, need I remind you we are at war Sergeant. My response was, Bull Shit and we've quit, we are not taking heavy equipment down into those wetlands war or no war you nutter. I told my guys to go back to the Brits and I was leaving the army. The colonel frothed at the mouth and I told him to do his worst but I will do my best to expose you for the idiot that you are, he never fought back or reported me as far as I know. I went back to my house in Bad Oyenhausen, made a fast request to go to college and got a quick approval release and I went over to Dover in England and awaited my discharge and college grant including a civilian suit and a pair of shoes.

Demobilized

Being now a civilian, (civvies) as we called it in British army jargon, came as a strange experience after five years of military service, mostly spent overseas. I decided to go home but it was not the home that I had known years ago. My dad was now retired and he and my mom were living in a little village outside of the small town of Millom. I got a train out of Euston, London up to Millom having to change a couple of times to stay on this west coastal route. There was a rail stop at a place called The Green, no one alighted but me and I walked up the grassy lane to their new home in The Green. It was an emotional meeting, especially with my mom, mothers are normally that way, and she had not seen me since I went to Africa except for 24 hours stop off on my way to Germany. I was not sure how to process it all as I was a half hard bitten soldier and even more so with my 12 months in Germany and all that insanity going on, I had to settle down somehow and it wasn't going to be here at what I now called home. I stayed for a few days and also rented a car and went up to the college I was going to attend in a town called Penrith in the Lake District. It was pleasant old country market town but I could see I was going to be the old man to the rest of the new income who were only in their 18's and 19's and I was all of 23. It seemed like a big gap at the time but as I look back it is nothing. I met one of my student colleagues to be and he was most refreshing. He was from a large family estate that had several farms and needed some scientific knowledge he said. Like me, he had grown up on farms and needed no practical experience although we had to endure that too from young women instructors who had nowhere near the knowledge and experience we had in the practical area. However, they were very scientifically knowledgeable in areas we had yet to discover, The Science and Practice of Agriculture, we had the practice. I had eight months yet before showing up for classes and I was amongst the fortunate who had accommodation on campus, God Bless the army.

I was wondering what to do about a job to fill the months I still had on hand before going to school. I said Good Bye to my new student friend and went back to a part of the north I was familiar with. I attended the next auction cattle-mart in a place called Ulverston back nearer Millom where I was born. I met several farmers that I knew at the regular coffee house after the auctions, a place where many farmers hung out for a few ales after the sales and a big country dinner as it was called — not lunch. I was talking with a young farmer I knew from a retirement and tourist area called Grange over Sands, he had a big dairy farm down in the flats where the grassland was unbelievably prolific. He needed an all round man especially for managing high production Friesian dairy cattle. Tending cattle that were high milk producers is a very specialist and dedicated job, one almost has to grow up in it and I did (animals producing 4 gallons per day) these animals are worth a lot of money and vulnerable to infection because of their delicate condition due to the high production of milk. They require balanced feeding which has to be off-set against their production and good records have to be kept and studied. We talked some and I signed on for a trial as his dairy manager. Within two weeks he offered me the job and I settled down to 12 hours per day 7 days a week and was quite happy about it. (Sunday was only 8 hours) As the weeks passed I became more than the dairy man, I became family and baby sitter allowing them to go to a movie occasionally, a very hard and dedicated life for all of us but it was in my blood from youth and early on after leaving the sanitarium. The weeks flew by and I was fit and healthy again. As we did the milking together in the early mornings I told him about my life in Africa and he was fascinated and told his wife Rita about me and my experiences and she wanted to hear it from me too. However, by the time we finished our evening meal both Tommy, her husband, and I were asleep in our chairs in front of the fire she said, what a life I have two handsome guys and they have no idea what happens after 8 p.m. We worked so hard, Rita was a beautiful lady and became my friend for life. I lived in the house and was as much a family member as it is possible to be, more so than with my birth family. I stopped by my home occasionally to say hello to my mom but that was the extent of my family connections.

On the land we had sheep and a couple of wonderful Border collie work dogs I often realized that without these dogs we could never have raised sheep. Even during lambing time these dogs would quietly herd the sheep so that I could inspect them and see which ones were ready for lambing that night and I would have to stay up and go out into the pastures with a lamp to make sure they got rid of everything. Amazingly the dogs hung way back but they were there and there eyes glinted from my hurricane lamp as they watched, these dedicated and beautiful dogs were always watching. I respected them immensely, one has to work with them and know how to work with them to realize how inherently intelligent and devoted that they are.

Our closeness as family was so good I didn't want to go to college and neither did Tommy want to lose me. I hardly ever drank beer and never went out at nights we were a tight knit group in all we did. On the lovely English summer evenings, on the level ground outside the cow barns, I showed Rita how to play games we had learned to play that my dad had taught us as kids and she loved the distraction and fun of it but it was not Tommy's way of life as Rita and I laughed and enjoyed these childish pleasures. One we played the most is called Guinea Peg, you take a clothes line wooden peg and sharpen the knob end. Then lay the peg on the pebbly surface of the ground, hit the point end with a short stick and it will leap up a few feet you then strike it for all you are worth, it doesn't go more than about ten paces or so. You give your opponent the number of strides to make it in and the fun begins. One always estimates as much as possible a number of strides just short of what it actually is then the strider runs and puts into it all they are worth to win the points. We had slips and falls and twisted ankles but we had fun like the kids we still were at heart that is Rita and I did. I think I was secretly in love with her a little but I guess she knew that. Time just flew past and I said to Tommy and Rita no, I wont go now this year I will apply to go in the following one but Rita said, Frank, you must go now and come back afterwards if you wish, but this is your opportunity to better yourself and you served in the army and took risks for all of us so get going Frank now, (Tommy died following a knee replacement) in1996 and Rita died last year 2009 The daughter I used to nurse on my knee was now with her own family, she emailed me and said, one of the last things Rita said was, tell Frank.

Newton Rigg Agricultural College

I went to Newton Rigg Agricultural School in 1954 and thoroughly enjoyed it, especially the scientific learning and study. I certainly did not need the practical experience and trips to big well known farms in the area but it was all part of the college way of life, teaching and learning which was especially good for me as I was lacking in this essential area of life which I had tended to pooh-pooh before becoming a college student myself. I needed bringing down to that level which in fact was above mine until I graduated. As I mentioned, I was the odd man out, the old man but most of these kids had been in school much longer than I had and were a terrific asset for me and generous in their helpful ways. A college dorm life was also something I had to learn about and how to live in it. I met many nice girls who didn't seem to mind that I was an *old man*. I had dates but always took them too seriously for whatever reason and the girls helped me to handle it in a more fun like way. A military career was always useful for breaking the ice and I was introduced to a new time and a good time and I also applied myself diligently and learned. In my past I was a very poor student unable to learn or apply myself but now I was enjoying it and doing much better at studying. Strange to say, I never drank alcohol during that time in school and yet I had been a drinker in my army life but I just didn't want it or need it. How I wish that I had continued through life without it but it was not to be as you shall see. We studied Land and their value this was our President's a Welsh man's favorite subject and we therefore knew we would be tested on that. Welsh men are Gaelic, of course, and emotional tending to emote but we liked him and his inherent acting. I was introduced to genetics for the first time in my life. Mendelsons Law of Segregation and all that related stuff and had to apply myself diligently there. In grains and grasses until it is a study one has no idea how involved this can be and how it developed through time. Dairy especially milk production for commercial purposes is another very involved study and important if you are going to manage advanced dairy stock. The study of diseases in sheep and cattle turned out to be most valuable for me when I went back to Africa as an Agricultural Officer. This study was most extensive and we had a veterinarian who took these classes twice weekly.

Many students came from big wealthy farms in England and Scotland and they felt it was not necessary for them to do these studies because they were successful farmers, more like playboys, they had super cars to commute in too important to be in the dorms and they were great boozers and made lots of noise discussing it in class. I asked them to shut up or leave and they said, what's wrong with you soldier boy and I insisted quiet or out so they left and complained I shut them out but the instructors knew better however, their dads were big contributors to the college so we had to suffer them. I got friendly with a couple of them and they asked me out to party. I went and had two drinks so I was not a blooming pal to be. I told them that they were going to fail as I said, it takes all the hours I have to keep abreast of the studies and the work but they were not concerned and they failed to great guffaws – what a shame as I felt privileged to be there at army expense. My results went to the army but that is not why I got my certificate, I wanted it desperately and worked for it. I wanted some of those girls too but had to close them out temporarily then college was ended and I had to face life again.

I was able to shut out for a time while in college all the worries and struggles of the daily grind of a normal working life and give myself over to the studies: diseases and pests in crops and how to recognize them treat and eradicate them; virus and bacterial infections in crops and animals and their differences. The genetic development of wheat, oats and barley particularly the shortening of the straw length to avoid lodging (going over with the weight of the corn head) and all the different grasses their advantages and disadvantages These were but a minor tip of all we covered in those years, I was a long time farmer and I realized I knew very little when it came down to it. For me it meant going back into farm work 12 hours a day 6 !/2 days a week sometimes 7 days a week depending on the season but that is the life I chose and mostly enjoyed, I could not work an eight to four routine, I needed the more free in a sense different life, I had to be out struggling with the elements. I went back to Home Farm, Tommy and Rita we had grazing stock, dairy cattle and sheep and most of all my two sheep dogs I had left behind, Border Collies and they welcomed me back with open paws and tongues My mother said, with all your learning why are you going back to work as a farm laborer down in the Grange. Poor old mom, getting a small proof of studies certificate didn't really change things it only opened the horizon a bit. I could have gone more towards a college life by going on to one of the many college home farms, most of these agricultural colleges had home farms and to become the manager of one of them was considered a real achievement and it is but I was drawn back to the wet ocean climate.

I brought with me lots of papers to study and work on. I was eligible to go on to Durham University, one of the more popular English colleges, and get a year off of a full four year college degree. I never made it, much to Rita's dismay. The Lawrence's had now become my family and there were quite a few of them in all, and most of them had farms and I was now considered part of this family. But, Rita was constantly whispering in my ear, are you keeping up on what is happening outside of this life and are you looking to see what is available to you, and she would pass all the farming magazines and newspapers along to me. I started to see in the Positions Available columns jobs in Africa and I would draft an application and then Rita, who had a grammar school education, would look it over for me. Tommy would say what are you two up to now and Rita would say, Oh Frank is continuing his studies. It eventually paid off and I got a position with the Agricultural

Department in Nigeria as an extension officer amongst the very native of natives, the nomadic cattle herders.

It was not with the Provincial Administration, each province (read state or in England county). Each state had its own administrative department that was typically bureaucratic and most cumbersome to deal with. At that time, era, the administration top echelons were managed by all British white people appointments many with an over exaggerated opinion of their positions and appointments, resulting in many delays the inability to make decisions, for fear of accountability, and failure and this, of course, caused more delays along the way. Things never got done on time or were not done at all and I came up against this bulkhead.

5

West Africa Again as An Agricultural Extension Officer

Kano: I could not find the Northern Region Production Development Board offices.

In England, I received all my sign-up papers for the Northern Regional Production Development Board position in West Africa, while living with Tommy and Rita Lawrence at their Grange-over-Sands, Lancashire mixed dairy farm. The Northern Regional Production Development Board (NRPDB) was essentially about developing a way of improving the life of the indigenous natives by introducing alternate crops and culling their herds of cattle, especially the old and seriously diseased ones. The (NRPDB) were a quasi government group, operating in a Federal like capacity, supposedly without interference from the Provincial Administration. The PA, however, was extremely possessive of their control over their territory (Provinces) with their own (AO) Agricultural Officer. Subsequently this outside position of authority I had did not bode well for me within the provinces.

At the farm, where I was employed, it was becoming uncomfortable for all of us. Tommy, Rita and me over my pending departure and when Rita, my dear friend, got the opportunity she suggested I quit and go home to stay with my mother to complete the remainder of the application paper work essential to my new Nigerian position. She suggested I be with my mom for a while before leaving the country again. Meanwhile, my mom was emotional because we had never spent time together since I was in the TB Sanitarium as a young teenager in 1943 We were bombed and blown out of bed so, they moved us away from the city of Newcastle, where the TB facility was into the country. Newcastle was a staging area on the River Tyne for moving arm laden ships out to Russia with all kinds of war use material and equipment. It used to be a ship building area pre WWII days. However, I was home again with my mom and dad, a rarity for me, but she made me very welcome and fussed over me as if I was getting ready to go to war. As it turned out, in many instances, it was more scary than war and traveling was an art and often difficult even for me who had spent many years traveling on safari in no road areas in East Africa.

I grew closer to my mom and she went everywhere with me in my car which I had to dispose of yet. I needed a kind of different wardrobe from overalls, jeans and boots. We went shopping in Preston, the closest town big enough to have small department stores. I had been in West Africa and had seen how the professionals were attired so we found whatever khakis we could, suitable shoes and suede boots, for my coming bush life. I had reams of documents with papers telling me how to dress and where in London to get such attire but I wasn't going to drive all the way down there and I knew how silly and often misrepresentative these bureaucratic documents can be. The entire vaccination and essential shots required were not available in those days in that locale anywhere close to where my parents lived. I had to go to the city of Liverpool to receive them all, from where I would be shipping out later. The area in Africa I was going to was well known for many diseases: malaria, dysentery, yellow fever and several more. It was rife with malaria because of the rivers and swamp areas but of course, one can take prophylactic for that, they said, but at that time the prophylactic didn't protect me.

From Liverpool where I got my shots I went back up to The Green, in Cumbria where my parents lived in retirement. A lovely rural village in an area mostly made up of sheep and beef grazing lands up in the high hills. Very picturesque but lots of rain. In the evenings my dad talked about his army life in India and the Sudan and he and I drained the teapot every night. He had quit drinking many years ago when he came out of the army of WWII, and I wish I had too, but I had yet to learn how and why to stop. I did not drink while staying with them and it was not difficult for me to do that, I had to have drinking companions for me to indulge in alcohol. I am so pleased Rita Lawrence encouraged me to go stay with my parents prior to shipping out. I told my mom how difficult life had been for me, especially in the earlier years and my time away in the TB Institute. I told her what it had all done to me and how sorry I was over my diffidence towards them, she hugged me and told me she understood it all. It meant a lot to them my being there as I had been sort of a lost child initially, much sickness growing up and missing lots of schooling, and then away into farm work for several years living with another family who kind of adopted me and took great care of me, periodically driving me back to visit with my mom for a few hours. I still had my car and we took drives into the Lakes. The Green, my parents village, being adjacent to what is known as the English Lake District, a popular tourist attraction in the summertime both for the lakes with their many trails and the rock climbing on many famous mountains in that locale. It is an ideal jumping off place for The Lakes. We just visited some famous spots within easy driving time like Bowness on Lake Windermere and Hawks Head on the other side of the lake and several more like this. They lived in a very beautiful area of northern England, remote and peaceful. In the wintertime, however, in those days one would believe everyone had fled the towns and this village. There was a little grocery shop which was also a post office, a small hostel nearby and an old dry stone-wall built Anglican Church. If it wasn't for the fact my life was ahead of me and had yet to be lived I would have stayed put with my old mom and dad but I was moving on again and finally, it was time for me to head out. I had been over to the farm and bidden farewell to my dear friends Tommy and Rita and now I was dealing with a very tearful mother but she had said goodbye to most of her three boys on many occasions.

I then had to first attend a 4 day seminar in Liverpool to learn about the tribes in that area of northern Nigeria and introduction to Islam and Muslims, and how to comport myself towards them, and the Senior Administration's Provincial Officers also various department senior officials who were serious about being recognized formally by the rank and file. We went over the diseases again and some history of colonialism as it is now and how not to get into difficulties with the Muslims and how to respect and respond to them. We went out partying every night until the early hours of the morning and created chaos at the hostel where they accommodated us for the seminar. Later in life, and to this day I am embarrassed and regret that behavior as I eventually did with many more such like instances. I returned to The Green again, the village where my parent's lived, and then finally, everything was set for my departure within a few days.

I walked down the lane to the railway station named, The Green, and caught a train going to Ulverston about 30 miles away. There I had to catch another one for Lancaster, Carnforth and get finally a direct run to Liverpool. That's how one train-traveled in the North West in those days. I was able to board the ship and was taken to my birth which I shared with another guy but the cabins were spacious and provided all one needed for the 10 day cruise. We unpacked and stowed our gear then wandered aft to the bar and sat down to get to know one another and for a welcome drink, always welcome. The voyage itself was, for me, a wonderful respite and pause in life. A life that had had its sicknesses, disappointments, hard physical labor, military experience and dangers but this was a blessing amidst it all. There was more trials and danger to come.

When I boarded they had not crewed up by any means but certain hands were already on board and took the time, of which they had plenty at this stage, to tell us about the port of Lagos. Lagos is a big port in Nigeria where we would be arriving and docking, it was the best information I got so far. The ship was a one class only, more first class rather than any other. It was comparatively small carrying less than 500 passengers. A low keeled ship, enabling it to go carefully into some of those shallow water river ports on the West African Coast like Lagos up the river, being one of them. However, the low keel had a big liability. When the seas were rough and that is a big percentage of the time in those northern waters, particularly after leaving Las Palmas in that group of Islands on the NW corner of the African Continent before going north into the Bay of Biscay and on up off Portugal, we rolled and tossed like a cork. Those great little ships were eventually put out to pasture and not because of passenger flying which was now taking over but people couldn't handle the tossing around, I was one of the few that loved it. We had well trained first class stewards and the individual attention we received was incredibly good to experience.

We sailed along serenely after leaving Liverpool; the weather was in our favor. The service and meals were excellent, something I had never experienced or had no idea even existed at all and I had yet a lot to learn about dining and eating. Finally, the wonderful voyage came to an end and we docked in the heat and humidity of Lagos (pronounced laygos) for you Americans, not largoes. I had to find my way around because there was no one to meet me and, all I knew was, I had to get a train to Kano, the Capital of Northern Nigeria. (I later discovered that the interesting tribes were in the West, the Yoruba, and to the south mainly the Ebo's who were more westernized and commercial-like in their ways, and made up of many small businessmen). The trains ran only twice a week and I was so fortunate one would be leaving later that evening; I just stuck around literally, and got a berth that evening for the assumed two day journey. The only cooling were fans in the better class carriages where I was seated and of course window open to catch all the soot as well as the days heated up. The distance, as the bird flies, is only 500 miles but in those days on that railroad, time was not taken into account and there were many extended stops plus the train speed of about 15 to 20 mph was frustrating to a person from a different world, I had much to learn. When we arrived in Kano I discovered the company offices were in Kaduna a station we had passed through. Fortunately, I got a ride with a Nigerian government guy heading out to Kaduna and he took me to his Nigerian offices. They said I had to go to the local Provincial Offices – bad advice; I was still a new guy and didn't know the nuances. The Provincial guys nabbed me and sent me to Abuja in the south to take over the resettle-ment of a failed British rice scheme. When I eventually arrived there in an old truck after 10 hours of awful track riding I complained bitterly and said, I have to report to (NRPDB) in Kaduna but the new boss just laughed and said, you are here and get out among the tribes. I learned later, that the English Provincial Administrating people had a plan to discredit and ruin The (NRPDB). They feared it because of its success, and it's projects success. After a week or two I was very unhappy and disgusted how my anticipated return to Africa had all turned out. I had a small bare hut which was away from the base where there were several empty, excellent small bungalows, providing accommodation dating from the rice scheme days but the manager simply said, these are not for you. I also discovered later that they were trying to discourage me and chase me back to England. I was very naive and felt trapped but unable to do anything about it as I had no transport of my own and they were not likely to provide me with any. One morning, I was standing out on the rail tracks as that huge brass plate of a sun rose in the hot humid early morning air and I thought, this damned rail track has to go back up to Kaduna so, I packed my gear, what I could haul, and made my way to Keffi a rail stop where I finally boarded the train again this time getting off in Kaduna. I told my sad tale of woe to the chief (NRPDB) man and he said, they're at it again and we apologize to you for this nonsense. That was it, they too were walking a fine line and I had to get used to it as it was as problematical for them as it was for me. I believe they used this situation also as a way of assessing ones character and ability to manage adverse situations and succeed. I had to put up or shut up and, I chose to soldier on after all, I was a trained, true and tried lethal soldier.

My Particular Duties as a Northern Regional Production Development Officer:

After a month to familiarize myself with the department I had to go out into the most remote tribal areas and get myself known and acquainted with tribes very much as they had been since the beginning of time and improve their methods of farming such as, (animal husbandry and crop rotation husbandry) At that time, over 90% of these tribes had never seen a white man, imagine how that improved my appearance in their world. Improving their methods meant stopping them from growing Guinea Corn, their staple grain, and replacing it with another alternate grain crop to avoid centuries of monoculture of the land that was reducing the crop yield by a big percentage and naturally now diseased. This was so ridiculous it was almost laughable, interfering with their livestock or crops was like signing your own death warrant. Their herds of cattle too were rife with disease namely Rinder Pest and Anthrax (I had seen Anthrax in cattle in England) I knew this was going to be the biggest task of my life so far, and maybe the end of it, to these tribes cattle was their assets and savings.

I recovered my optimism and felt good again. I had a huge breakfast of bacon and eggs with my boss, I noticed he didn't have any, I think he had eaten already but just told his servants to serve breakfast again. I slept in a room that night in a comfortable bed with sheets under a huge fan and a mosquito net that made it cool to my knew acclimated condition. After a few days to meet my colleagues and get acquainted with the area I was about to leave for, and learn more about the provincial administrators. I was warned about their sensitivity and to avoid differences with them but know that I was not directly under their jurisdiction, however, it would be easier for me, was opined, if I could sort of work with them, it was only later I discovered they didn't work at all. My new boss told me I would eventually have my own vehicle and if it was an emergency he said, he trusted me to know about one following my initiation period with them there in Kaduna. I can't tell you how much better I felt about it all even though I knew my work was not going to be easy irrespective of the provincial gangs inhospitable behavior. He said, I take it you are accustomed to driving African dirt roads and I assured him I had that experience more than most for many years in East Africa. He said, I think this will be our last night before you head out and tonight I have invited a few friends and we would very much like to hear about your experiences in East Africa. That evening in a little comfortable clubhouse I gave them better than a thumb-nail about the Radar Air Survey Liaison section, my life as a geodetic surveyor attached to the RAF and what our purpose was and how we achieved it. I got a round of applause and I didn't get drunk because I knew if I was to make it to Yola in one day I had to be alert and strong, these people were real gentlemen and treated everyone accordingly. I got the after shock when I arrived in Yola, Adamawa Povince and linked up with the pseudo Brits again, what a self serving group they turned out to be.

The rainy season had started already and my boss warned me that I would experience some very bad patches but don't get off the road to detour or your vehicle may be stuck for the remainder of the season in the black cotton soils along that stretch. It was bad in places but it wasn't anything I hadn't experienced and I made it in fair time, 7 hours known as a 10 hour run they told me. I am not a fast or crazy driver, one just can't do that alone out in the middle of nowhere. I just didn't know what to do when I arrived; I went to the provincial offices and got no help at all. It was incredible, I was stunned, and back in Jebba again on the Niger in my mind. I finally found the trader's depot, the company that brought in and supplied the provincial people and the small traders in the territory, Taylor-Woodrow. I made fast friends with them and was invited to dinner and a bed for the night, thank God. (For the life of me I can't remember the guy's name). He told me all I needed to know so, I felt relieved He too was not mighty enough to attend most of their soirees but, he put on some wonderful ones himself on behalf of his company, sent out invites and many of them did attend that. I was allowed to move into what was known as the small guest house, I was given this information by a Black Muslim indigenous employee of the administration. He also told me that there would be no service for me in the way of servants or provisions; I had to obtain such for myself. Provisions were available in a local shop and, for me, at the Taylor Woodrow Depot, they also loaned me two guys, a cook and a houseboy. It was disgraceful because other trades people came into town while I was there and they were given all the facilities of the big guest house which was like a hotel, it was hard to take as I was a professional. I could have cried to my company in Kaduna which would have taken at least three days to get a message through and what then? I let it go and decided to do whatever I could on my own initiative which was right then very limited. My Taylor-Woodrow friend, let's call him John, was extremely helpful. I was informed, indirectly to go to a place called Numan on the confluence of River's Gongola and Benue about 20 miles back along the road I came in on. There was a "hut" there that was to be my home, no doors or windows and only bats above an old rotting ceiling – it was unbelievable and I felt crushed, not because I had to live like this but that they, my brothers, could be so resentful and nasty.

I had very little money of my own at that stage and was not able to do a lot in upgrading my living quarters or employing someone to help me. I knew the big picture of what we were trying to achieve in the province but naturally, I needed to liaise with the Provincial Agricultural Department. Their job was to provide me with transport to get out to Numan, my base, which they eventually did but the jeep then went back to Yola, the capital, leaving me stranded. I was extremely disappointed with it all but, following a few days of trying to establish myself, I did manage to find a general factotum man in the area who had previously worked for a white man and I hired him at a slave price arrangement until I was richer and able to reward him better for his services. Meanwhile, he was very happy and busy going about whatever we could do to help me make the one roomed hut bearable.

I caught a ride on the mail truck owned and run by Arabs and went straight to the Agricultural Offices and demanded to see the AO. (Agricultural Officer) He had done this to me purposely in cahoots with the CPO (Chief Provincial Officer) to make it virtually impossible for me to get around and have me to complain and hopefully leave the area. I was aware of this, however, and maybe I should have got the Mail Truck in the opposite direction back to Kaduna and attempt to have it as to where we were in regard to the PA's attitude towards (NRPDB) officers. However, I thought better of it and decided to remain for a while, take it easy and see what my options were. First I needed to fix up my living quarters and got to work on that with my new man and a local Ebo contractor. The job was mainly repairing door and windows with shutters, no glass allowing free access to deadly mosquitoes and clearing around the area to define the homestead. This was necessary because the local girls going to market with their head loads of mostly curdled milk from their tribal cows and vegetables like okra trekked right through my house grounds. I mostly slept outside in my camp bed with mosquito frame and net. These market girls with their uncovered breasts would stop right by my bed to see if I wanted any of their wares, I needed just a little privacy.

Meanwhile, I was learning about Numan and the surrounding territory that of course was mine as far as my assignment was in getting to know the tribes and covering my beat so to speak. Numan, an ancient city and a one time important stop for the river traffic traveling from the crop growing southern cities on up to the northern desert towns adjacent to the country of Chad. The Benue when in flood was navigable as far as Garoua and sometime as far as Bei Bouba. These towns were in an area called N'Djamena, squeezed like a slit, between Nigeria and Chad. It used to be huge canoes navigating up the shallow bankside waters, now it was flat bottomed paddle steamers and when they tied off at Numan the excitement rose to a fever pitch. These boats always had kegs of Creek Gin which was stilled in certain areas in the more southern provinces and the boat captains purchased plenty of it for all occasions. Numan had out of town professional prostitutes who mostly made their living from the passengers traveling to the desert towns in N'Djamena. There was shore partying at nights and I think my home had previously been a rendezvous for some of this activity.

Many of these girls made them selves known to me and let me know we could be closer friends if desired. AIDS had not yet started but I was not available for trysts. I went to some of the night activities and introduced myself to these half Arab ship's captains and drank creek gin. There was a dancing group of men and the first time I experienced their acts I was on the alert. Their warrior dancing was incredible, they were all drugged on Ghat, a leafy plant cultivated and grown in the northern regions, and leaped and danced through huge flames from the big prepared fires. One landed, purposely, immediately in front of where I was sitting, some kind person gave me a chair. He had a spear and looked ready for a kill, his eyes were glazed and he was not all there, he looked at me and thrust the spear forward, one of the captains was sitting next to me and he said, be still, and of course, I was, because I was frozen still in the chair. These dancer/warriors never mixed with the crowds so it was not possible to know them or their origins but they were southerners. The southerners were more negroidal in appearance in contrast to the local semi nomadic tribes in my domain which were like half Arab-like in appearance. After a time I became an acceptance in Numan. Many people traveling to Yola, only about 40 miles more, stopped by to say Hello and get the local gossip and information on the action in Yola.

It was time now to spread my wings, so to speak, and my options were to go into the local cattle grazing tribes immediate to the north of Numan or canoe up the Gongola River, a big fast flowing tributary of the Benue flowing past my door. Some of the administrator's staff came to Numan just to picnic on the sandy river banks and watch the steamers come in if they were lucky. I got to know some of these people and thereby learned more about the higher level of administration. These positions were good postings for the PA's staff and although they had their criticisms of the management and activity or, lack of it, they did not want to rock the boat and jeopardize their own positions,

Nevertheless, what I heard reinforced what I already suspected, that the senior administration lived a princely life and the lower echelon assisted them to protect their own appointments – a very insincere and bad situation. There were alcoholics within the senior ranks which were covered up and ignored for the same self protective reasons and the rounds of partying were endless.

I decided to take my first run up the Gongola River which took a huge bend below the Jos Plateau. The plateau being higher by several thousands of feet and consequently much cooler unfortunately it was not my territory and I had to stay below in this hideous humid climate of above 90F degrees plus, I hated it and dreamed of the lovely East African climate particularly Southern Rhodesia where I planned to live one day. Navigating these rivers against the current is a laborious and tiresome method of getting around. However, the vegetation along the river areas is very dense and most of the vehicles of that time had never gotten in there. We made about 12 to 20 miles a day working up against the current in the backwaters, bank side waters and shallows. The method of travel was by poling, I had three men (polers) with huge poles to move the canoe along (paddles were of little use in these circumstances except when coming back down stream), with huge poles that they worked constantly about 10 hours a day. After three days of poling and putting up my camp bed and frame with mosquito net every night we came to a well worn track down to the rivers edge. I have forgotten the name of that village now, no name because I never went back there again. It was a Pagan village and I mean pagan, no missionary had ever been in there to carry the gospel message to them, they were as basic as tribes can be, virtually no clothing, particularly the women and all they had was a herd of pigs that slept right in the village center. The smell was unbearable, not only piggery but many decades of filthy build up from these people themselves. (one district officer had put up a sign: "This is the filthiest village in the province"

My job was not to be a social worker improving the lives of people directly, and this was to be one day a huge undertaking, whether it was to be by foreigners or Africans, one could only conjecture at that time. I met the chief, said Hi and fled back to the canoe and moved on. We eventually came across another pagan village more advanced looking people at the riverside. They just took, unloaded, all my gear, head loaded it and set off up the trail, there was little I could do but follow with my right hand man and polers, the polers evidently trusted the village men to pull up their big canoe. (This canoe trip yet had to be paid for out of the provincial administration budget I expected problems)

After about thirty minutes walk along the trail through the heavy vegetation we came to a very large village which was clean, no smells and there were gangs of boy's playing soccer in the cleared area in the center (town square) I was intrigued. We passed through the village with little or no excitement and that was strange to say the least but soon we came to an obvious mission with a church building with the inevitable Christian cross atop and more soccer fields this time with goal posts. My porters went right up to a big house and set off my gear. The house had a long wing on one side. Two priests came out and welcomed me and said come in don't worry about your gear, it will be in your room and your crew will be taken care of. It was mid afternoon – hot as always, but we had tea which was a normal thing to do in "British' Africa. I told the priests who I was and that I was taking a survey of the area along the river because I had no other transport. They told me that transport would be of little use in any of those river areas because of the jungle like growth and the deep black cotton soils were treacherous. They had a big American car, a Desoto, given by one of the priest's brother now living in America, and they had made a road out to what we called the mail line. The mail road, and only dirt road, coming in from Kaduna, my head quarters but very far a-field under my circumstances, and to phone was always most unreliable and the line was always in use. Of course, following tea I was shown my most welcome room and, after the way I had been living I threw myself on top of the bed and had a welcome sleep. Sitting on a hard wooden cross board in a canoe day after day, believe me is tiring, I had no pole but I did try it. I had plenty of strength in those days and was physically strong but no poling skill and I never practiced, it required skill and strength. I stayed for two nights at the mission and even served at morning mass being an old altar boy from my youth. The Father's had built a big frame on a concrete sort of patio area and had covered it in mosquito netting with an access door. What a gift it was in those mosquito malarial ridden areas. The houseboy brought us large bottles of beer and it was a "blessing" maybe? But, I think I emptied too many bottles. We had a terrific meal of beef, cassava, yams and what was described as spinach, tiny tough leaves grown on a strong stem, difficult to chew and swallow. I don't remember if we had a dessert but I am sure we had something.

I traveled up that Gongola River on several more occasions during my time there in Numan, but it was a laborious and time consuming trip, had it not been for the Mission I would never have taken it again. I was never successful in establishing contacts along the old Biu cattle trail that I discovered, with my traveling being limited in those areas higher up the river under the Biu Plateau where cattle was grazed on the lower slopes. The plateau rose to over 6,000 feet AMSL and should have been the Administrative Head Quarters in my book for health reasons. With that valuable hindsight which we all come by too late to be of use I would have not moved too far away from that plateau and made my home half way up the slopes. I was not secure enough in my self or in my appointment, it was all very vague. I hardly had any contact with the NRPDB and yet the Provincial guys wanted to keep me in sight and tried to manipulate me for their own advantage, a worrisome situation for a young man starting out in the bureaucratic web.

I always dropped off crates of beer at the river bank edge track up to the mission, (a crate being 24 quart bottles) there was always someone there from the mission I knew and they knew, of course, when my canoe was coming long before I arrived. But, it was not expedient for me to spend valuable time doing those trips up the Gongola. On the reverse run with the strong current, the river flowed rapidly with all the rain waters coming down from the Biu Plateau. The trip back with the paddles was delightful and we covered three times the poling upriver distance in one day. The danger was at the confluence with the Benue River, the merging turmoil was like a rapids and dangerous for our 20 ft long canoe craft. On the first time back into the Benue my crew boss asked how I wanted to cross the Benue River, I lived on the other side, the east side, and I said, paddle through. They looked at me a spell but went ahead and we ended up way down river on the Benue following a magnificent display of canoe control watched by a crowd along the banks on both sides of the Benue, we had to pole back up the shallows to my landing stage.

Following that grand display of paddling, in all future crossings we tied up along side the ferry, at a price, I kept my head down and let my crew boss haggle the price but he was at a disadvantage with a white man on board. The ferry was a wooden built raft on petrol drums with a rope adjustable ramp on each end. It could load two ten ton trucks (Lorries) and several cars at a crossing. There was a huge rope from shore to shore but when leaving the ferry and going up the steep ramp onto the river bank was always a tricky adventure and a novice often failed the first several attempts, one had to throw caution to the wind and roar up the ramp and the slippery steep bank side, I watched many failures as we tied up there. There were six operators on either side of the ferry who took turns pulling on the huge rope, a painful task. There were occasions when the ferry was out of operation firstly, repairs to this rope or welding to the float drums and on other times at Ramadan, the ferry crew was Muslim and passengers had to wait until sundown and the crew had eaten.

After my initial introduction to the Gongola River, I turned my attention northwards on the east side, my house side. I would request a vehicle from the Provincial Public Works Dept., wait at there convenience until it arrived and I could head north. They wouldn't allow me to keep it and once I arrived at my first village of call, so to speak, there the driver and vehicle left me and returned to base in Yola town. Initially, I walked from village to village, staying there for several days, introducing myself and getting to know the chief and his cohorts but, it was hard going in that climate and painfully slow progress. The trails were navigable in this area and a jeep would have been a perfect solution and help on my journey into this territory where few had bothered to penetrate. As I became more familiar with the territory I could see and visualize many places where I could easily establish a vehicle track, I had done that for years in East Africa. West Africa is an ancient civilization and yet we still knew very little about these particular areas. I believe they have a rich history and although reputedly, no white men had traveled my routes. I definitely believe somehow contact had been established and then lost in those gone by days

Extending myself out into this area was essentially a risk, even my local bureaucratic Maalam (my Muslim aide) from the Provincial Administration, upon their request recommended we don't progress any further into this unknown territory. I asked him why, and his answer was kind of devious but basically they had never had contact with white officials or any white-man for that matter, and their reaction was unpredictable also, we might disturb the status quo. I said, the status quo is exactly what we are trying to change, any cattle coming out of this area is riddled with Rinder Pest and in some cases Anthrax (an animal with anthrax is not comparable to a reduced lab form of concentrated poisonous anthrax). He shrugged his shoulders, he was a Muslim, a bureaucrat and probably not over concerned about going further and later, as I pushed on, he deserted me and returned to Headquarters in Yola town. This alerted the PAO (Provincial Agricultural Officer) who sent me a message on a scrap piece of paper with the driver, (an insult) to drop in next time I was in Yola Town. When I did stop by there he told me to stop moving into those areas, we don't want an uprising, I responded: why would we have an uprising? He said interfering with their animals would disturb them to the point of anger and then there is no telling what might happen, I told him I would take care, how could I cull contagious sick animals without the aid of the chieftains so, I made no commitment on this matter which disturbed him. He may have been the Provincial Agricultural Officer but he was unwilling to inspect stock, said he was afraid of contracting diseases. I asked him what his job was but he became difficult and arrogant towards me so. I left him to do what? I have no idea what they did in their offices.

I had been "renting" a horse from one of the friendly chief's closer by as I went into the more or less "safer" traveled areas. It was against his tradition and Islam to outright charge me for the use of a good riding horse so, on my arrival at the village he would send around a nominal gift to my lodging (a mud hut) this obligated me to having to give him a very large gift when I asked to "borrow" his horse. We both knew how to play the game, a game known as Rikitshi in the Hausa language of Northern Nigeria and a description adopted by all including the whites. I rewarded him substantially as I needed better than foot travel. It worked well until later on when one of my new Chieftain friend's father along into the *danger* area He had also become a very personal friend the original advances being made from his side, and was a substantial aid in my opening up that worrisome, map warning dangerous territory. Upon meeting with the first few Chieftains as I progressed I realized these were not dangerous people, a misnomer applied by some commissioner traveling in style and not meeting with them on a more comparable level. Also, not wanting to proceed into unknown territory and listening too much to porters (load carriers) who did not come from that area and were nervous and afraid..

— ..Speaking of traveling in style there was a very senior District Commissioner (SDC) it doesn't matter now, time has long gone, and his name was Bacchius. For some unknown reason he had no specific territory to administer but he traveled in a huge limousine with about three very pretty Fulani Arab type girls dressed like wealthy whores, which is probably what they were by now. The powers that be turned a blind eye to his idiosyncrasy because he was from a British aristocratic family and a well known wartime decorated army officer, no excuse! But, he survived as long as I was there and caused much gossip and eye rising when he came into a town with his "aides" and attended a meeting.

This special Chieftain friend asked me about my horse, he said it was too old for me and I told him the story. He told me to leave it with the other chief when I returned to Numan, my home and base, and send a runner next time before I left and they would return with my fresh horse, yes, *my horse*, he made me a magnificent gift. These half broken Arab horses were gold to these chiefs and I was exceptionally privileged. He also told me the runner would be told how many hours he could ride the horse in any one day and not to push it. From then onwards I had a great ally and it was through his friendship I did so well in that task and meeting more chiefs who accepted me in good faith as a friend. This chief also had a smattering of English which was a tremendous help since malam Ibrihim had freaked out on me and returned to Yola with some fascinating stories, I later discovered. I think it was when I accepted the gift of the horse named, da'n serki (son of a chief) that was the last straw for him, not that I didn't always get a horse for him too but he was a poor rider. However, for some reason, he spread the word I was taking bribes – for what? In truth, he resented the white-man's friendship with these chieftains and he had been told to keep me out of there I later discovered. After I became accustomed to my big horse and the Arab saddles I was expected to ride with the local horsemen when they went out hunting and that really was a ride, as we say. They went out to find whatever little buck (deer) was left in the plains, they carried their spears at the ready and picked up (stuck) big iguanas en route to the hunting fields and putting there tails through a slit in the throat they hung them around the saddle horns to roast and eat later.

I was learning of these territorial Fulani tribes who have covered very large tracts of Africa and this section now named Adamawa State since the British became their Protectors. This particular area was once known as the Gongola State but the Germans became involved – German West Africa — After WWI when the British took over and, they like to use the geographical terminology of Province, they also adjusted the boundaries. Whether the Germans or the British ever specifically entered this part of Adamawa is unknown. The Benue River is not too far west of this area and inland access must have been essential for these tribes to do the minimal business they would have required. I am sure there are various trails out to the river to pick up on boat traffic but I never knew about them or thought at the time to ask for the tribes help in identifying them. Had I remained in that job it would have been high on my list to do as river traffic connection is essential for these people and if and when a cash crop really got started close by markets and transportation are necessary, this was all part of my extended work after being accepted and becoming friendly in the area I had already made a large inroad on friendship. That isn't to say I didn't have some fears and scary times and wondered about my longevity. However, after several moths and many visits spending time with these particular chiefs I was moving forward with my mission in regard to animal husbandry and also crop husbandry that was also an obvious failure. I had not yet investigated the other "dangerous" area to the south, inland from the Benue River. The area I wanted to see was down the Benue and inland on this section of the Plateau slopes where large herds of cattle were known to be. I somehow got the use of the Provincial Administrator's travel barge. It had a mosquito screened-in bedroom and kitchen as well as a living (drinking) area. My handyman and I lived well on this journey down. We took two paddlers with us and arranged for our poling crew to meet us down there in ten days time allowing me to make a survey inland either walking or maybe find a horse to rent. We had three days traveling down with the current and covered good mileage. The paddlers and my man at the helm worked on into the late night hours, I could hear them talking quietly as I went to sleep with absolute confidence and security in my crew. We eventually tied up on a little dock at a small village in the Jatingo area this was where my men said I could move inland to the dangerous "Cattle Chiefs". The villages were Muslim and clean as a result of their way of life. I got temporary accommodation in this village and someone brought me a nondescript horse, I was spoiled now owning the fine Da'n Serkie, my horse. However, I rode out with a couple of locals who ran alongside; they didn't have to run much as it was very hot and humid so I walked the horse. We eventually came to a village with a few milk cows standing around and I assumed there would be cattle grazing out along the slopes somewhere. I did not have inspection authority, I doubt anyone had it or wanted it, and I needed to make friends first. I later met with the chief who was hospitable but not exactly outgoing. He wanted to know why I was here so I took the bull by the horns, no pun intended, and said I would like to walk with him amongst his cattle, I explained why but he turned me down. That night there was a huge party and the drums rolled on and on. I had fears, because of blurting out my intention of looking at his cattle herds that they were getting ready to come for me. It is not easy going out alone into these remote *new* areas but it was what I undertook to do and I knew the Administration would not help me. I met with the chief again next day and asked him who was the next chief inland and could he let me have one of his men to go along with me which he kindly did. I met the next chief about another 12 miles along the way and had a similar meeting, I decided, if I had the time and wanted to open this section it was going to take much more visiting and gifts to get going with them This meant I would have to find a kind of base to operate out of. I returned to our temporary base on the river and my houseboat with a comfortable bed and decided to go farther down river looking for a place to establish an outpost.

We found it at Jatingo where there were provisions enough for me and my gang; we lived off Cassava, Yams and Sweet Potatoes, occasionally rice from the plateau there were varieties of these and other plants and crops I never learned the names of but there were many and we didn't starve and sometimes we could buy chickens. However, for a white man who had never lived on this diet it took a little while to become accustomed. But I did and rarely opened my stash of canned food. My man could catch a certain fish from the river simply by letting his hand dangle there with a semi open fist and one would venture into his hand then he would throw it into our boat, they made a good breakfast with fried previously cooked cassava in peanut oil. I began my usual routine of trekking and riding inland to meet with the chiefs, it was slow progress but given the time I knew I could make an inroad to cleaner cattle management.

The Provincial administrators sent malam ibrihim (a Muslim bureaucrat and ordered me out of there which I ignored and told him I worked not for the Administration and I would be back soon to talk to them. I decided the time had come for a face off and I wasn't going to continue in this ridiculous way, they had to put up or shut up. I made several more sullies inland successfully meeting more chiefs, they were only too ready to meet me and find out my intent. I realized as, a partial stranger, I could not yet jump into discussing cattle and their diseases. However, we talked about grain crops and replacing the sick dying strains with alternate grains for local trials. But my time was limited and the administrations agric department could have done a lot of good in this area and be a great help, however, they were not interested in a project like this that required a certain type of life with it's inherent discomforts. Why were they there claiming to be agricultural department? The AO had an elite problem and a class attitude which was going to get him nowhere if he wanted to eradicate disease and improve the sick herds. Nevertheless, I intended to do as much as I could. Recently, I had been suffering from fevers most likely malaria and needed to get back to Numan and Yola and see someone. There was an MD came at times but he too didn't seem to want to put himself out in any way. So, we caught a "ride-along" with a paddle steamer going back up to Garoua which was about as far as these boats could go because of the shallows. *By ride along* meant to tie up along side if the paddle was rear mounted or aft if the boat had side paddles. They were steamboats and had to pick up wood for firing and consequently had contracts with locals for supply depots en route. They also stopped somewhere south of us in Benue Province for Creek Gin illicitly brewed and had the nomenclature of "Creek" However it was illicit and distilled in some secret places along the route. The boat skippers picked up many flagons of it and they never ran dry, they used it for usual entertaining purposes and all kinds of deals including exciting girl's en voyage. After we tied on and I met the captain and he invited me up into the wheelhouse to sample the gin and it was very good and *on ice*. I got to know these skippers well and always had an interesting ride back up to my hut in Numan.

I did have malaria very often and in fact, I had it so bad one day I just passed out in my hut in Numan. The Irish veterinary officer was on his way back to Yola and my boys waved him down and showed him the semi conscious NRPDB man. He got me loaded up and took me to the little kind of local hospital (not the white-man's one) in Yola Town and watched over me himself, an animal doctor bless him. He medicated me on what he had and monitored my fever and condition, he put a girl on to swabbing my head and face with a cold compress and that was about all they did in those days. Except, if one of the senior administration persons got it bad they rushed them through to Kaduna where there was a hospital and doctors – class distinction. After I came back into the land of the living Paul, the Taylor Woodrow Supply Company area manager took me in to his home. He had several servants and I was well cared for as I recovered. On that part of the river were huge monitor lizards, about 18" high and two to three feet long. As I was recovering I would lay out on a cot on the veranda under the trellis foliage covered shade. One day I opened my eyes to find one of these creatures checking me out, I don't know what it might have done but I yelled for help and it went lumbering away, I thought I had died and gone to a bad place. The Malaria hit me bad on many occasions and this was one of the reasons I decided not to return to Nigeria and my now very friendly delightful chieftains on the north side. Sometimes, when in a very far off lonely place with no one really to look after me I thought maybe I was not going to recover from it and didn't care if I didn't, but prayed the end to come quickly and take me away from this incredible sickness and pain. I once came to in one of these lonely outposts where I traveled and couldn't figure out where I was or what was happening to me. I was laid in what was apparently a shallow grave and covered with leaves. I felt better, yelled for my boy and got out. He told me I had been there a few days and that was how they treated their own bad cases and he said you were already dead boss. Evidently the leaf is important, it has to be the branches and twigs are picked fresh and then have to wilt for a day and then they covered me to re-cover once more. It always left me very weak and shaky for a week or more. In Yola town when they had a malarial attack they would go to the cottage hospital until able to get around again then rest up at home for a couple of weeks, not me I kept moving. This constant malaria was not good for my physical condition, or even my mental status, and I knew this was not my place in the world, in that Africa.

I had begun culling sickly diseased animals by having the chief's cattle attendants do it under my guidance, this way they were managing it rather than me but I was subtly putting on the pressure. We took them to a walk-in ditch, cut their throats and then burned the carcasses, you would not be able to do that today without a veterinarian, an EPA witness and god knows how many others in attendance. I also got an alternative grain for them to try in a newly prepared field I had the women prepare the field; men don't dig up land, that is a woman's job. I didn't want them to plant new seed too close to the old grain patches and be contaminated by disease. I also explained this to them but it was very difficult to have men be concerned over women's work unless there is no food. However, my grain grew well and they were now interested whether it be women's work or not. I was also getting them involved in growing cotton; I wanted them to have a cash crop for the women. We barged it down stream to a cotton market and got some money with which I then persuaded the women to purchase bolts of cloth. This was an intense and careful matter which took a lot of time but, that's all we had, time. Only because I was white, a special friend of the chiefs, was I allowed to be involved with the women and their evolution. We all, the women and I, went back to the villages and stashed the cloth away. I then persuaded the men to build one shop front under the big trees under my guidance and what a great success it turned out to be, we had a market place – they were on their way to capitalism, don't say it doesn't work. Many years of provincial government control (socialism) had done nothing and in that very short period of time I was there we were on the go by the power of the ladies with no government investment and they, of course, the administration, were furious but I knew it could work. Had I stayed around it could have become a flourishing enterprise branching out into other fields but alas, I decided to leave. I needed to get well again in my own climate. I never heard if they kept up this development but knowing that administration they would shut it down if they could. They wanted to bureaucratically control all happenings only in office by micromanaging so that nothing could ever break out and start. They were not prepared or able to get involved with it and a new enterprise like this needed momentum and help in the field and the villages but I know they could not do it with their mentality. I felt guilty but no one cared and no one had ever come to my rescue or provided me with the basics of a white man living and moving around in that environment in that area. I did it regardless and got no thanks for my efforts from my own employers or from the local administration.

Maybe during the last four months of my time there in the Yola Province I was accepted into the white community but not by the official government administration. However, this began to change after the CAO saw my map. By this time I had a desk in the corner of the large general office and mostly worked on my map there annotated with local Chief's names, the date and all other related progress. The PA was fascinated and asked how I was able to make such a useful and official looking topographical map. I told him I was a qualified topographical land surveyor and he replied, my god, why didn't you say something we need someone with these abilities. He then continued, what about this map, it should really come to us but I told him that they might copy it, not so easy in those days. He also invited me to their home for a party night, I was flabbergasted but I learned a lot that evening at the grand house. I met lots of people who knew much about me and congratulated me on what I had done fearlessly and against bureau-cratic obstacles. They wondered how I had stuck it out but it was balm to my shattered nerves. I found my host and could tell he was alcoholi-cally influenced; he greeted me like I was Livingstone on the Zambezi. The big shock to me for some unknown reason was that his wife was a complete troubled alcoholic. He finally had one of his subordinates take her off somewhere. Of course it was a well known circumstance and I imagine most embarrassing and very difficult to handle. I had no sympathy because I knew so little about that condition of which I later succumbed to myself. After this soiree the other government employ-ees always included me in other parties when I was in Yola, fortunately not often, but often enough to build my own partying reputation which was getting worse, I was more at home with the steamer skippers and Creek Gin.

I eventually did a tour through a portion of my territory and gave the news of my imminent departure to these good chiefs. We had eradi-cated hundreds of diseased cattle, an achievement that has never been equaled to this time among semi nomadic tribes like these. I was a protected man in a dangerous area where others still refused to en-ter even with me. They said, one day Frank you just won't show up maybe, but it would not be through any harm from these loving new friends of mine.

Eventually, that day came, I was all packed up the little I had worth taking away with me and I was finally in a Provincial (government) Rest-house in Yola Town. I gave all of my household effects to my general factotum man, my cook, camp manager, trail boss, interpreter and more. He was most upset because of my imminent departure and came on over to Yola in the event I might need him. These rest houses are normally to accommodate visiting officials government or other-wise I was not accepted but now leaving I was okay to spend my last days therein. They had servants including cooks and meals were provided. I remember there was a nominal fee of something like 25 shillings (Sterling). The Chief's from my areas sent word that they were coming in to town and I decided to inform the Agricultural Officer and the Administration. They did not know how to react, I told them not to get alarmed but have an open area where they can assemble. You may not know it but they are most familiar with Yola and know how and where to go and they are very important people, and you should formally meet with them and I will also be present.

As the time came there was a cloud of dust on the horizon and about 100 Fulani Tribesmen came into town at full gallop. The administration had put out the police units but I put the word out quietly for them to stand back and they were very happy to do so. I quickly went to the riders and they surrounded me completely. I managed to squeeze through and tell an official that the Provincial Administrator should be meeting these people but he finally sent a lesser official as did the agricultural officer. I don't know if it was fear or a deliberate insult, in any event it was stupid at the least, a wonderful opportunity squandered. I think, possibly that there was a lot of envy in their lack of reaction. I thanked these chiefs and wished them a great and Godly life then turned over my gifts, a small herd of hand picked sheep which we there divided amongst them; I think it was five chieftains. They spoke a lot about what they had learned in regard to cattle management and I was amazed at their humility, a people who had herded cattle for centuries thanking a lone intruding white man for teaching and helping them to have healthier herds. This was a magnificent gesture and should have been applauded by the authorities and followed up on with zeal but the opportunity was squandered from the fact it was not the provincial administrator's glory. The Chief's went on to laud me and have a good time together; I had to hangout with them until sundown when we made our long farewells. I gave my lovely Arab horse for safe keeping to the chief who had given it to me; it was not polite to return it although he knew I had. It was a very emotional and a hard thing for me to make this farewell with a people who only wanted help on how to improve their lives. I was extremely limited in what I could give other than my knowledge and friendship which I gave freely and without fear. Any fear on my part would have upset what I was trying to achieve and I know how strange it was that these people trusted me implicitly.

The NRPDB should have investigated what was happening, how much progress had been made and what had been achieved and then equipped me as I should have been equipped in the first instance and asked me to extend and develop the successful project so far. I still had to report in to my company in Kaduna from where I headed out from about 18 months previously. I had submitted several progress reports and problems which were never acknowledged but I knew they had received them because I asked the Arab mail truck driver to deliver the envelope personally and he told me that it had been handed in as requested, these people were all friends of mine I had been back to head quarters in Kaduna on two occasions only in that period I was in Yola Province and I could hardly find anyone interested in what I was doing. The department had been taken over by typical bureaucratic type degreed guys who wanted to expound in front of blackboards and maps but would not, or could not talk about the facts. I finally pinned down one I knew well and asked him if he knew what I had been up against from administration and what I had achieved in spite of it. He replied, you have done very well and we should discuss this on a different occasion and come out with another contract for you. Then I talked with some of the ones doing similar jobs to myself, some had gone what we called *native*, married a tribal girl and lived pretty much like them and cared little about what their task was. Others met opposition similar to mine but were close enough to whine at the establishment and got concessions I could only have dreamed of.

I was staying in a big comfortable guesthouse belonging to NRPDB and was fairly comfortable so I hung out to see what was going to happen to me, did they know who I was and that I was there at all. Eventually, a couple of them came to talk with me and I explained in more detail what it had been like. They commended me for doing what I did in front of the opposition and excused themselves of having been busy getting NRPDB established. I responded with, it needs to be established over there in Yola and Bauchi they then asked if I could do that and I said, of course, if I have the necessary equipment and wherewithal. They then left me with, put your proposal forward and we will let you know how we will proceed. I wanted an answer before I departed for UK but I got tired of being put off and waiting, it didn't bode well for my future.

I requested traveling documents: train ticket, boat ticket, my final salary and traveling letter, which was usual in those days. I then made my way down to the Kaduna railway station to get Lagos train times, the office didn't know and there were no such things as phone checking and, of course, no email on-line sources. Six days later I boarded the train with my boarding pass and bunk reservation. The first class carriages had big overhead fans in the ceiling but no air conditioning so the windows had to be down about six inches to keep cool and ventilated but black coal dust and ashes sucked in until we looked like coal miners ourselves. There were not many passengers in the first class so there was no uncomfortable crowding until arriving in sweaty Lagos. It was a three or four day journey depending on what delays transpired along the way. Sometimes we were run off onto a side line and ignored for hours except by mosquitoes, however, nets were issued in first. Getting from the train station in Lagos to the docks was another fiasco and an ongoing cab fare fight with the drivers whose main intention in life is to rip you off by any and all means at their disposal. Some people actually find it exhilarating, I found it most annoying. Finally, I got to the right dock, as if my driver didn't know but went to another area and then said that is where I told him to go and another fare had to be negotiated. When we arrived at the correct shipping line I recognized the cleanliness of the dock area and the boat tied up in dock, I had traveled on it previously. I was early but allowed to board and make it my home. Having made friends with the Boson I tipped him generously and had my pick of a good cabin. These ships only had one class which was a kind of first class and everything was as good as anyone could wish for. I doubt ever again was sea travel as good as that was and it was soon afterwards it all changed as flying was becoming popular and taking over. One of these ships was sold to a private Arab group and the other one was refitted and hauled different classes of passengers up and down the West Coast. I experienced the last of the Colonial Era in Nigeria. It was one of the last of those countries in West Africa to get independence because it was so successful. Local state and tribal fighting was held in check by a handful of dedicated District Officers (discount my Adamawa Province experience). This was the last of this kind of sea travel and an incredibly fascinating train journey that continues to this day only now using diesel locomotives.

That sea voyage is with me to this day. Somehow everyone lets there hair down and becomes semi ribald and bacchanalia. I needed no encouragement in either of those areas although I liked to keep a sort of decorum, I think it came from my mother. We ate in a most splendiferous fashion and setting and drank much too much of wines, beer and liquor. Made several friends and girlfriends whom I vowed never to forget and did as soon as I passed under the Mersey Tunnel in my new car awaiting me at Liverpool docks. We put into Las Palmas in the Canary Islands where I was to board a bigger ship later with Louise my future wife. I went to the café's and fell for Spanish dancers and dancing music, those beautiful dark haired girls that stamp their feet and even dance on big drums. I met some of them and was having the time of my life and would have liked to spend a year there in Las Palmas alas, we had to sail on into the Bay of Biscay, a sad ending for many ardent imbibers and seafarers. On that trip we hit the Bay of Biscay or, in reality it hit us and those waves were many times higher than our little ship and we rolled and pitched and slid down waves until I was sure we were going down ever to come up. The fun was over 80% or more took to their cabins for the duration and 50% had very bad sea sickness. They swore they would fly after this last experience. We had the decks to ourselves not that they had ever been busy or crowded, and the crew kept one bar open on the aft covered deck for we brave drunken would be sailors, and a small portion of the dining room and the lower bar. The ship had lost its charm and all we could do was act brave. The troubled seas continued up off Spain and Portugal and remained gloomy as we went up into the Irish Sea but then that wasn't anything unusual and finally we docked in Liverpool and the dull cloudy west coast of England. Now what!

FINI

Back in England Again
What to do with Myself Now

Having returned to England and once again to my parent's home that was now in a very lovely, North Country area, in Cumbria village, The Green. I moved in with them once again but could see that any extended stay would be inconvenient although my mom never made any remarks about my being a nuisance there. However, she was sleeping on a pull down bed in the living-room, I was using her room and dad had health problems now and she was taking care of him. I decided I would have to find some alternative accommodation soon meanwhile I needed a month or so to get myself together health-ways.

I had temporarily taken a job with the Cumbria Estate people as a woodcutter (lumber-jack) felling soft woods for commercial use, Larch, Spruce and other fast growing trees. A good man could fell one of these mature trees in less than three hours by himself, I was not a good man initially. I had used an axe plentiful in my farming days previously but this was entirely different and I needed to learn some new skills at felling timber. Our crew had an old woodcutter who hung out keeping the big branch fire burning and sat around with what appeared to be whittling. One day, after a short time and my struggling to fell trees so as to be like the other guys, he said, bring your axe over here Frank and he stuck it in the fire and burned the halve (wooden handle) out of it. Then he had me hold a shaped wooden handle he had made while watching me, he made a few adjustments and by evening I had a new totally different axe. The following day I was paired with the crew boss and learned to fell timber, what a relief, I thought I couldn't do it but it was all there inside of me and with a bit of coaching, encouragement and a new halve (axe handle) I knew I was going to be a master, I had the build and the strength. That winter of tree felling and topping, after we had laid it down we ran along the trunk loping off the branches with the razor sharp axes that the old man kept honed for us. This was in the days before power saws yet we achieved a mighty lot. I was so fit and healthy I didn't know what to do with my-self. I enjoyed the work, my life and forgot about drinking and its dangerous pleasurable feelings. I eventually bought a fairly big motor cycle for that time, a Tiger Triumph Twin, a royal blue. How I loved that bike and rode it with heavy frosts on the ground and snow falls. The forest was huge, empty and quiet, it was our domain and we felled and slewed until 10-0-clock tea break from starting at 7:30 a.m. in the dark then a half hour lunch break whatever was in your bait box (lunch box) and that was it for the day until 4:30 p.m. and already dark – long hard wonderful days.

Spring came and as soon as the ground was soft enough we stopped felling and took a sack cut it half way through and turned half inside out forming a Kangaroo pouch and this we filled with tree shoots. Then we walked lines around the hillsides planting shoots (young sapling trees) as we went at about 20 pace intervals. We had a short sharp special spade and that was how we spent the spring months planting thousands of trees. A back braking hard job and one had to be really in top shape for this work but we were woodcutters and what better men to do this task. Eventually summer arrived and our work was seasonal, and it was over until autumn when woodcutting would commence again, I looked forward to it. Our pay was meager and would just keep a family alive but, I had no family and no commitments I was staying with my mum and gave her some but I was still flush from my African salaried job.

I did self checks such as, what do you want out of life? Do you want to go back to Africa? What if I just worked on like this or back into farming as a manager on a big farm. I just had no answer to it and I was not all that perturbed over the unmade decision. I was lonely for feminine company but had never been much of a success at finding a girlfriend. One of my close friends, a house painter married the girl I had always admired secretly and I think I was in love with her so, consequently I was very lonely. For me, finding a girl was not easy at all. One had to attend the dances where the girls all lined up on one side and the guys on the other. When the band struck up you went over to get the one of your choice and if she got paired with another guy who was quicker than you then I would be mortified and slink away so, I was not very good at that game, the only one in town. I did have a pretty girlfriend for a while; she was the only daughter of the huge local inn keeper. A big frightening man even for someone with my physique, but we kept going out and he kept warning me to bring her back safely otherwise…One spring evening we were going to the local dance held in that village hall. I was on my big Tiger Triumph 650 twin motorbike and not in my car, her dad said her riding on my bike with me was a no-no but we went on it anyway. Those narrow country roads had build ups of fine gravel on the corners and bends in the road which could be very dangerous and I got into a wobble-skid. We would have survived had she been a regular pillion rider but she wasn't and she went rigid upright instead of laying into me and she held back stiffly scared and made the wobble worse and the bike went from under us. She received terrible gravel and road burn and I not so much. She was spring dressed for the ball and had no protection at all and what she had was torn to shreds. Fortunately one of the guys was following in a car and he picked her up and took her back to her dad at the inn and he got the doctor. She was scarred and had to be watched for infection but she turned out not too bad but not me, I was forbidden to see her and almost banned from the inn. He eventually allowed us to meet and talk at the bar but it kind of faded away. I saw her in the village about two months later and she asked me if I wanted to go out. I said, what about your dad and she said, it would be okay if I used my car. Evidently, she had been crying every day and wouldn't talk to him, I didn't know that. He eventually caught me and said, you get around there and see that lass of mine. I did and used his fine big American car but it just didn't work out.

My old friend Tommy of Tommy and Rita knew I was in town again so I went along to visit with them again, and was invited to stay for a few days. After a day or two lazily hanging around, getting early morning coffee in bed Tommy came up one morning with my coffee. Staying a while and asked me if I would come back and work with him and we could improve the volume of milk again, I said yes. There I was, once more, in that busy demanding 12 hour a day lifestyle. I started immediately, and began the following morning by getting up early and making the coffee myself as I starting the morning with the milking routine that was all so familiar to me.

We also had a large herd of big sheep that required constant attention, clipping and shearing rolling of wool into bales for sale, clipping their coats annually but otherwise regular attention. We had two Border Collie sheep dogs and these did most of the running about and rounding up of the sheep for inspection and maintenance. Keeping sheep healthy and clean requires constant vigilance and constant work. Most of the land was low deep sand silt and it produced big crop yields, crops for fodder such as oats and wheat. We had a lot of grassland pasture for grazing cattle and sheep but also meadows cut constantly for silo and hay. It is not my intention here to write an agricultural novel, only to show, what I gave up my lazy freedom for. However, I loved the work and could not just sit around idle while my good friend worked hard alone. So I joined him in a life that I knew so well.

What is my future, how long will I do this. I am qualified as a land surveyor and a field engineer yet I am here working as a farm worker with what future? Understanding and becoming efficient in all aspects of farm work is good but has no future. However, I was doing this job to help out my friend, and I had to take the time to decide what my future was going to be. I said previously, my heart was still in Rhodesia from my time there as a Radar Air Survey Liaison Engineer which will be described in the chapters which are due to follow.

6

Going To Southern Rhodesia

Introduction:

It is not easy to describe the life of a Geodetic Trigonometric Land Surveyor (prior to GPS) whose main job is to define the whereabouts of any piece of land in relation to its location on the earths surface by what is known as Geographical Coordinates (The origin of these ordinates is the equator and a selected meridian such as, for instance, Greenwich Meridian. However, for measurement laterally on or around the earth's surface we use a much closer big circle going through both poles. In the case of Rhodesia where the system is metric several of the odd meridians have been adopted as datum lines). This is a lot of information for the reader to have to absorb in a short time, particularly if your own career has not taken you anywhere close to this criteria. However, it was work that had to be done at the time and this intro is simply to clue you in as to why a few guys were out there spending their lives in this manner. Attempts have been made, especially in the starting portion of the book to describe, in some detail, other aspects of the work and the various people involved. Knowing this, one can read on without wondering what some of the story is referring or relating to.

Catching the Train for Rhodesia

In May of 1957 I finally made all my farewells to family and friends then boarded the train out of Millom a town in Cumberland (later re-named Cumbria) with my belongings in a large suitcase, and headed out for Southampton en route for my long desired immigrating trip to Rhodesia. Millom, on the north-west coast of England, is a small town on the north side of the River Duddon that forms an estuary emptying into the Irish Sea. Millom Railway station is a one track railway station with no more than one or two people at any time waiting to board the train; and everyone knew, of course, that I was leaving for Africa but they didn't know Rhodesia at all. I had to change trains in a place called Carnforth, a change station for several different rail routes north and south and from where I was able to get a direct line to London. Changing again to catch a train out of Paddington, London, going direct to Southampton, from where we would head out to sea in a ship named Cape Town Castle. It was a medium sized liner that sailing from Southampton to Cape Town the immigrant runs of that period with the majority of immigrants going on up to Southern Rhodesia. I was able to board the ship a day ahead and that saved me hotel accommodation for the night. I met my cabin mate with whom I was to share with and we got settled in for a three-week trip to Cape Town. He was a Mormon, a very quiet individual returning to Utah, and they don't drink alcohol. I had not known or met many Americans especially Mormons but I was sure he was not a typical American. He spent a lot of time in the cabin reading his bible which was troubling for me to have this quiet godly living man sharing a cabin. I decided to go up onto the main deck and explore, then aft to the ships bar where one could maybe meet others and make voyage friends. I met a couple of guys in the bar and we had a few drinks together sharing our stories so far of our lives and why we were now headed out to a country called Southern Rhodesia. These men were also going to Salisbury, the capital city, to take up positions in Government Service.

I was also kind of Government but on a renewable project by project type of contract depending on that projects longevity. I had previously been in Southern Rhodesia involving the aerial survey work when I was an army engineer and I was so impressed with it I decided, at that time, to return one day and settle there. I had made up my mind to leave England behind hopefully finding full time work with a private survey company in Southern Rhodesia. This would be not easy for me because I did not have the standard required four year college degree for practicing survey in private Township Surveys which was the bulk work of private survey companies in Southern Rhodesia at that time. A position in Land Surveying required a four year degree to register with the Government Surveyor General's Department to be licensed as practicing land surveyor. I had my Army Engineers certificate in surveying, photogrammetry and aerial photography but, at that time the Society of Land Surveyor's were very insistent on that four year degree qualification. Later, as aerial survey became more available outside of government, I was able to register as a private surveyor but by that time the Federation of Rhodesia's and Nyasaland was about to dissolve and separate to go their own ways into independence. This would mean all land surveying and geodetic survey in Southern Rhodesia, my expertise, would cease. However, South Africa recognized this surveying certificate and I was able to re register in South Africa as a land surveyor. *(I will expound on the status of these countries that were instrumental in the breakup of The Federation later as it becomes relevant).*

However, I was now headed out en route Cape Town, South Africa then on up to Southern Rhodesia by rail on board the train for a three days two night journey up to Salisbury the capital city of the then Southern Rhodesia. I met up with some friends in the bar aft and it all had the makings of a good time. Within three days we docked in late morning in Las Palmas, Grand Canary. Meanwhile I was on a relatively pleasant well managed liner and making new friends. I went ashore to explore and found a café where we saw and experienced Spanish dancing and singing for the first time in our lives. A woman dressed tantalizingly and singing in a style that was so exciting we just couldn't leave and there were plenty new drinks to sample. It was all so exciting for a young man reared in the depth of the countryside with folks who had never traveled, and whose life was sheep dogs, sheep, cattle, milking, growing of crops and reaping grain and grass in showery Northern English mountain weather and spending 12 hours per working day in this environment. I was now having an experience in a new world. *We returned to the ship in late afternoon and found quite a crowd of guys gathered at the ships swimming pool. On inspection it was obvious that the attraction was a beautiful dark tanned Caucasian girl who had obviously boarded while we were out exploring the Spanish attractions in Las Palmas. The buzz went around that she was American and had been living and working in Morocco, she sure looked good. The thought passed through my mind that maybe I could meet this lovely girl but then reality took over and I told myself, you have no chance. You don't know how to talk to someone like this under these circumstances. I didn't have the suave easy way of approaching her and I would misspeak or not be able to speak at all, and then I would be the laughing stock of all the smart guys around and a fool in front of the girl. I realized my short comings and put the whole idea out of my mind but I could not erase the picture of her in my mind. That evening I saw her at dinner and a couple of guys were with her already and I felt sad and disillusioned by my inability to know how to act and handle myself in a situation such as this, particularly when I was wanting to meet a nice girl. I had had a couple of girls in England where I worked but one fell off of the pillion seat of my motorbike, a big Tiger Triumph 650 twin, and her father forbade her meeting with me, she was semi skinned on her back and her rear end. The other one I made a mess of talking with her and she finally gave up on me so my history with women, so far, was not to be bragged about. I had a wonderful adventure with some beautiful brown skin tribal girls during my army years when in the Gold Coast in West Africa but that was somehow different and I had no problems relating to them but it was not the same as this situation. However, I couldn't get this girl out of my mind and I thought, damn it, I will now have to watch all these handsome capable guys hanging around her throughout the voyage and it put a bad aura over the happy time I had anticipated and thought I was going to have on this voyage to my new home back in Africa.

I went off to bed fairly early for me even my Mormon cabin mate commented on it, I would be reading his bible next if the trip went on like this. I told myself, if I was going to enjoy this voyage, and I surely wanted to, I had to push off this mounting doting attitude about a girl I could never meet because of my own inadequacies and negative self evaluations. The next morning I was awake bright and early, no alcohol in my system to slow me down so, I went up to the swimming pool deck, it was early for swimming pool attendance but there were one or two there already and then I saw her, alone! I had to speak now or forever hate myself for not taking advantage of this opportunity so, I said, hello! And she said, Hi! I had to say something else, I am so happy to see you. I was almost ill with my own unconnected remarks. She replied obviously with. Oh! Why? I was almost speechless now but I struggled on and said I was going to ask if we could get together for dinner tonight and she said Sure! What time? She came and sat near me and introduced herself. I told her my name then we shared a little more casual information and then we had a dip and she said, "See you later at the first sitting this evening". She was at the entrance when I arrived at the dining room with a couple of guys, of course, and I was disappointed, I didn't want to share this evenings event with them but she got rid of them when she saw me and we dined alone. I was so fascinated by her and I was also, nervous. This lovely girl as my dinner date that required I entertain in an interesting and somewhat amusing way, was I up to that with my timid approach with women and inability to make the required small talk. I was also troubled with the thought that I was going to have to curtail my possessiveness that was ever present in me when being with a girl I hoped to influence and charm. Nevertheless, I was absolutely ecstatic, I never dreamed I could get this far with the most desirable girl now on board so, I decided to just tell her who I really was as we talked and shared that evening, and I had those years in Africa as a soldier to fall back on, for sharing in new meetings or later for story telling. She appeared so interested in me and my life in Africa it amazed me and it was not so hard at all to talk with her after all. She was a good listener and she also shared about herself in a very natural way, her own life and future plans from here onwards. It seemed we were good together so far so, I asked her if I could give her my cabin number. She said yes, that will be handy and she gave me her unit number too. She was on a higher up deck than what I had in a much larger cabin, in fact, two adjoining ones the other for her mother. Her mom had flown out from San Diego where she was living, joining up with Louise prior to leaving Morocco so as to be with her onwards to the Far East. During this journey Louise was going to select where she wanted to be for her next assignment as a civilian Club Director for the US Services. Between us we had no shortage of experiences to draw on so the big gap, always a disaster for me didn't arise this time and I assumed she was from a much higher place in society than I ever was. However, I was reticent about my family, my earlier home life, and I think she was alert to that kind of omission but I avoided it because I was embarrassed over my poor origin in life.

We had put out from Grand Canary the morning following our dinner and evening together. I was already fascinated by her and heading towards the phase of obsession that I wanted, at all costs, to avoid with her. Before our first dinner night, one of the forward guys who had met and talked with Louise earlier was a demobilized British sailor, a Welshman, on his way home to Cape Town, South Africa. He was married to what we used to refer as, in those (apartheid) days as a Cape Colored and I felt he was embarrassed over having a wife classified as a lower class of person We later met up with her when they emigrated from Cape Town to Rhodesia where there was no apartheid but the stigma in his mind was there too in Southern Rhodesia. Meanwhile, we had a wonderful voyage and became so much occupied with each other, the 13 days simply floated past unnoticed. I had only ever dreamed of a situation such as this and I was flying high. I drank probably too much because I was on a sort of paid vacation and because that is what I liked to do, I enjoyed the confidence it gave me. Taffy, as a Welshman is usually called, attached himself to us and he was sharp, witty and a bit of a comedian so we didn't mind having him around, He showed up a lot at Louise's cabin as did others who attached themselves to us forming a sort of small group. However, I was no longer afraid of losing her and they all knew how to make themselves scarce at the right times. Unfortunately, time ran out and we were due to dock in Cape Town within 24 hours on that last night of dining together. We never went to bed that night but hung out on the upper deck with other people there with different emotions to see Cape Town most of us for the first time. There was some coming home, others immigrating and anticipating their first impressions of that most lovely of harbors. And other's, like us, romancing away their last night together up on deck.

By this time there was not much that we didn't know about one another and we had developed a familiarity that no longer needed a lot of explaining when saying something or asking for something or other but, what I had in mind was maybe different and mind blowing. I realized with a pain in my heart, and believe me it is very true when someone who is now so dear to you and is parting for an unknown whereabouts and time, I was bereft and decided I had to let her know how I felt, as if she didn't know already. However, I sucked in all the air and courage I could muster, realizing she might think me odd to say the least but I said, Louise, will you marry me? She almost looked shocked and said many things about it being difficult to give me a straight answer. She said that she was honored to get such a proposal and we should think about it deeply and seriously over the months to come. I was a comparatively low paid surveyor and she was a well rewarded US Government employee – a very big difference. However, she did say that she was not saying, no. She really loved me too and she said she would stay in touch with me at all costs and then see what the outcome would be about this big step. I was very happy with that rejoinder as we sailed into Cape Town and began to think about our onward journeys, Taffy had simply disappeared, "a sailor's farewell" I honestly believe it was because he did not want us to see him meet his wife Glenda. We did meet her later in Southern Rhodesia after Louise and I met up there again and married and she was a beautiful woman. I am not very conscious of race other than obviously I recognize the main races and colors but some white person with maybe a dash of color it was not obvious to me because, I wasn't looking for it, as so many whites did in those days even in non apartheid Rhodesia. He even bought a home down in what one might describe as, the other side of the tracks. I asked him, what the hell he was doing and he said you've seen my woman! and I told him he should have his ass kicked such a lovely girl and you are treating her like a pariah. (More on this later with our pal Taffy)

The train journey north was uneventful, it was a comfortable coach with sleeper bunk and I relaxed and watched the unfamiliar scenery speed past my window. The Great Karoo in the Northern Cape which extends northwards to the Orange Free State Province where all the gold was discovered and subsequently, the well known South

African gold mining industry. The train stopped in Kimberly which is the place of the famous Kimberly diamond mines. We got off the train and looked around but there was not much to see, so we stretched our legs and boarded the train again for the long wait before the next move onwards where we changed trains again in Bloemfontein east of Johannesburg. We then continued north across the Transvaal and on up to Salisbury in Southern Rhodesia The journey took two days including two nights on board the train and it was a weary man that arrived in (Harare) Salisbury. I made my way to the Federal Department offices (Federation of Rhodesia & Nyasaland) then, and was introduced to my new colleagues, mostly Southern Rhodesian men. They were most welcoming but took the mickey out of my North Country English accent in good natured fun way. In a very short time we got to know each other quite well and I knew that I was going to get along with these new Rhodesian colleagues of mine who were mostly likewise minded. However, I had not yet met the Senior Surveyor who was to be my partner, supervisor and as it turned out, my mentor and my friend. He had returned to South Africa (An Afrikaner is someone born in South Africa of old Boer stock, mostly Dutch). I gathered that he was a quiet and serious man who kept to himself and not much was known about him other than he was an Afrikaaner. The chief surveyor and head of the Department of Surveys also an Afrikaner and acquaintance of De Wet by the name of Oggie Reitz and I met him too. He confirmed my contract and told me to settle in somewhere and find accommodation until De Wet returned from South Africa. De Wet and Reitz were ex army Buddies and fought up in the North African Campaign against Rommel. Reitz told me in confidence, because I was a bit short on qualifications, my application was passed on to Brigadier Collins, our Director and an army Engineer, as am I, and I was accepted as a Geodetic Land Surveyor, not an easy appointment to get in those days, Wow! The guys told me that there was a place outside of town known as Mount Hampden where I would find a temporary place to put out my bedding roll. It had once been an old army base and there were barracks still kind of furnished i.e. iron cots and various shelving and boxes. I went to our store and collected some of my bush camping gear which included a small mattress, blankets and basic cooking pots and I made this my temporary home. I had very little money, and certainly could not afford to stay in any kind of a hotel so this was to be my home while I waited for François De Wet to return. This may all seem hard and shocking to an American that we had to provide and fend for ourselves like this but this was typical both in England and the Colonies. Very little was provided for the junior type employees, even a professional, in the way of any accommodation or meals, not even an allowance under these conditions.

I took out maps and plans of the area of where we were going to establish survey control so as to get an appreciation of that particular terrain and topography before leaving civilization such as it was, so to speak, there was a small town named Gwanda on the railway which was the main track connecting South Africa and Rhodesia, small trading/ranching town on the railway and here is where I assumed we would head out from into the bush. There were no roads at all indicated on these maps for this area that we were to survey. This mapping was from the aerial survey work I was involved in flying and producing back in my Army days in 1952 and I had confidence in them that nothing was there in the way of useful navigable trails. So, other than this, there was very little information on this area but I was able to study the shown topography such as hills, mountains, dry rivers and their sizes also bush density knowledge valuable to Bushmen going out into new territory. Our task was to run a network of triangles. (for the uninitiated, these triangles are only visible on paper in the form of horizontal angles and lengths of sides all calculated from the angles read on the theodolite by the surveyor). north west along the Shashi River area and provide coordinate control to fix and establish the International Boundary between Southern Rhodesia and Bechuanaland (Botswana). To "fix" a boundary means providing coordinates on a known map grid system that can be then connected to the physical geographical line of the border (I am trying not to get too much involved in describing "survey" but this is what I did, I am a surveyor). Further up the Shashi River is the Tati River, which runs south emptying into the Shashi all joining with the Limpopo the boundary between the Northern Transvaal and Rhodesia and finally empties into the massive coastal swamplands of Mozambique.

Bulawayo is the main town in the south of Southern Rhodesia where Cecil John Rhodes is buried underneath his statue in the Motopos National Park, which was full of wild game then, Bulawayo was a thriving industrial town and a center for all the big ranches in that lowveld where huge farms grew wheat, and oats, it was the bread basket not only of Rhodesia but also the poorer surrounding nations like Mozambique and Botswana. Back to the bush: Many of these remote and mostly unoccupied areas have no means of geographical reference without some geodetic land survey being carried out to establish local grid coordinates referenced to the earth's surface. In some countries geodetic surveying is not done at all. Any development is simply ignored as to how it relates to the earths meridian and lines of latitude so it is simply floating, so to speak, and not located accurately at all on the earths surface. In those countries that want some sort of survey control they form a simple local grid-work with a hypothetical reference point with the hope that in some future date it can be connected and transformed onto the geographical system. If industrial, and remember, that in those times there was no such thing as a GPS all reference and identification had to be done by triangulation and trigonometry initially referenced by an astronomical fix(using the stars) to establish where one is on the earths surface. This had to commence with primary triangulation and at a later stage, a secondary breakdown of triangulation. However, this work could only be carried out in what we called the Dry Season otherwise all of these ephemeral rivers would be in flood and traveling would be impossible because many swamp areas are also formed. The angles within these triangles had to be measured most accurately and then locating of the points of the triangles was a very crucial part of the work. Obviously it was an advantage to locate these triangular points on high ground and this involved difficult traveling in hard terrain, both in vehicle and on foot. Having completed a reconnaissance and confirmed the positions we would then spend hours measuring the internal angles to an accuracy of no more than a two-minute misclosure within any triangle which sides varied from 25 miles to 45 miles long and in some cases 55 miles long. (Once again I am trying only to explain enough for the reader to get an idea of, what is a geographical surveyor – Geo = geography, graphical = what it says all making a map of the earths surface shown related to graticules (grids) of the earth. Knowing exactly where one is like a navigator at sea only many times more accurate.

I am trying to give the reader, at this early place in the story, some idea and appreciation of what we were doing in these remote areas and territories so that one can then get with the story in relation to the task being done. It is not necessary to know your trigonometry other than to know most of this work involved forming huge triangles on the earth's surface to provide graphical coordinate control for all engineering and other forms of big developments planned for the territory and also to establish the *real location* of the International Boundaries. Obviously, this was a particular and specialized type of work requiring qualified and bush experienced surveyors familiar with all related calculations and abstracts because this had to be carried out in the field to prove that the work was accurate. One just can't walk away "hoping" it is right when you consider the relative costs of keeping a party out in the field. You could say, then how does one become a "Bushman

Surveyor" if experience is part of the qualifications. Some young men had bush experience in other ways such as being born and reared on one of those outlying ranches and they had all the hunting and bush type of experience necessary. They came and started as survey technicians, learned a lot about the calculating and applications and could then go on back to college and qualify if that was what they wanted to do. Some did but most simply enjoyed that way of life and wanted no other. The operating costs were equivalent to operating a Big Game Safari and we actually met up with and knew several of these "White Hunters" as they were then known and described. Great hunters they were with comparable egos. Their clientele came from all around the world and particularly from the USA I can not remember ever one of their clients being mauled by a wild animal but they always got their quota as allowed by the Department Game Warden. Some clients I know, never actually shot the lion that they took home as a trophy. It takes a lot of courage and shooting skill to stand there and let a lion stalk you and move in on you. The killing shot always, in these instances came from the Hunters rifle. The game licenses were costly and the Safari fees ran at about anywhere from one hundred Pounds sterling to one hundred and fifty Pounds, and these Safari hunters always got something like a $1000 tip on completion of the safari with all the bags. These were mostly very wealthy clients and some great lasting friendships were formed between hunter and client, some white hunters were even invited out to the States as guests of the client. I tend to write a lot about these Hunters because I was very friendly with several and our work often overlapped and it was essential, especially for them, to know what areas we were in frightening off their game. We occasionally had a supper with them and their clients if we met out there giving the entertainment aspect of the Hunter's life a break with us taking over relating our life, however, they are naturally raconteurs or they would not be there, hunting alone wouldn't cut it.

I knew two of these Hunters very well from my earlier years in Kenya and Tanganyika. They always rendezvoused in one of the most well known and expensive hotels where they often found new clients. These hunters also had to be very good socially and entertain because that is what their clients came out for on these expensive trips. Not only the hunting, but they were close to and with their client all day long and every night a fine meal put on by the Safari Team Chef (a real chef) and naturally drinks with entertaining conversations around the camp fire. I am afraid I would not be good as an entertainer night after night, I might have to drink too much to be social repartee. If there was a single woman in the safari some flirting was expected as well. Even some of the married women wanted to be *noticed,* I speak from first-hand stories told to me by these White Hunters. Back in the earlier days in Nairobi, Kenya their hotel was the famous or infamous Torrs Hotel and The Norfolk, both well known worldwide by the Hunters and clients alike. I had several hard drinking nights with some of these hunters up in Kenya and again down in Salisbury and also in the well known Victoria Falls in the Falls Hotel on the Zambezi River. I never drank after I went into the bush on the job, so to speak, but usually had a few parties prior to heading out for several months at a time and again upon return to "civilization". If they had hunted the area we were about to go into they would give us some valuable information on navigable trails and features to avoid such as deep river crossings, where not to camp because of lion territory, trail runs out and information only useful to those temporarily living in these desolate remote areas. There was no such thing as communication, no radios. Once we were out there we were on our own. It is most remarkable that no one was ever seriously ill other than various fevers contracted which were never treated and we developed immunities, however, there is not much immunity for malaria. In those nine years I was doing that survey work we only lost one young surveyor and that was in a semi civilized area consisting of a motel with a phone line hook up and a ranch. He and another man sharing a tent went to sleep following a night in the motel bar with the Tilley Lamp (Hurricane) lit and unattended it fell over and the tent burned to the ground, one man crawled out but the other died, it was very tragic. We treated ourselves for sicknesses and it is remarkable that none of us was ever seriously ill in all those years, in or out of the field. It must say something. We ate sparingly because there was not much to indulge in unlike the safari groups, except game meat, rice and corn meal by the sack full which was for the "boys" (laborers), *it did not matter how old a black laborer was he belonged to the gang known as boys.* We stocked up with canned goods initially before going out but if our time was extended we soon ran out of "luxuries" We shot, ate meat fresh and then cured some of the game meat known as Biltong (Afrikaans for jerky) as we were granted game quotas by the Game Department to kill to feed our labor force (boys) and ourselves, certain game like Kudu, Eland and Roan however, were off limit to us We soon got tired of it but we were all very fit men and boys and worked all the daylight hours and burned the night oil doing the necessary calculations to be satisfied with the work we had done before moving on. If we knew we would be moving frequently like only being in a camp for a few days we did not establish a big camp, we just slept on the ground beside our vehicles with no tents only a Baobab tree maybe for good shade and shelter. Baobabs are like upside down trees, and looks like the branches are in the ground and the roots up. They are huge trees, do provide shelter and shade but a big 500 # limb can drop off with no warning. They are also safe from elephant if you can get up the lower limbless bole.

By the time De Wet showed up I was relatively settled in at Mount Hampden, this place was about 8 miles out of town and I was fortunately able to use my Bedford ½ ton truck to commute. These ½ ton trucks were built for the military in the WWII years and we had an allocation of these vehicles. They were really unsuitable for the kind of work that we did which really needed a 4-wheel drive jeep for this kind of work which we did eventually procure and what a difference, what a relief for covering that type of terrain, those Land Rover's were incredible reliable little vehicles capable of going Most places we wanted. These 1/2 Bedford's (always known both in the army and with us as ½ ton) They were conventional rear wheel drive and required skill in the bush to avoid being bogged down in marshy wet spots or stuck in deep sand. On the other hand they were large and spacious compared to the Land Rover but when we could, we always brought one along as a work vehicle and left it in camp. They were capable of carrying a big load of equipment and gear and two or three black helpers.

This first sortie that De Wet and I were about to undertake was to be initially reconnaissance and establishment of the network of triangle location (points) to be observed from at a later stage. In Southern Rhodesia at that time the main roads between major towns were called strip roads. Two parallel 18"strips of paving set a standard distance apart to fit both wheels. These roads were the main lifeblood of the city interconnection for many years there in Southern Rhodesia When meeting oncoming traffic both vehicles had to move off with one side only on a road strip, and at 50 mph this could be a feat although these strips did not seem to be the cause of many accidents, they were certainly better and cleaner than the dirt roads of which there were many The cities usually known as towns were also interconnected by an excellent railway system and the main heavy loads and equipment were transported by rail leaving these strips mostly free for lighter vehicles. These strip roads were only in Southern Rhodesia (SR) as the country was becoming prosperous with all of the industries, SR had become 70% self sufficient. Tradesmen were emigrating mostly from Britain with a sprinkling of other European Continentals. Fire Cured tobacco was grown and Salisbury was one of the worlds biggest markets with a huge demand for Rhodesian Tobacco. Sugar Cane was grown on big extensive farms in the lowlands 1,000ft to 2,000ft AMSL Hundreds of thousands of acres scientifically grown and managed by third generation white farmers. These Ranches employed thousands of laborers, well paid with standard schools on the farms and excellent provided health clinics with transport on hand and communication to the ranch owner. These sugar cane ranches were small countries and incredibly well managed and provided (Today, they are just "scrub" bush-land again with the clinics and schools burned to ashes and never rebuilt under Mugabe, the ex terrorist now president. However, all he has done is to rob the bank and get International aid which is not used for the benefit of the people. I know those people before and after Mugabe came with his "Freedom" and they cried to me afterwards and said, those were wonderful times Boss Frank All the big main towns before Mugabe had become industrial and produced much of what was needed on a day by day basis except for specialized equipment that had to be imported. However, many international companies and banks had already become established in Salisbury in the north and Bulawayo in the south. Rhodesia was going forward like a house on fire. I repeat, there was no apartheid which the US Universities in particular constantly beat the drum over. These elite professors never came to see it or experience the life but from their ivory towers knew all about it, they thought. These elites were trying to compare (SR) to what they believed America would have been had they been running it when slaves were brought to America. They seem to have a big problem over that instead of moving on. However, they made it clear that the white man must get out and let the native Rhodesians take over. It was so ridiculous we laughed at first but then realized it was going to happen and the country would become derelict and it did. But, these people don't relent nor repent in their arrogance they believed it was all for the best. Thousands of people were starving and dying and the hospitals were now inadequately staffed with doctors and nurses and had become dangerously dirty. They commandeered the huge farm lands which collapsed in the first season. The irrigation system was not controlled and disease and dryness finally killed the crop. They took over the tobacco farms having killed the white owners. Then because of ignorance and drunkenness most of the tobacco fired barns burned to the ground. All those productive lands are now just scrub dessert. Many of the children returned to their old ancestral villages but there was no food and the distribution systems no longer existed. I could go on and on but I hope you get the idea. A sophisticated developed country can not just be deserted and all will be well, that is not how it works and now we have chaos, but political correctness and the bad foresight of our grand masters created one of the biggest disasters in Africa. Huge grain crops grown in Rhodesia fed all the neighboring countries, keeping them from starvation. There is much more to reveal about what happened when these terrorists took over the country which they had no idea whatsoever how to manage. There was no apartheid in Southern Rhodesia and it was a modern country suitable to those circumstances and was and should have been show piece for Africa. Their interests, the American elites were egotistical and hyper political with a swash of some kind of guilt that many of these elites love to grovel in to the detriment of others. Just because you have become a teacher does not mean you know how to do the work of many workers, tradesmen, professionals and government officials of another country, particularly in Africa. The Brits had already pulled out they said because they couldn't afford to keep it as a protectorate. They never protected it at all; we had our own more than capable army with specialist units far superior to the Brits in that part of the world. I have found that some of the biggest liars in the world are politicians.

There was one other man staying out there in one of the other barracks buildings by the name of Edgar, He had himself comfortably set up there too. If one was not a fussy type of individual and could manage with semi camping like circumstances it was a good deal, no hotel bills and there were no water bill or electricity it was all still connected. They were now the responsibility of some government department and as long as somebody was using them they did not intend to close them up at this time of promoting immigration. Several months prior to my coming and moving in, there had been quite a number of immigrants passing through and using this as a jumping off place while finding accommodation in town. There had been a big push to get new specialized trades British Immigrants into Rhodesia, Edgar had a 4-wheel drive 7 ton Bedford truck with high side rails because he was a beacon builder and he nursed and cleaned it daily. The work of a beacon builder was to follow up a reconnaissance group like ours and build 4' high 18" diam. cylindrical concrete pillars with a 2" G.I. pipe in the center to take a 4' high — four finned removable vane on the quadrants and the whole beacon as it was known was built accurately over the steel pegs we left driven into the ground, if it was solid rock we would paint a circle with a cross inside of it. We also made a page of access instructions and a good sketch. If we were being followed up by a builder which was unusual but happened occasionally, we would leave a sketch in the nearest school or similar place for them to pick up. This system worked very well yet communication was virtually non existent for us as you will see later re Louise and me.

By the time De Wet returned from South Africa I was settled in at my ex barracks and not suffering too much by deprivation. It was my choice to come to (SR) and I knew that further along it was going to be good, especially if I could get Louise to come. One Monday morning I went to the offices and a tall leather grained sun darkened faced man strolled out into our big room where we had about 8 engineers and looked directly at me and said, you must be Frank, I have a description of you and a small smile touched the corner of those rugged features. He introduced himself like the gentleman he was to us all and then asked me to come back into his office. He first of all gave me a brief description of himself with a little history attached. He was not happy with the apartheid in South Africa although, of course, he was an Afrikaaner born of Dutch stock. At first I thought, I will never get used to this man, this Afrikaaner. And it took a while, but as he talked on my fears began to abate, this was an exceptional good man and I was becoming relieved about our coming life together in the bush. He knew more about the bush life and it's animals than I ever would and I conceded that to myself right away and was pleased to be going out into the wilderness with such an individual. He had been in the process of bringing up his family and his household effects to a home he had purchased in (SR). He was not an impetuous man and I imagine it took him some time to make this decision and move his family here to a new life and country which was very English at the time. He left a beautiful big home in Pretoria's, the nation's capital city including all their family and friends. It was a very big decision at their time of life, Frank and his wife were in their 50's and two of the kids were at college age with a girl late comer. They were somewhat strange for me at first but I was often around to their place for evening dinners and weekends. Pat, his wife was appalled at the way I was living but Frank told her not to worry because my friend Frank has a great future here in Southern Rhodesia.

He asked me how much pre work I had done and I pulled out the plans and maps that I had been working with and showed him my proposal for new trigonometrical (trig) points, as we called them, based on the mapping contours. I had also been into our records department and enquired what surveys and coordinates were available for that area and these were ready for us to withdraw and take with us, I had even plotted what I could on these maps. As a matter of fact I considered these maps mine, They had been produced from the military aerial survey work we flew in 1949 it was now 1957 and these were the only available maps in a 1:30,000 scale which caused Frank to raise his eyebrows, both the scale and the fact that they were virtually "mine" he expected a 50,000 series and I explained to him how the larger scale came to be used.[Having two Franks is a problem here although we kept our nom de plumes however, I will name De Wet Francois, his real name].

We were now making our final preparations to head out to the remote south western Southern Rhodesian/Bechuanaland (Botswana) border area of the country for a most likely six months trigonometrical safari. This entailed many trips to the stores taking out, checking, and thoroughly testing equipment to ensure their suitable condition. We had looked at the camping equipment but the technical equipment required careful testing Instrument tripods have many clamps and wing nuts and arriving in the back of beyond with missing pieces does not bode well for a responsible surveyor. The precise measuring equipment such as theodolites needs a lot of checking to see that the level bubbles are accurate and the vertical and horizontal plates are adjusted. The theodolite we use on a survey safari such as this one is a Weld T3, Swiss make and the best for the job at that time Trigonometry is a triangle if you remember your Trig., we establish a network of triangles on the earths surface with length of sides anywhere between 20 to 50 miles long, we did have one at 57 miles long on this particular job to establish one triangle. Of course, the points of the triangles are usually located on the high hills or mountains making access difficult in the bush with no roads with only game trails and to compound the challenge we had no communication with one another, nor back to base. Things did change later but for the first three years we managed well without communication point to point. We had solar mirrors which could be mounted on a tripod or a beacon pedestal and with two mounts could send signals in the direction of the suns rays. I knew Morse Code from my early army days but we devised simple numbers of flashes for aspects of the work such as; I am here, let's start etc... Horizontal angles are read to one tenth of a degree and estimated to one hundredth, obviously level bubbles have to be synchronized and plates read left and right circuits in agreement. Also for our comfort, we got two new Indian Pattern tents. These were exceptionally good tents made in India, they were lined with amber colored fine cotton and the fly sheets were lined with blue cotton and they had bamboo end and ridge poles. We grew to appreciate these rugged, good looking tents particularly in the hot times down in that lowveld. It does not do any good to get a way off out in the bush and discover that any equipment is faulty, although during the course of six months many repairs are made. Good surveyors carefully check out and take exceptionally good care of all of their equipment. We had been to Françoise new home on the outskirts of Salisbury (Harare) several times and I had come to know his wife and children and this was a blessing for me because I had no one there in Southern Rhodesia. Finally we gave our vehicles. a careful final check out and we were now ready leaving Salisbury early one Monday morning and headed south on the main strip roads through Chagulu, Kwe-Kwe (frogs), Gweru and finally Bulawayo, a famous town dating well back to the time of the British South African Company who came up from South Africa and had many skirmishes in this area prior to conquering Bulawayo over King Lobengula. Lobengula was a Zulu Chief of this Ndebele State which in time became part of Rhodesia. Strangely enough, Bulawayo is an Ndebele name and means slaughter, not from the war with the BSAP but from a tribal war of his own which he won. (My memory at work), Bulawayo's history is now well documented and covered on the Internet for those who want more than these few words.

We drove on south for a little way in the direction we were to go but turned off into The Matopos National Park, where the statue and tomb of Cecil John Rhodes stands. His body was later removed to Oxford in

England but at that time he was still in his beloved land. We camped that first night off the trail near his statue. It is also a wild animal park but we were left in peace with Rhodes. We had become short on time to make the run through to Gwanda where we had to meet with certain government officials re our entry into game areas and to get a hunting license and allocation and kind of animals could kill so we needed at least one full good day in Gwanda. Gwanda is a mining and farming town on the railroad and has the essentials we needed and to fall back on in the event of any minor emergencies. We also had to set up a mail collecting place and the pub was always more reliable than the Post Office which was often closed when the pub is open so, our mail was delivered to the local pub in Gwanda for collection, a common practice by those living and working in the remote areas, there are one or two ranches on the edge of the game reserve. As it happened we had to stay over for two nights to complete our tasks. François had a relation in Gwanda town, a niece who had married a Southern Rhodesian born man who worked at the local Power Plant including the power lines network. They had a small ranch with some citrus trees and we camped there for the nights. They insisted we stay in their house but only had accommodation for one without shifting the kids, a boy and a girl and Francois wouldn't take it alone. We pitched one tent and had meals together with them in the house. We all became quite friendly over that season we spent down there in the Shashi and Tuli River area and Francois Johnny and his wife were able to catch up on family developments. On the third day we headed out west in our Bedford ½ ton pick-ups and looked for our first site where we could do sufficient reconnaissance and take some good theodolite observations without having to move camp. We early on saw evidence of elephant in the area but were not too concerned as these big wonderful animals are not in the practice of chasing anyone minding their own business. Nevertheless, we used their trails to get about through the scrub brush.

After some time, through constant use we established our own useful trails and identified then on our maps for use by others, particularly our beacon builder's who would be following up later in the season but, before the rains came. Until we established how much line cutting was necessary we worked with our crew of eight boys (I have explained that in the jargon, all native workers were boys when referred to in total). However, we used their names when referring to them on a daily basis but, how many laborers do you need was, how many boys do you need? This was how it was and had been since the days of Rhodes and the BSAP [British South African Police] in the early 1800's). We took our time pitching only one tent and then on the following day covering as much terrain as possible using our binoculars to identify possible beacon sites on the surrounding hills. Making camp in the sort of center of gravity and in a useful, from the point of view of nearness of water and a clean cool site, was important to those living like that and would save us much time having to move too often. In this event, where we finally settled on to make camp, water was not too close and fortunately we had several 10 gallon milk cans to bring enough into camp for several days at a time. We also bathed ourselves down close to the water source whenever time permitted otherwise it was sometimes just a lick. We had little 2'x 2' by 12" deep canvass container that clamped onto a expandable frame but we only used these for times when we had plenty of water. This early in the season, water was not too difficult to find other than the huge wide Shashi River which had no flowing water now but many pools. The closer pools that we were using were roiled, muddy and trodden by lots of animals the elephant, of course, making a big mess. We dug holes nearby and the sandy soil filtered it to some extent but it was hardly fit to drink but not likely to be a problem and I had drank much worse in West Africa. We were able to get it clean enough this way for brewing tea and we had candle charcoal filters in aluminum containers for drinking water. We allowed the water to filter through the chalk encased charcoal filters overnight and filled our Joe-sacks, (canvass bags), to hang on the Bedford radiators keeping it cool while traveling. Amazingly, we developed a manner of drinking little during the daytime even when it the temperatures was high, (Bushmen style) we drank but one Joe-sack each which was plenty. The "boys" had theirs in a clean 4 gallon jerry can. For eating we mostly carried hard tack, Rusks (hard dry biscuits – SA/Eng word), sweet biscuits (very English) and maybe a small can of sausages to heat up, we didn't usually eat much between the morning and evening meals.

With our camp site established, our tents up and the cook's kitchen arrangement set up, a tarp on a pole frame braced to a big tree we were ready to head out and survey the land. We had made our plan of action the previous night; I was to head for the furthest hill through some rugged terrain and De Wet would occupy a closer hill and commence taking horizontal readings onto other hills in our network we could see and occupy readily from this camp. I set out early that morning after coffee and rusks through what turned out to be fairly dense shrubbery and trees, elephant had apparently and unfortunately not entered this area for eating, stripping down the trees and pulling them out. Our trek was circuitous, ponderous and slow, putting me on edge because I needed to give Helio light (sun reflection by mirrors) from the hilltop to confirm identity by including it in the round of observations Francois was taking with his theodolite.

I knew returning was going to be extremely difficult and we needed a lot of luck to retrace those eight miles back to the Bedford in that dense 12 foot high brush. I took a last compass bearing from the hill top and we started down in the deep dusk and very soon loosing all chance of any directional aid other than our bushman senses. Trying to use the compass on short legs not knowing how far one had drifted can only be confusing. As soon as the stars appeared I picked one and kept more or less oriented to one but I did not know when it finally appeared if we were going in the right direction. If we didn't go altogether haywire we would hit the river bed where we left the Bedford in about 3 or 4 hours, 5 at the worst. It was 6 p.m. when we left the hill top and should find the Bedford about 9 p.m. We made good time to the river bed, 2 1/2 hours under the circumstances was good. We were moving too fast to worry about wild game leopard are the only thing to have to worry about at night in this type of terrain and we were too anxious to get back to the Bedford, our canvass sleeping bags and grub (food). We split up into two groups from where we found the river and trudged in that sand in both directions a 20 min time spread and if they see it holler, sound travels loud at night if you know how. We did not see it, I had left it nosed out into the sand for easy seeing because I had anticipated it was a throw of the dice finding it and we didn't have a spare man to leave with the vehicle to keep sounding the horn every 15 minutes. I waited and they came back their length and mine and now, it was a dice throw I said we will go the same distance on my leg and if we don't find it we will light a fire and just sleep the night as we are. Even with daylight we wouldn't know where it was we trudged on and I was about ready to call a halt and find firewood when I caught a dull metal glint in the now moonlight, I thanked God for my sense to leave the Bedford nosing down into the river tree line opening. I just knelt down and kissed the mudguard while the boys collected firewood, an easy task, and fixed a little camp clearing. I brewed tea, of course and forget what I ate but it wasn't of any consequence and we stretched out immediately falling into a genuine healthy earned sleep, we weren't worried about game as we lay close together next to the Bedford truck. It can happen and has happened that a lion or a leopard will come and drag the outermost guy off but we were Bushmen (this term Bushman is not, of course, the native real Bushman, we lived and worked in the bush – an accepted African term for this life) and relied on experience, luck and instinct, both needed in this kind of life. I was back in our main camp by noon that day and Francois was working on his map with angle observations he had taken while listening to our story. He said, Frank, I have told many departments that do our kind of work to only employ experienced men and you have just reinforced my advice. Yes, people have to learn but it has to be in a big group where they can stick around and see if they have what it takes and what is required to live like this. To you it is in a days work, to an untrained person it can mean panic and death or parties having to spend days looking for someone, I am pleased to be working with you.

We moved south repeating this kind of work until we found ourselves at the Limpopo River and realized we were somewhere on the South African Border. Francois said, we should find established beacons just over the border because South Africa was already well surveyed. Checking our maps we saw what would be a hill in South Africa with an established beacon on it and we went there to discover we were right in our assumption. We tied our network into this good trigono-metrical point check and then moved back north and west this time crossing the great Shashi about 3000 feet of sand to cross with only conventional rear wheel drive vehicles. We crossed the Shashe River at a little Dorp (Afrikaans for town) at Selebwe-Pikwe it contained a pub, a couple of stores, a store sells anything that might be needed in a remote area in the kind of life in existence, mostly government type contractors, employees and cattle rancher's They constantly fight and kill lion marauding their cattle and then fight with the game depart-ment who say the ranchers must call out a warden before killing a lion. You work out the details of this for yourself. We camped close by for the night, had a couple of beers in the pub and checked out the store items. We moved on up the west side of the Shashe keeping an eye open for another ideal camp site as we were in a location where we wanted to radii out and do more survey and theodolite observa-tions. In the quietness of my mind I decided I would avoid somehow the problem at my first hill on this survey. We had been out about two months now and I was edgy wanting to see if there would be a letter from Louise, I had written a few and they were all with my papers. However, until we crossed back over the Shashe there was no chance of mailing or picking up any. We came across a large opening spreading out for far enough with beautiful big canopied trees following the route of the river's natural grassland. One would never find openings like this anywhere, it was magnificent used by every kind of game that were hanging around and drinking at the large ponds and natural dams, and enjoying the grazing. We fixed our camp back into the tree line so as not to disturb these lovely creatures, it was not our territory we were visitors passing through and we didn't want golf courses, holiday camps , motels etc, just this magnificent wildness. It was even hard to leave this paradise to go about our daily tasks but what a magnificent site to pitch a camp, Experiences like this came only in the remote wilderness, a gift to wandering Bushmen both the indigenous and proclaimed.

While in this location we must have seen just about every type of animal that lives in that environment and all day long something was there taking its turn to drink and play. It is remarkable that the three weeks we camped at this location we never saw a kill in that open area. We heard the lion grunting around at nights, always curious, and they were checking us out too, it takes a bit of getting used to but we were both experienced with the life and lions so we were not over disturbed but alert naturally and kept our rifles handy. Unfortunately, I was not a photographer and never thought to take advantage and record such a wonderful opportunity to take a plethora of animals in their natural environment: Elephant, Zebra and Wildebeest, (these two groups travel and graze together), Kudu and other big buck and the Roans and small deer all in this opening with the lion and wild cats. In retrospect, of course, I am ashamed of my laziness in this area of opportunity. Not so special now because we have all seen them on TV but that is not a good excuse. My supervisor, Francois took pictures and was a great authority on the animals we saw, he knew them all from a lifetime in the bush and a practiced interest of identification. We reluctantly departed from our paradise and moved on to a new camp site, further north as we were working our way back along our network of triangulation. Our next site was just typical bushveld because we were pulling away from the River and working our way back now in a north easterly direction. Our location was easy for us but sometime breaking a new trail in the high bush can lead one on a winding path.

We had now been out for about six weeks and François decided we should take a run into Gwanda (a small town on the main route) to pick up mail and get fresh provisions. He was also concerned about his family newly resettling into the Rhodesian life, the kids at school and his wife managing and getting into the changed routine. For some families in our way of life it is kind of like the military and he needed to know what was happening because we had no contact whatsoever during those away periods I also wanted to know if I had any mail from Louise now in India somewhere or I thought so, we used one vehicle and discussed these family like concerns of ours as we picked our way through the trails back to Gwanda. Our camps were easily struck so we loaded up one tent and headed out leaving two boys to take care of all our belongings and expensive equipment. There was no fear of anyone going off with stuff it only required someone to keep inquisitive animals away. We finally hit a trail we recognized and soon made camp just out of town. We went to the pub and had a beer and picked up our mail, François had several letters from home and I had three from Louise, I was over the moon because the possibility was in my head that Louise may have come to her senses and thought better of keeping in touch with me let alone the idea of coming back and joining up together. She gave me her itinerary so far and her itinerary forward. Their plan was to work their way back to Tokyo and catch a direct flight to San Francisco. Louise was born on a big hop ranch north of San Francisco, unfortunately, there was a fire, they lost everything and the insurance was expired so they moved to a house in Ukiah and from here Louise went into her Club Services for the military and was seeing the world. She did not yet know where her next assignment would be but I think she wanted Japan. They had taken a *freight ship* to Calcutta, India, a flight to Delhi and bussed and trained up to Kashmir. They were now in Kashmir and their schedule was to make their way east across those countries bordering on China into Hong Kong and finally Japan. Louise's twin sister's husband was Army Intelligence, a Colonel, and had given them contacts in Japan where they had been for an extended tour. Meanwhile this poor Topographical (Topo) Surveyor was longing for her to be here with me in Africa. I was so taken with her that she was now my all and I was afraid of losing her in so many ways. Francois' wife was apparently struggling a bit with her new life and this put some stress on him but as an old soldier, WWII Northern African Campaign, he held his head high and said she will pull through. He then consoled me and said, Louise will come over Frank, she has gone to the trouble of informing you of her whereabouts and itinerary so she is going to keep in touch and by the time they make Japan she will be ready to come, I was not so sure.

We took Francois relations out to eat that night in the only restaurant in Gwanda. Southern Rhodesia had some of the best beef in the world. They had imported White Faced Hereford cattle from England and some very knowledgeable cattle farmers were breeding and rearing them for beef. Hereford's are a natural strong ranging animal and can take care of itself and thrive. As long as they get food and are not allowed to take too long to mature, they are late maturing cattle; the meat is of the best. Southern Rhodesia also was, by this time, exporting beef to South Africa and flying it to countries on the Mediterranean that could afford beef from these exotic animals. Anyway, we had some delicious beef stakes and the usual typical English type food to go along with it but we all enjoyed the evening and his niece and husband commiserated with him about his wife Pat having to take over the home life at this stage. At that time in my life I did not understand what she was going through and why so much talk was involved with simply running a home, I was to discover all about it later in my life as well. The next day, we (posted), mailed our letters, and stocked up on some fresh produce to take back to camp with us. We left the main trail again on instinct and headed in the direction that somehow we knew where our camp was located and we soon found it again. I think here it needs be said that we had that instinct that only those who spend most of their lives in the bush (outback) develop or possess. I don't know what it is but the maze of trees and scrub do not present to us a scenario that is all the same and there is a sense of direction that invariably works. It is just not convenient except under certain circumstances to mark the trail for such relatively long distances and neither is it a good idea to start "tracking" under these conditions, you will never get there. We have taken visitors, both informal and officials, to our camps way out in the bush and they are amazed, and nervous as to how we know the way but how it works, they don't know. These official visitors are more often than not professional men, even land surveyors but, they claim, there is no way that they would be able to find my way in this maze-like set of conditions, what are you looking at? How do you know where you are? Well, it is our job, that is why we are here doing this and we are few and far between. Our department manager's are very much aware of this and hope to find the right people for the job. My back ground, my resume when seen by Oggi Reitz, the senior department surveyor, and Brigadier Collins, the Director, was a little bit of a puzzle for them because my professional qualifications just didn't add up for the position but my background of a survey engineers life in East and West Africa tipped the scale and this aspect out weighed the other which was not in any way inadequate but let's say, thin. There is a large cost involved in equipping and putting geodetic surveyors out into the field, and a big responsibility to mapping and future land development control so, several factors come in to the mix. It can be said we were hand picked and as far as I was concerned I had the best job on the planet and I knew I was very fortunate to be there having this gift of, *knowing where you are!* The Military Engineering School is a very tough course from the point of view of understanding and managing the complex angle measuring systems and equipment and it was attended by army officer engineers from *"The Empire"* Strict also, from the ability to apply, in the field, the mathematics: trigonometry, algebra and geometry and such applications to check the accuracy of the work done at each station before proceeding to the next location and adjust ones progress on the spot. In my 9 years with the department, we were only contract guys. I recall only three who were asked to find another life and the selection of these special surveyors "Bushmen" was stringent. Very few, at that time, were what you might call new comers, they were mostly at least second generation Rhodesians or South Africans who understood that way of life, and applied for the position knowing what to expect. There were some Polish guys we became friendly with, they had moved to Africa after their service in WWII One man had made his way through China and India where he got a ship to Africa before the Russians came. He was a surveyor and obviously had proved himself as a good bushman which he was and he and I worked together later in Northern Rhodesia (Zambia) where he eventually became the Surveyor General for Zambia.

With the receipt of Louise's mail I became unsettled again and it took a week or two for me to get back into the state of mind for practicing and producing reliable and accurate work. We were both aware of this and carried out only reconnaissance work until we were ready again to observe angles:

I will take time here to describe the theodolite observation work because it is the core of the work that we did when laying out a network of triangles on the earths surface to provide geographical coordinates which, in this case, were to be used initially for establishing the border line between Bechuanaland, as it was known at that time 1957 and Southern Rhodesia. There was a practice known as a border commission which was set up between government officials from the adjoining countries and senior field experienced qualified land surveyors. Naturally, these bureaucrats do not like hanging around in remote areas under our safari conditions, so along with the commission group there is another group who physically demarcate the agreed to lines of location by means of stone cairns and/or steel pegs. Another field bush survey team follows up on this and connect these agreed to positions to the network established in advance of the commissions work. Following all this a copy of the calculated documentation along with maps and sketches is provided to party representatives from both countries and the opportunity is given to inspect the final establishment of the border, the invitations are rarely picked up, no one but survey bushmen seem to want to live in this manner. In a way it is like the army too, marriages are affected by this way of life. My marriage lasted because my wife was with me in the field as much as was possible for our life and time together doing that work in Africa.

The previous chapter will provide some idea of what and why surveyors like me were out in the field doing this kind of work for governments. Most governments had their own surveyors who did township layouts and monitored from only an office bureaucratic aspect what trigonometrical geographical field work needed to be done, what it entailed, and who was available to do it; those experienced geodetic wandering contract surveyors such as me. Meanwhile Francois and I were busy winding up the reconnaissance network to establish the adjacent border and a route for a major dirt road to be built along that boundary. Roads that were essential yet did not have a lot of traffic in that time were usually maintained dirt roads. The building of a dirt road is a lot more scientific than the uninitiated may think. The route has to be selected by the use of aerial photography, if available and gravel pits found and marked for future maintenance as well as initial construction. The current dirt status of the route proposed and many more road building characteristics applied. As a surveyor and roads engineer I usually logged this information while in the area for the Government Roads department. We belonged to the Ministry of Lands and Mines and somehow this soil identification work fell into our sphere of work under certain circumstances, if of course, one had the experience and qualifications.

I digress, but it is hard not to, I feel that some of the work and life of a Bush surveyor requires a bit of explanation and technical description. We were now again at the relocated camp in nowhere land, only high desert bush every which way. One of our nuisances of which they were many was ants, big black Matabele ants so named after the Matabele Warrior and tribes once in that area. These ants had an awful sting which would pain for hours. The first thing we did in grassland was to clean off the grass where we were going to pitch the tents and one could smell their warning by moving them. Then we would cover the area in DDT, which is a wonderful repellent next, place our ground sheet down on the DDT and life would be void of these fast attacking fighters of many kinds some causing considerable pain and discomfort.

On occasions it was advantageous to use one tent as our local field office and the other for sleeping in. Before moving away from a completed section a considerable amount of, on the spot, paper work had to be done i.e. checking and abstracting all recorded observations from the record logs (the logs themselves, of course, being the record that was submitted to the office computer department) These log books are never altered or tampered with. With the abstracted information we would calculate geometrical-trigonometrical sums to field fix the position of the new beacons located. All instrument observations had to be compiled and reduced in such a way as to ensure triangles closed within the allowable geographical limits. For two Bush surveyors working in a tent this was a lot of paper work and it was done along with the other field work after suppertime, we would work until about 11 p.m. on this. It was not considered as overtime, there was no such thing, we signed up to do a project and we gave it all we had. During those 9 years with that department we were reassigned over and over saving them thousands of Dollars in most ways.

While catching up on our paper work on this leg of the survey and sharing a tent we always left open the tent flaps at night. We were not afraid of roaming animals and we liked the fresh air. On one of those nights following a late night field office work I went to bed and fell immediately asleep. We worked from before sun up to sun down often returning to camp in the dark spotting many animals along the tired journey back to camp: lion, leopard, hyena and others. Francois sometimes had a shot of brandy but I was not a regular drinker and usually did not drink alcohol when out in the bush doing field work. I was a party drinker and would wait for my opportunity. Francois said he did a bit of a patrol with his rifle before turning in because he heard a leopard snooping around, a low growling sound, then he too hit the cot and faded away as well to a well earned sleep. He awakened suddenly as the leopard he heard walked into our tent; we had our cots one on either side of the tent, and this snoopy leopard, most likely a young one, sauntered in between the cots and passed through and out the other entrance with hardly a notice of us. He had awakened as it was entering and carefully grasped his rifle and waited. I don't know what I would have done as my 1075 was right there beside the cot, I may not have been so stoic but Francois had a lifetime as a field surveyor and knew the animals well that we worked amongst and he used his gut best judgment any sudden move would have startled it and the outcome of that will never be known, We carried that tale for several seasons and it was well known in the department, but we never did close the tent flaps.

Once again we completed a section of our network of trigonometrical triangles and decided on another run into town to check mail, stock up with some fresh foods like potatoes, any other root vegetables and some greens for a few days. We were now well north up the Tuli River area and would have to blaze a new trail eastwards to hit the main road somewhere near a town called Plumtree with a train station, a store, a government Public Works Department and one or two other bureaucratic offices and private houses – not much to get excited over. However, having found our way out and hit the road south of Plumtree we headed north on the strips (parallel 18" strips of paving placed a distance apart to fit the vehicle wheels. If you had a Land Rover the wheels were much shorter axel length and difficult keeping them on the road strips, we usually just kept one side of the vehicle on a strip in this event). We headed for the inevitable pub, showed our ID's introducing ourselves and yes, we both had mail, mine fro India and Francois, of course from his wife in Salisbury (Soweto). Louise was out of India in a freight ship headed for Thailand and the Malay Peninsula ultimately Japan to fly home to San Francisco. (If not in a big hurray these freighters had good deck side cabins) We found a campsite just out of town and got all set up then headed back to the pub for a beer and some supper. One always met others traveling the country in the nature of their work and we shared interesting tales about our lives. The best stories usually came from the guys working out in what we called bush territory and these were the ones most likely to be at the pub which was also a kind of motel and gathering spot. The following morning we mailed our letters scribbled the night previously and pulled into the PWD (public works department) yard where we were able to fill our petrol tanks and a 44 gallon drum to haul back to camp. Picking up the trail again was not too easy and we just had to leave the main road at the approximate distance south of Plumtree. It seemed as if we were heading through ranchland although there was no sign of a ranch house or domestic animals. Had there been one we would have stopped introduced ourselves and explained who we were and what we were doing passing through their land. We switched on our innermost direction finder and kept going hitting a tributary of the Tuli which had too deep of a cutting to cross there where we met it without much digging slopes, a major task so, we headed south, we must have crossed this tributary south otherwise we would remember it. As soon as the cutting leveled out we crossed and then headed slightly north of west and soon recognized the area we were survey-ing, certain high hills and distant mountains and it was then not long before we hit our camp unfortunately, we can't patent these direction finders. Another few weeks and it was time to cut back to Gwanda area, where we started, to begin the complete very careful observa-tions. Francois said, we now needed a second pair of observers to complete this network before that rainy season in November. He de-cided to go back up to Salisbury and meet with Oggi Reitz, the Chief Surveyor to assign two primary experienced observers to assist us with the completion of the job. It was now September of that year 1957 and we had only two months to complete the precise observing of all the reconnaissance and preliminary observing we had done so far. He also wanted to spend some time with his wife and family and see how his new home was turning out, kids, schools etc. Pat, his wife, had not been too happy about coming up to Rhodesia knowing that Francois, as the senior field surveyor was going to have long spells away from home, it was a constant bone of contention in an otherwise happy family. Meanwhile, I was to commence the observing and see how my readings were coming in. I was an experienced field surveyor also of primary triangulation but not at this extension so it was an opportunity for me to get familiarized. These T.3 Wild theodolite cost, at that time, about one thousand British Pounds, they were made in Switzerland and the horizontal plate on which the angle is read off can be read to 1/10 of a second and estimated to 1/100 All angles were read calculated to the 1/100 and were read many times from different parts of the plate. All these observations had to be what we called abstracted to give the best result for that angle. (Remember, any completed triangle in the network has to close to less that 1 minute and the average of all to be under 2 minutes) to obtain this accuracy requires not only experience but total dedication as well. I got busy with my lonely job.

Two weeks had passed and Francois had not come back, I was back north as I had worked my way around on the eastern edge of our network. I decided to have another try at going to Plumtree without having to circle around southwards to find the river crossing so, off I went on a new trail probably not the smartest decision going it alone breaking a new trail. I came to that deep cut in the river again but this time worked my way northwards and came to a wide game trail where they had broken down the banks on both sides of the river bed. It was all bone dry, hard and lumpy at this time of the year and the elephant spoor where they had sank into the mud when it was wet had dried out like concrete leaving deep holes in the ground. I was not afraid of getting stuck but more concerned of being hung up on my differential and that can be a real pain to dig out from in these conditions, nevertheless I went on through and up the other side without amiss. We always ran our tires about10 psi below the recommended tire pressure for moving better over the rough terrain. Unfortunately, if there was any distance of main road traveling involved it meant inflating the tires again, we somehow didn't always do it and tires tended to wear more quickly and it could cause a blow out at higher speeds. After making the crossing successfully I headed for more open land slightly to the north and I made very good progress across this section. I decided to stop after a while like an hour or so and take a look at the range and my suspicions were rewarded, a rangeland with cattle droppings but no sign anywhere of cattle or homesteads. I continued in the same direction keeping a sharp outlook for any buildings and I eventually saw in the distance a homestead and headed in that direction. I came onto a Jeep Trail and recognized it by the narrow wheel width and followed this to the house. There was no sign of anyone around, I opened the door onto the very big veranda surrounding the house and called and called, but no one came. So I sat down at a huge bare topped eating table and in a little while a rough looking individual entered, rough being a torn khaki shirt and pants and an old Boer Trekker hat, a character. In that locale, the ranchers are predominantly Afrikaners, a number of whom moved up from the Transvaal to purchase these ranches offered by the Bechuanaland Government and this man was typical of these South Africans who came in to Bechuanaland. They were rugged and had been reared in this kind of life (existence) and were in the process of developing land that had not changed in a millennium. They built Kraals to protect their cattle which had to be brought in every night for safety against marauding lion and leopard followed, of course by hyena which also attacked once the lion pulled down the cattle or even, in many cases, scaled the kraals and carried the cattle out again to kill and eat them. If this became a practice, and it does, the rancher would lie in wait under the kraal fence and shoot the lion. These kraals were often built of old railroad sleepers planted in the ground and laced together by strong tree logs, they were formidable and yet the lions could get inside. I spoke to him in English, but he only replied only in Afrikaans which I did not yet understand, it was becoming difficult and then he smiled and asked in good English, are you hungry? and he threw a side of beef down onto the bare wooden topped table with a knife stabbed in beside it. At this point, I guess he thought he had gone far enough and he smiled broadly and we introduced ourselves. They were the Maxwells, and they became my greatest friends. Two brothers aged around 30, and one was married to the girl called Kathy and that was John. The old man their father was also around, having his siesta. He had worked in the diamond diggings in South Africa. There was also an uncle and an aunt who I do not think were directly related to the Maxwells or to each other, but old friends of old man Maxwell from the diggings. That side of beef was put away and Kathy brought out tea and scones and we shared who we were. Meanwhile, I had to move on. But I assured them I would stop again on my way back in a couple of days and I did. We now had a ways station along the trail and the beginning of a great friendship. These two boys spoke excellent English but had gone to an Afrikaans school Old Max was from Ireland at a young age but he never learned, certainly never spoke, Afrikaans, and yet his wife, Aunty Ruby barely spoke any English.

In Plumtree I found mail from Louise and she was now in Cambodia, she also said that she had sent me a book to my office address. I stayed at the pub that night and wrote her a letter with all my news, especially about the Maxwells. The next day early I got supplies and filled up with petrol then headed out to visit my new friends and I spent the night there, we had become close friends in a short time, I was almost a family member and later became one. Meanwhile Francois returned with the two additional surveyors to join our team and we got down to planning our approach to observing the network of triangles that we had reconnoitered in great detail to meet the strict closure requirements. I do not want to spend any more time on making you into a surveyor, I will assume from what I have said so far that you have a good idea of what we were doing out there in that far country, remember, this network would be the framework for establishing the border between Southern Rhodesia (Zimbabwe) and Bechuanaland (Botswana). In Africa, most of the border areas are wild country, nobody wants it or likes to be there other than hunters, game rangers and surveyors. Should there be villages and locals in some of these areas then there was also certain government agents like health officials, educationists and others but generally no one but the wild animals whom we knew and loved just as they are.

Going into this phase of the work means more time is spent in one location as opposed to being moving constantly and far reaching to find and establish more hill top points to balance the triangles. We could now establish good well set up camps with a separate sort of office area under light weight tarps where we could gather, usually at nights to complete the abstracting and reduction of all the observing, it can be a frustrating, boring and yet most essential part of the work we do to assure ourselves that all we have done is within the limits of this extremely precise primary surveying. It usually turns out that certain people have a bent towards the reducing and calculations and it is wise to allow this to develop and facilitate these guys in getting on with it. We also have some who are natural hunters and they bring home the meat for the pot and for making biltong (jerky) anytime you come across a bush camp of this nature you will usually find biltong hanging and curing. For the first few days it is covered in mosquito netting to deter the blow flies from laying eggs in it. The hanging meat initially attracts all kind of night visitors like hyenas and other smaller animals so the curing rack is usually on the edge of the camp but not too far away or it will all be gone in the night. We sometimes have watchmen detailed in these bigger camps and they keep an eye on it because some of it is their ration. We all eat great quantities of game meat cooked in a variety of ways that guys learned from their elders as they grew up with it from childhood. These guys that grew up in remote areas on ranches or their fathers involved in remote work for government agencies are mostly quiet types who get on with their tasks quietly and without any "look at me" involved, they are excellent people to work with and have as a friend.

We usually had someone go into town every two weeks to collect mail and get some fresh supplies like any available greens, eggs and stuff one can't store. I went whenever I could and stopped overnight in or out with my new friends, the Maxwells and sometimes if free enough I just went for weekends and cemented our friendship. I was there once when John asked me, do you have your rifle along? Is it heavy enough for lion and I said yes to both questions and he said, early tomorrow morning we will get it, it is a big old one I have seen its spoor (tracks). Old man Maxwell was sitting quietly drinking coffee and said, come over here Frank, I went across and he said very sincerely, we have not lost any lions. He was telling me you don't have to go with those boys but we went. It was a big black one snooping around the cattle kraal John's brother headed off around the kraal and John and I laid in wait. In a little wile we heard one shot and Mike walked up smiling and waved us across and their it lay dead. This lion had caused a lot of damage and killed several younger animals. It turned out that the government had tried leasing this stretch of land out previously to new European immigrants, mostly Brits, but they just didn't have the background, experience or most of all determination to see it through, they moved on to settle in better managed and controlled Southern Rhodesia. During that period of doing that network survey down there we shot and killed four lion on Maxwell's spread. Their neighbors, also Afrikaners, Duplesis, and they killed six lion. A number of years later when Louise and I were down there visiting I asked how many lion had they killed and it was only one in a year, and they were happy about that. This is what the authorities had hoped for, that the ranchers would kill and or drive the lion back into the wilds and thereby enhance the range for more settlements. It never happened, independence began and white settlers, especially from South Africa, were not encouraged to come in. At that time Botswana had a good chief, President, who had been educated at Oxford in England. It was a period when someone with his credentials was needed, there were many white immigrants and they needed support which, coming from the chief of the Bamangwatu tribe, the biggest and main tribe in the country of Bechuanaland was a blessing to these immigrants, many of their grown children are still there ranching, no lions.

The weather was heating up into around 34C Degree's we had the metric system in Southern Rhodesia. We were in low-lands (low veldt) only 700M AMSL and it was getting nasty and it was only September yet and we had much to cover. We could observe horizontally from just after sun up, as the sun rises all is a shimmer so one has to wait until that stops. Then we had a band or window of about three hours after that visibility was too poor for seeing over those distances of anywhere from 20 to 40 miles sides Seeing a six or eight foot high target over that distance requires experience and skill some guys never were able to do it. It was also possible to observe later in the evening but usually for not as long. It was essential to catch the point to be seen as soon as it began to cool about 5 p.m. and one could continue for about one and one half hour. If you were out on a far point then you had to spend the rest of the day up that hill waiting for the evening observing. Most of these hills were mountains and the access at the foot was thick and difficult to penetrate, certainly not a conventional road vehicle access. The climbs were hard and demanding taking on average two hours to climb and find the point then set up a target if the beacon builders had not yet been through. If you knew someone was observing your point then you gave them the target centered over the point and you did what is an auxiliary set up requiring additional abstracting and calculating to reduce the observations to center (I stated no more survey lessons) so just know when you do this considerably more work is involved with abstracting and reducing all that has to be done in the field. And in those times prior to all the hand held calculators it was a laborious effort requiring dedication and care.

We had now been out four months and if we got early rains our job was doomed and we would lose a lot of momentum and costs to have to return to complete the network observing in a later season, Francois also had this weighing on him his first project with the department in Southern Rhodesia. At his time of life, He was then 48 years old, he had taken a big stride to leave a much higher position in Pretoria, South Africa where they had a lovely big home to come and commence this field job usually for the younger men. Our office in Salisbury, the computing section, were anxiously awaiting our results to layout the proposed borderline to be established by a team and later observed and fixed all from the work we would have achieved if all went well, a large burden for Francois. It is not such a burden for an experienced younger man as he doesn't have as much at stake. Francois wanted to arrive in this Southern Rhodesian Department and it involved him, initially, being top man on some of these projects. He later, to Pats delight, (his wife) practiced a more balanced job between office and field. He became a senior field man participating in what projects to do and assigning the staff. He loved the field and was one of the best, so disciplined and knowledgeable on all that was involved in this way of life but, he was a married man with a family and he honored this and was torn between his two lives.

Meanwhile, we progressed steadily with this project and continued the observations with the pairs we set off with. Francois mentioned that maybe I would rather be the lead observer with one of the other two as I was senior but I declined and remained with him. He did the lion's share of observing but he allowed me to be involved in it as well. A good pair of observers not only are fast but an experienced recorder can reduce the readings as they are read out and thereby know at the end of the set that they are most likely accurate and will reflect good results with the final closure. I had come to respect this man and was privileged to be working along side him. He had an endless store of knowledge on life not only bush wise but in general. He was modest in all his ways and yet strong, a Christian of a sorts I had not yet come to terms with and I grew to like him the more I was with him. I needed someone like this I could respect and in some ways emulate. He was filling in some of the blanks in my life. We kept going and the humidity increased as we got closer to the rains, the long arduous climbs to many of the hills was taking a toll on me but Francois acted as if it was all in a day's stroll. I was never robust in the sense of keeping up a walking grind like this day in and day out and I was always glad to get a break. We were not all that far from the Maxwell's and whenever I got the opportunity off I would go. Francois also liked to pay them a visit and then they all spoke Afrikaans except old Max and me, I was learning but old Max always said one language was enough for him and I got the hint to talk with him in English. Come October Louise was now in Japan following her visit to Hong Kong, they sure had quite a trip and a lot to talk about whenever, if ever she got here. I was so looking forward to her coming and my anticipations went up and down like a yo-yo. I was afraid she would change her mind, in retrospect, many years later when I had matured a little I realized what a leap of faith she made. I had lived a rough basic (bare necessities) kind of life ever since getting out of the TB sanitarium Louise, on the other hand, had a more normal American way of life. I certainly did not initially give her the credit she deserved for adapting to our ways without one complaint and I had many in regard to equipment, especially our inappropriate transport but, we were a very new department and funds were not all that plentiful we did, however, get our Land Rovers towards the end of this project. We also got a big 4X4 7 ton load Bedford with long rang petrol tanks and a big built on 50 gallon water tank, this was a tremendous help in loading and moving equipment and transporting labor.

On one of my trips into town for supplies, using the new big truck, I collected the mail and there were several from Louise including a book she had sent. It was about the Man Eaters of Tsavo. A game park in Nairobi, I knew of this book but had not come across or yet read it. However, I had been through the Tsavo National Park west of Mombassa, Kenya. The event took place at about the turn of the 18/19th centuries during the time of the building of the Kenya/Uganda Rail Way. Col Patterson was in charge of the work and two male lion carried of many Indian Coolies who were the workers on the railway, he also finally shot them both. One of her letters said that she and her mother were getting ready to return to the USA in October and that they would take a direct flight from Tokyo to San Francisco. I was very disappointed because I had been dreaming of her coming direct to Africa and not going to America first. Somehow, I felt that if she returned to America with her mother and be with her twin sister then it might take precedence over her joining me here in this my life, it may be that being home had more to offer. I learned later, some time after we were married in Gwanda; that she had provisionally decided to go back to Tokyo and take up her career again as a club director for the American Services. She had a long time friend, Helen Berry; they had been together in Germany for three years and had also covered a lot of touring together around Europe. Helen was a wealthy girl with her dad's money and also had a high position with the Red Cross, of course, I did not know about this plan, they were the best of buddies and Helen was going to have herself moved to Tokyo and the fun could begin again for them. From where I sat, time was running out so I wrote right away, not always the smartest of ideas but I told her I wanted her to fly to Salisbury and not San Francisco, put her mom on that flight and then for her to get one for Southern Rhodesia. I have regretted that spontaneous action many times over. Obviously, I should have allowed her to take her mom back and then correspond with me about how we would proceed from there. I was young, foolish and immature but I wanted her with me and didn't consider anyone or anything else. I mailed it and went to the Maxwell's and told Aunty Ruby about it. Aunty Ruby, old Max's wife, spoke virtually no English after all this time with Max who said, he knew no Afrikaans, he certainly never spoke it. Mine, on the other hand, with the help of Francois was coming along so I struggled to tell her, she could understand English but would not speak it. However, she called for her son, Johnny Boy as they called him, and had me relate the tale again. John said to me, you should have let her take her mom home, she will come back to you Frank and you will feel better about it and that disturbed me because I knew it was the right thing to do but it was too late now.

One night Francois and I were re occupying some far stations for magnetic bearing checks and traveling light to get in and out quickly without having to break up the main camp. This area was rife with game although they were beginning to move on due to water holes in the river beds now virtually dried up and the grazing was all but cleaned out. The Elephant, Buffalo, Zebra and Wild beast (Blauwildebeeste in Afrikaans) and other big game like Kudu and Eland had all left the area now, migrating to what is called the Okovango Swamps, a massive wet-land full of wonderful life. I later worked in this area and had the opportunity to travel through the "swamps" by canoe along the trails made by hippopotamus and elephant, a somewhat dangerous trek but the only way to get through the rank vegetation. Nevertheless, Lion and Leopard were still around looking for weaklings that could not follow out, these were easy targets. Some of the cats always followed the herds as they moved and pulled down the stragglers and the weaker ones. The lesser game can survive for much longer without water but they also know when it is time to go. It is a precarious life for the buck and sometimes to we who think different to animal's, in fact, we think they just live and survive on instinct given to them by God each after its own kind. God put into mans soul, on the other hand, the breath of life and a mind rather than instinct with which to function entirely different to what he gave the animals. Our job was to understand and manage it all what He had created and put under our management, unfortunately, we have bungled it and failed. However, some do their best and God is pleased and helps those to see and understand His ways (end of sermon). Sleeping out on the ground at night in these circumstances under the stars is always a wonderful experience not easily described. You are vulnerable and insignificant in the way of things, big cats could sneak up at any time and we would also be food for the changing and ongoing scheme of things and yet, we never thought of giving it up or wondered why we were there so insignificant and susceptible. In all those years of being a "Bushman" surveyor I never wondered why I was there it seemed like we too were in the scheme of things and maybe we were. Obviously Francois had the same sentiment as he had been doing this kind of life for a lot longer than I. We slept soundly with our rifles and a flashlight (torch) between us on the banks of a river, we were also close to a game a trail from which we moved off but the morning brought many fresh spoors and they had been around taking a look at these strange humans. In this life you live from day to day and sometime moment to moment, and I found that it brought me close to a Creator. Francois was what later I knew as a born again Christian but I had not at that time realized what it meant nor had I yet been called but later, God decided I had drifted long enough, sometimes into useless ways, and He called me out from it, what a relief.

7

News of Louise & Onwards

I told Francois that night as we slept out on the sand at the Kafue River bank under stars, I believed Louise had a decision to make, whether to go on with her career or walk away from it all and join me here in the wilds in this far way remote life of ours. I said I had done my best to describe this life because I wanted her to get a good picture of what she was signing up for, not only with me and our marriage but also a new life on an entirely different plane to what she was accustomed. The life, customs and environment was so different and I may have gone too far and scared her off and yet I felt she had to make that decision now for herself without further delay or any more input from me. She had to want to be with me as much as I wanted her with me here in the Bush in Southern Rhodesia. Some weeks later, after we had returned to the main camp, one of our surveyors came back from a town, Plumtree, with the bundle of mail from the pub, some for François and some for me. In those days when you wanted to get a message to someone quickly you sent a "telegram" and there was one for me inside the large envelope from headquarters. A telegram could be sent on the wires from Japan say, to Africa in a day but then to reach someone in my circumstances it still had to depend on mail pickup. I saw it was from Louise and chills ran through me, not of joy but sadness, I figured she was telling me of her decision to extend further our getting together again but when I opened that well known telegram colored envelope and the few lines said, leaving Tokyo on November 23 which was now three weeks back, and will be staying in the Norfolk Hotel. She would already be in Salisbury, wondering what was up. I quickly told François I had to go and find her. He said, one more night is not going to hurt and I want you to calm down and we have to talk now about something else. He said, please come back as quickly as possible because we must finish this project. I promise you as much honeymoon time as you want then, meanwhile, we will move camp now while you are gone, back close to Gwanda. We have a brand-new Indian pattern tent which I will have setup comfortably for Louise, and I will also asked Nancy, (his cousin), Johnny Haggard's wife, to make all inquiries about wedding parties, etc. then one of the Catholic guys will go along to the mission church and get all the details about the marriage service, reading of the banns etc. I considered that to be a very good plan and I was also sure he was correct about not rushing off all excited and unprepared about everything, a wise old man. (He was considered an old man because he had about 20 years on any one of us and we already knew he was wise.) So the following morning off I went alone for the 550 mile run on the strips up to Salisbury and Louise after all the longing and doubts about her really coming. I remembered her, of course, only from our delightful ocean ship voyage now it was going to be much different to America and I was apprehensive all the way up to Salisbury. 550 miles of road traveling is no big deal but I had bush road to Gwanda, dirt road all the way to Bulawayo, about 80 miles and then strips (as earlier described) to Salisbury. It was getting dark as I pulled into the outskirts of Salisbury but I knew it well. I had a sports coat and long pants at Francois' house, no time to go there now so, I continued over to the Norfolk Hotel on the other side, west side of town, I know the Norfolk and in my real bushman attire I doubt if I would be allowed in the lounges or inside any public bars.

One can dress smart as a bushman-hunter and be allowed into these hotels but it had to be a recognized attire, bush jacket with a cravat at the neck and long khaki starched pressed pants that only one of your boy's know how to do properly. I was a long way from anything like this so, I went into the outside back bar and asked if I could send a message for the lounge. Again, in those days, a chalk board was carried around within the lounges nailed to the end of the broom pole with a bicycle bell on the bottom, and message was chalked on the board and it was carried around ringing the bell in the lounges. Fortunately, Louise was sitting waiting for dinner and glanced up for the bicycle bell and saw my message, Louise I am here in the bar and in a short while she was there beside me, Oh! My Lord! And what a wonderful experience that was. After all that time and concern she was right here with me and I was never going to let her get away again. (I didn't, we were married for 49 years) There are many things I have said, I don't want this book to become and I don't necessarily want it to be a love story. However, I was in love and the love of my life had just arrived from across the oceans after eight months of wondering and waiting, so there's a lot of love here right now. We checked with the bell captain at the front and he confirmed I would not be allowed in as attired. I told Louise to pack again, I would wait in the bar and then meet her at the main entrance, load her gear and we would move to another hotel where I would also be allowed in as dressed and we could plan from there. I knew many good hotels where we would be admitted and have a peaceful night. We had a good meal and went to bed happily. The next morning at breakfast I told her that we only had this day in Salisbury and then we would have to head out directly, and I explained why. I told her, of course, that we would have many opportunities to explore in Salisbury later on in our new life together. She was smart enough to know that things had changed, we were no longer on a voyage and I had to get back to our extensive observing project at the border. She was now the apprehensive one hoping that she would fit in with the bush survey group. I was sensitive enough to realize this was a big decision that she had made and a huge step she had taken, and she wanted to do it well. It was not only our marriage yet to be, that she wanted to be a success but she also wanted me to be proud of her on the job. Not many guys in those days took their wives out on the job with them, we were the mold breakers and Louise wanted to do it just right.

She was so happy and interested in all that we saw as we traveled back down to Bulawayo. We went a little way into the Rhodes National Park to Rhodes tomb outside of Bulawayo and I explained to Louise, who Cecil John Rhodes was, and what he did and then we had our snack and hit the road again for Gwanda. We went straight to Johnny Haggard's house on arrival and Francois was there, as it happened. We left in a little two vehicle convoy and went straight to Louise's new tent off-loading her gear beside her cot. François had had a great job done for her and I believe she would be fine until the wedding. Each tent group had to have a "long drop" hole dug with a little pile of dirt for covering the droppings and a little seat trestle built and our "boys" had excelled themselves for Louise. Later, we showed her how to operate her Tilley Lamp, a kerosene pressure lamp and, of course, she had a couple of good flashlights and a hand gun, the latter if she wanted it. She was not too far from me but formally far enough, Francois said, you two are not married yet!

François and I had a couple of beacon points to revisit then afterwards we needed to be in camp for a few days checking out observance recordings. This gave Louise and me the opportunity to go meet with the priest and talk about our wedding arrangements. There were in-structions to attend and certain prayer functions to have with the priest as well as view the procedures for the wedding day itself. One thing I still had to do was to purchase a car and I found this old banger in

Gwanda. Unfortunately, we did not know just how much of a rattle-trap it was, it sucked in all the dirt, especially of course on dirt roads where we used it the most, as there was no seal left beneath the floorboards and the noise forbade conversation, not a very good buy. However, without having to go up to Bulawayo, there was virtually no choice available to us. So I closed the deal and made the best of it. Meanwhile, Nancy, Johnny Haggard's wife, had been making wedding reception arrangements and all was well, except for the cake, which was coming down from Bulawayo 80 miles distant. The vehicle, which was bring in the cake turned over on the side of the road, but the iced cake survived more or less intact except for a little straightening up by Nancy, we were so lucky as the wedding was to be that weekend. Johnny Haggard was my best man and the owner of the pub's, wife stood up with Louise and we were all gathered at the mission waiting for the marriage ceremony to begin when a group of local people trooped up to receive communion and I will always remember that with a smile. We were married with a typical Catholic service in this mission church out there in the Bush and then we all gathered at the pub for the reception. It was a grand occasion and I had many people to thank for it. However, I had not yet told the Maxwells that we were married and that was trouble ahead for me. Our wedding was on this Saturday and we did not leave until Monday to drive up to Bulawayo and then on over to the Zimbabwe National Park, where there was a large group of ancient ruins. These structures were built of dry stone and patently dated back approximately 500 years. Not a great lot was known about who built these structures but there were many theories and the pamphlets were there at the park center. We stayed in a hotel there for three nights visiting many parts of this strange land before returning to Gwanda. I thanked Louise with all my heart for coming back and making me that happiest guy alive. I told her that I could understand what a difficult decision she had had to make and I loved her for putting her trust in me yet hardly knowing me or much about me.

I told her, I will never let you down, we are together now and your life is my life so let's live it to the best of our ability, and that was my real wedding vow. She told me that she had no hesitation about coming to Africa and beginning a new life with me but she wondered was it just a passing fancy on my part with an attractive American girl, I simply told her no, it is an honor with a lovely American girl.

Upon our return to camp, we set up a large work area where we could carefully put together all the observations regarding our work here: observation record books, the abstracts, checks and the analysis and calculations. All these documents were to be handed in to the office and we were ensuring all was complete before leaving the area. The rains had started now and there was very little chance of going back into those areas of observations. However, our results all appeared to be in order and triangular closures were good. I know Francois was now in a hurry to get home and I told him to go and I would break up camp, check all our equipment and make sure we all got back to Salisbury together. Louise still had letters to write telling people about her marriage to me, the wedding and all, and she got on with that while we checked, packed and loaded the delicate instrumentation and eventually we were already to leave. Then Louise and I went to Haggard's and thanked them so much for all they had done for us and we hoped we would be seeing them again soon.

I told the gang to proceed on up to Salisbury and make arrangements with the Department store-man to receive all the equipment we had been using. I reminded them to have out all the withdrawal sheets for him to sign off on, be sure everything was received with "in good condition" comments and then take off for vacations leaving a list on my desk as to where everyone was going and for how long. Louise and I now headed for the Maxwell Spread. It meant crossing a river bed which was starting flowing lightly in the rock sandy bottom. The crossing was very rough and I got my vehicle hung up on the differential on top of a rock, I simply could not move it without a lot of digging so, I told Louise to sit tight I would walk the 8 miles and get Johnny Boy, a son of the Maxwell's, to come back with the jeep and pull us out. I told her to roll the windows down and relax; it was hot in the bottom of the river bed but tree shaded. As I climbed the far bank a Leopard crossed right behind me and I thought about Louise and the lowered windows, a target for a Leopard. I went back and said, on second thoughts roll up the windows to 9 inches open and I left again watching out for that dashing yellow shadow. I moved quickly because I didn't like leaving her there alone. I was hot and flushed by the time I arrived at the spread and only Aunty Ruby, the Afrikaner wife of old Max, was available. I explained as best I could in that language that Louise was in the car stuck in the bottom of the river and we had to go get her. She gave me a hard look then went to the other side and I could hear her yelling in Afrikaans, then an engine started up and around came John with two black boys on board, he said hop in she'll be okay but they had not met her yet. We were there in no time and the boys got a rope onto us and we were up the bank Louise smiling and waiting to be introduced. As it turned out they absolutely adored her starting right there with Johnny Boy. She told him we were married and he said Jarragh! An Afrikaans exclamation, then he turned to me and said, you are dead meat Ma has been preparing for your wedding reception here like you told her. I knew I was in deep trouble and John said we will just ride it out and have another reception. Then he told Louise a bit of the story of me finding them and becoming like another son of Aunty Ruby and Old (Max) Maxwell.

We arrived and tea was brewed, the introductions made and we sat down for tea and flap jacks. Aunty Ruby called me into the kitchen and John came with me. She was upset and said you are like mine and you went and did this thing. I tried and I explained to her how we didn't have much choice the way it all went down and John took over for me. She listened to him for a little while then said let him speak for himself whatever way he can so John left us to it. Finally she hugged me when I was almost in tears and said, my son you are still welcome so back we went to the others for tea smiling and holding hands. She went and hugged Louise and said she had been waiting for her all of her life, John interpreting, and it was all very good. We had a big comfortable room which had obviously recently been prepared for a wedding couple, I don't know who got kicked out. The following night there was a party like you have never seen, big barbecue known as a Braai Vleis in the Afrikaans language and lots of other goodies. The Du Plessis, their neighbors, and another old friend of Maxwells from the diamond diggings came too and old Roddy Barker, also of the diamond diggings, who spoke both languages fluently. There was beer, of course, and brandy, a South African liquor favorite, and some of us drank a little too much but it was a wonderful wedding gift to give to what had a short while back been a passing stranger now an adopted son and daughter. As I said, Louise's popularity only grew. We stayed several days and they were disappointed hoping we would be there for a couple of weeks John Boy said there were a couple of Lion we had to kill and the old man told me again he hadn't lost any, he didn't want me to be obligated to go Lion hunting. What a magnificent interesting family, Max had made a bit of money on the Diamond Diggings at Vereenaging near Germiston outside of Johannesburg and with the proceeds they bought a small cattle ranch in Tzaneen close to the Botswana Border area but they did not get along too well with the local authorities and when the Botswana ranch offers came up they applied and were accepted. So they sold their South African ranch and moved over. It was hard for us to leave them but we too had to get on with our job and get back up to Salisbury but we made many return visits during our time in Southern Rhodesia. On the way up to Salisbury, just Louise and I alone it was good. I explained to her how little of a salary I got and we would not be able to go into a hotel when we reached Salisbury, we would have to camp outside of town or maybe the Mount Hampden old army facility may still be open. When we were out in the bush we got an allowance on top of our so called salary but once off the trail we were back on basic salary. About 12 miles north outside of Salisbury, on new unincorporated territory, the town surveyors friends of mine, told me that they were surveying five acre land parcel lots which would be going cheap for those who could get in on it. I told these friends of mine I wanted one and they said they would give me a heads up with all the details. This is what I told Louise and consequently, we did not want to spend money on hotel life when in from the bush. We were trying to save up to put down a deposit on one of these mini ranches and build a house. It was unincorporated and there were little or no applicable building codes, it was perfect for us in our status.

As we came on into Salisbury we passed close by the old army barracks and I was hoping they would still be useable and we were lucky, one of the beacon builders in from the bush had also moved in there and that kept them open yet a while. We staked a spot and off loaded our equipment. Edgar said, he had two boys there one a cook and he would tell them to watch out for us and cook for us as well. We went on into town and the office. I introduced Louise to the guys who were there but was sensible enough not to take her around the upper echelon yet until she had a chance to clean up and sort herself out again.

When Louise saw how our life was to be for some time, she sorted through her gear and her possessions and put two footlockers into storage. Bless her heart, it moved me because she made no complaint and dealt with it like it was a routine thing which, for her certainly was far from normal. I never forgot those moments and almost every day she moved up one more notch in my estimation of a beautiful, courageous and accepting women We had a better car by this time which I left with her and told her to explore a little on her own, meet me for lunches and again in the evenings some time for a drink, everyone drank and drove in those days. It all worked out well and she was popular with all the guys and by this time knew the shakers and movers who, if they could catch her coming in to the office took her off to their own offices and enjoyed her company and her American accent and her life story. She had plenty to tell in that most delightful way of hers. I can't help but think that they must have wondered why a smart competent obviously well educated professional American girl had settled for a barely making it contract surveyor, but she handled it all with ease and aplomb.

Francois had taken another few days off and was helping his wife, Pat, catch up with it all, schooling for the kids, all the local activities with their many friends and planting a great garden. They were in the best part of Salisbury and Pat wanted a good garden, they had had a beautiful home and garden in Pretoria, the capital city of South Africa, where they had lived prior to coming to Southern Rhodesia. Our work relationship was over for the wet season and Francois was not going out again until the next field season. He had me in his office several times working on our records prior to their submission to the department. He mentioned subtly that I could remain in office too if I wanted but I simply didn't want to stay out at Mount Hampden for another four or five moths and we needed to save on the allowance that was paid extra when in the field and put it towards our own future. Employment in the off-season that is the rainy season, the work we do is of a different kind, and we were able to be confined to the more manageable areas close to navigable roads. In the rainy season many areas are very difficult to navigate and at times we would be semi-stranded. This was a certain set of circumstances that we were accustomed to and managed carefully but without insurmountable problems. However, living under canvas in the heavy rainfall areas required a lot of experience and ability to live under these damp conditions which were often trying of the patience. In a more progressive country where lots of development is happening it is essential to have good easily identifiable level marks known as bench marks. A level Mark is an identifiable elevation that is a known datum on a network of elevations carried throughout the country. These networks were constantly being extended and this is the kind of work we did during those heavy wet season. We would take a length of highway from town to town and build benchmarks at approximately 1 mile distance along these routes and main benchmarks at 20 mile intervals. This was in a sense a boring job but we settled for it during the rains and made the best of it by getting to know the landowners along the route and often making lasting friends. I will not go through another drawn out description of what is known as precise leveling, and it was very precise. So precise that leveling observations could only be read in the early morning hours before the temperatures became too hot or in the late afternoon hours upon cooling down.

We had a good portion of the middle of the day to ourselves and although we were under canvas in the wet season it was a good life and we enjoyed ourselves. My colleague was a Welshman and he had done a lot of this kind of work in England and was familiar with it. We struck up a good buddy friendship which lasted well on into our immediate future even to pooling our savings towards buying a home in Salisbury. The first section we did of this precise leveling work was along the section between Mozambique and Southern Rhodesia. About the 45 mile stretch from in the Inyanga south to Umtali and although we were on the main road it had a lot of bends and many hills. We had our usual group of boys and cooks and we were able to keep our main camps for long periods and this made life easier. The first land we made camp on belonged to a tobacco farmer, her husband was dead and she, Joan McFarland, carried on with the growing and oven curing of tobacco. In those days 1958 tobacco was a desirable product and the Rhodesian tobacco was most desirable on the world market and auctions, Salisbury, Rhodesia had one of the largest tobacco auctions in the world at that time. Joan had a very experienced manager who not only grew the best tobacco but also managed the farm in a general way leaving her more free time for herself and family. They were successful and made good returns on their crops. All big farms built schools for their laborers children which also included a number of local children in the surrounding area, as many as they could comfortably fit in. The educational authorities inspected these schools and gave them a rating and recommendations. The farm also provided clinics for possible injuries and sicknesses which included families and these clinics were staffed by experienced nurses and the approved authorities of the state.

that area for about four months We established another 40 miles of national level values, these benchmarks were valuable and used by surveyors and engineers doing government work and private township work in that area. We were in and made several new friends during this period. And a couple of these new acquaintances, being private surveyors, who had invited us to dinner and a game of Bridge regularly once or twice weekly. They said that they were delighted to have us as bridge players and friends and we sure enjoyed the invitations, being all surveyors the conversations at dinner-time were very interesting. Any long weekends we would go down to Beira, a big port on the coast in Mozambique. This town also provided amenities and good tourist attractions for the Rhodesians and the accommodation ranged from beach cabins to big Hotels and we tried both. Joan sometimes came with us on these expeditions and we had a wonderful time down there drinking plenty of wine and beer and eating cockles on the grand hotel verandas overlooking the beach. Returning to Umtali after one delightful weekend in Beira we stopped for lunch in an inland grubby looking bar however, we went in and had the typical Portuguese cooking of fish which was good and when we finished I went up to the bar to pay one of these two big tough rough looking individuals. After settling up he said, you go now! Then to Taff you go! But to Louise, he said, you stay! I said, let's get out of here and we left quickly. Those weekends were amongst some of the best short vacations I have ever had, we came back with many bottles of good Portuguese wine in our vehicle trunks, and as long as we declared two or three bottles the Rhodesian Customs levied a small charge and ignored what they were certain was stashed in the trunk, those days were wonderful memorable times. On one occasion coming back through the customs into Southern Rhodesia the guy in front of us said he had nothing to declare. They told him to open his trunk and there were 10 bottles of wine. They took them all away from him and he had to pay something as well, I guess he learned a lesson not to try his luck so greedily. Eventually the job in Umtali (a town in Southern Rhodesia) came to a close and we returned to Salisbury to start getting ready for our next dry season project in the Bush. Louise and Joan had become very good friends and were often in Umtali town doing whatever it is that women do when that out together shopping et al.

On this occasion while we were back in Salisbury we rented an old house in the lower part of town, (the other side of the tracks), it was built of mud, sun dried bricks, adobe's and we discovered, unfortunately, that they contained bed bugs that came out at nights to feed on our delicate flesh and we were not long vacating this old house. Instead of going back to the Mount Hampden accommodation, the vacated army depot, we pitched camp outside of town in a park called the Balancing Rocks Park and we found it to be very pleasant although a longer distance from our office. We cleaned, tested and handed in our equipment, this equipment is very delicate and expensive and we had to handle it with great care, and we very carefully handed it in to

the store-man. We now had to spend some time in the office reviewing and studying for our new job on the available maps, mostly the
30,000 series I was involved in producing when I was a soldier in East
Africa. The work was to be in Northern Rhodesia (now Zambia) close
to the Congo Border. This area that we were about to survey was going
to be very tricky, it was right up in the north of what was then known
as Northern Rhodesia. The area to be surveyed was the usual network
of triangulation up along the Katanga (Congo) border separated by the
wide fast flowing Luapula River. It is about 700 miles from Salisbury
what is now known as Zambia. All of the country's standards were at
a much lower level than that of Southern Rhodesia which rated highly
for roads, towns just everything. To get to this area one had to cross
the Congo Pedicle a leg of land protruding deep into the north section of Zambia almost cutting it in half and of course, controlled by
the Congolese army requiring visas and passports to enter and pass
through. My passport was a Southern Rhodesian one and I had to
quickly renew my old British pass-port, Louise thought she would be
okay with her American Pass-port. I was not so sure about that, however, we decided to go with what we had now. We needed more time
of course preparing for this big job which was so far away and out of
contact completely with our headquarters. Our now old friend and
mentor, François DeWet, had gone out locally with camping equipment to do a small job it was local but very far and he was out of
touch with us. He would be the party leader for this new safari job in
the North meanwhile we were getting together everything we needed for a project of this magnitude. Not only did we need equipment,
plans maps and data we also needed to be armed to defend ourselves
against wild animals and terrorists now roaming various parts of that
country and the part we were going to was one of these areas. We had
been hoping our new allocation of Land Rovers had come through and
we were told they would be available very soon. These land Rovers
are incredibly dependable vehicles and although smaller we preferred

them to the Willy's Jeep, the big jeep still had a lot of suspension problems in rough territory and we did not need that kind of trouble as we
would have no garage maintenance up there. We also wanted good
camping equipment and we were told a brand new order of Indian
Pattern tents had arrived that were ear marked for our job, we were
going to be gone for a long time and needed good tents. I tried to
talk Louise out of this one, Northern Rhodesia at that time was not a
very good place to be, they were beginning to have dangerous gather-
ings for independence and we would not be welcome in many places.
Already terrorist activity was going on there. She declared that she was
not going to be left behind, she had married me to share my life in all
related circumstances so that settled that one and we didn't discuss it
further although on the inside I was very concerned over the situation.
The days were long gone, unfortunately, when we were welcomed
anywhere in those British Protectorate areas. The people had been
willfully stirred up against the white-man they had been told that the
white men were robbing them of their heritage by a group of their own
tribal people indoctrinated for this very purpose. Consequently, it was
a shame as they were the losers, it was their own people turned terrorist who were robbing them and continued to do so. Their standard of
living dropped immensely after independence when the gangster terrorists moved into positions of power within the country, they simply
robbed the coffers. No accountancy was kept, they spent prolifically
as if money simply grew on trees and they lived at a fast pace at a
very high standard of living at the expense of all else. Of course aid
began to trickle in but it was considered bad form to expect them to
account for it or use it wisely for the benefit of the people, they didn't
care about the people. When the government was monitored and controlled by the white man funds were allocated, audited and a record
was kept as to how it was all spent this was never again done because
it would be a record of their pilfering of the peoples money.

Our next big survey safari was on the north side of the Zambezi River in a huge area marked off by a thick line on a useless map titled Game Reserve. This area of land was about 500 miles by 400 miles and it was a game reserve but not in the sense of being a tourist area it was, at that time, some land not defined or occupied but straddled the boundary between two countries not yet demarcated or "fixed" on any map (there was no map) We had to demarcate it, have it agreed to by all representatives and then leave it so that when the area was finally flown and mapped it could be plotted.

Kafue National Park 1958-59

The Kafue National Park is also in Zambia but in the south western area close to the Kafue River which joins the Zambezi River to the south of there near the big hydro electrical power dam we built in the Kariba Gorge. Our part as representative government surveyors (then Southern Rhodesia) in the dam construction was to define the high water level, the main high tide contour around the lake which would be named, Lake Kariba. The contractors needed this line to begin a huge demo-clearing of the trees on a 100yd. swathe for a clean shoreline. This was a massive task and the international general contractors, one British and a South African did a super job. They somehow got the old chain from the Queen Mary, that is now docked in Long Beach Harbor, and slung it between two Caterpillar Bulldozers D9's — the D 10's were not yet on the drawing board, but the D9's are monsters. They cleared a path and cut out big timber and burned the remainder as they moved on leaving a row of huge bonfires, the indigenous women carrying off as much as they could before the huge bonfires were lit and burned in the cleared areas.

This valley along the Schukmanburg Trail, (an Afrikaner explorer) the same route Livingstone used in his journey along the Zambezi.

Schukman, of course, an old Dutch South African (Afrikaner) pioneering in that area and settled there thus it got his name. In those days 1888 in that area along the Zambezi there were little or no indigenous tribes other than this one now that was following the bulldozers for firewood and useful posts for house building and kraals. Of course the government had to become involved and the bureaucracy immediately increased accordingly. This tribe, The Schukman Tribe, had to be relocated to higher ground and big government insisted that it must be done by truck transportation. This was a huge undertaking because the tribe was spread all along that Valley for over fifty miles. Had it been left to the contractors to manage it would have been a comparatively simple undertaking, but the contractors were advised that this was not part of the contract moving the locals to the higher ground on the north side. This was a lateral move of about 40 miles and they were compensated for disruption and supposedly enabling them to rebuild their houses in the new area. These very ancient indigenous people we assumed knew very little about the way modern business works and are transacted. However, they devised the idea of walking back down the escarpment and being compensated again to relocate once more in the high ground. No one knew these people or how many they were but they obviously were shrewd and I believe some of them were re compensated several times before the penny dropped in the bureaucrats mind. Evidently these "indigenous" already had us figured out. Later, having spent several times the budget for this relocation each village head was made responsible for the relocation numbers, Ah!

A new town was built in what became Kariba close to the dam wall and it was a real new well designed Township. Later, when the lake filled it was also a Tourist Ctr., There were Lake Trips which went out and had plenty of room for traveling along the 300 mile lake length and 50 mile across. However, in the shallower areas of the lake the trees were still there standing visible under the clear water and great care had to be taken not to foul the boat motors in them. The lake, of course, by then was full of crocodile along the edges and shallows which had already been there when it was the Zambezi River. It was a very successful dam construction and hydroelectric scheme built by a British contract.

We went there in that Kafué Game Park area to do another primary triangulation job and we were six white Rhodesians and our regular black boys of 10 and then hiring locally what labor force as we needed them. We drove northwards towards the town of Chirundu on the main road north then turned west towards Mazabuka, a farming town and area en route the historical named town of Livingstone and on to the Victoria Falls town-ship on the Zambezi River. Kalomo is part way between these two towns. It was a long round about trip but the alternative was south to Bulawayo and then north to Victoria Falls and cross the old Zambezi bridge into Kalomo, and is just as far in the south round direction. Kalomo was another one of those government depots consisting of Roads Dept (PWD); Local Veterinary HQ – there was a lot of Tsetse Fly over in that National Park area and the Veterinary Dept. had a sub group of Tsetse Fly control people with Special check points on any minor roads in or out the Kafué Territory. One has to drive into a kind of shed, the "fly-sheds" and the (operating boys) inspect for these Tsetse's and they have to count and record how many were traveling on your vehicle. Also, who you are, and on what authority and business you are traveling on in a controlled Fly area. Eventually, you and your vehicle, including the load and possessions get sprayed with the fly killer. Another animal control sub group is watching the movement of wild animals to protect cattle ranchers in that area. There were also resettled tobacco farmers from South Africa growing sun cured tobacco, not as desirable on the international markets as the Rhodesian flue cured but good for the local markets and sales

Tsetse Fly are unable to fly distances greater than 500 yards some veterinarian worked out so, a massive bush clearing job was undertaken to the south and partial east side of the game reserve to protect these farmers cattle and stop the Tsetse from spreading. The government wanted to encourage farming and therefore undertook this clearing project that was in effect when we went in. One of our guy's Land Rover became lodged in a huge rock right in a12" deep water at the river crossing (a poor driver) and I was following him. Of course, we got out of our vehicle and went to help free him. While doing this we were bitten dozens and dozens of times by this swarming Tsetse's and it is a vicious bite. Louise came to help and I actually ordered her back into our Land Rover and keep the doors and windows closed. She was allergic to bites and these would have killed her, not the Sleeping Sickness, the allergic reaction. There are, supposedly two kinds of Tsetse Sleeping Sickness one affects animals and another humans. I never believed this because young black children in that area came down with the disease and eventually it kills them, any time one of us got a flu-like condition we said uh-uh the sickness. The supposedly laziness that comes with it well, we often had that. Our employers knew nothing about Sleeping Sickness but made certain they never went anywhere near where Tsetse were reported to be. They reminded us that we were contract guys and we had work to be done in this area, *if we wanted the job,* goodie for them. In today's world this would not be allowed or possible the people in charge would be held accountable to at least understand the situation and the danger of working in areas where Tsetse Fly exist. They would also be held accountable for sicknesses so, they had better have the insurance coverage on behalf of their employees contract or otherwise

There was also a motel in Kalomo, hotels in these areas consists usually a few round thatched roof huts with water piped in and, of course, locally built wooden beds but to us it was a luxury and we made many friends there at the hotel and bar.. There was one South African who had a garage, a petrol station and he owned the hotel which his wife managed the running of. The South Africans were very good entrepreneurs and you would always find them doing something in these remote areas far away from home. They love the wild life away from government and its controls and we were very much of the same ilk. After introducing ourselves and staying over for one night getting all the valuable information that these people knew about the area we moved on into the Kafué Wild Life Reserve the following day. We passed through the ranch lands and the tobacco growing fields then the wide cleared line and eventually a high fence, no Tsetse check is necessary going in obviously but we introduced ourselves to the Tsetse boys and told them we would be in and out occasionally and they smiled happily in there lonely existence. However, they had already established a little village of wives and families and were apparently organized. Revenue Monies for all these operations which, of course, benefited the local inhabitants all came from a most prosperous thriving industry of all kinds both from big farming and major township industries. All this was lost after independence was gained and then taken over by Mugabe and his ex terrorist thugs.

Meanwhile we pushed on identifying our whereabouts as much as possible by distances from recognizable features on the maps made by my group in my army days. When we figured we were somewhere towards the western side of the park, we had two groups working independently to check our initial position. Of course, later once we began our survey with an Astronomical Fix and orientation we would know exactly where we were. The topographical features on the 1/30,000 maps were fairly accurate because they are photogram-metric interpretations of aerial surveys which we did in 1949/1953 This was the only accurate topographical mapping available at that time, it was also used by the dam builders in locating the Kariba Gorge where the dam is built. They did however carry out some low level flying to enhance the clarity of their critical dam wall areas. To continue, once somewhere in the center of the area we were interested in we split up into two groups to look for an ideal campsite seeing that we would be in that one location for at least four months. We knew that at times we would be away from the camp when establishing new points and observing from them. This was par for the course so to speak but it is always good to have a well established base camp, if possible, in the area of operation.

To briefly summarize again this is what we were doing in this area. Establishing points on the earths surface with accurate coordinates (a reference) so that anyone using them now or in the future would know exactly where they were in relation to all geographical positions on the surface of the earth (We had no reason to believe GPS was in the pipeline to one day appear) These points we were establishing would be used by a team made up of representatives from the abutting countries to agree on and establish a permanent international boundary between these two countries, Zambia (Northern Rhodesia) and Angola. (Angola, after their wars was divided into many smaller countries of which I have no knowledge)When these Commissions are conducted, they are made up of senior government representatives from the Departments of State and selected surveyors again, who are entrusted with provisionally marking the new boundary until they can return to fix (calculate coordinates along the boundary) by use of points we were now establishing and later additional traversing along the new boundary. These boundaries were new only in the fact that they had not been agreed, whereas previously, they were floating and problematic uncertain areas. The Commission didn't care about these out of the way hard to reach places and many times would not go to the areas telling us we had the power to do it as we showed on the mapping and aerial photographs and they signed off on that.

This area around the granted Kafue National Park which, of course, was not fenced off was one of the best and densest game populated areas since the well known parts of Kenya now virtually depleted and wild animals all killed or, in the case of the elephant, destroyed. After these Game Departments and Rangers became indigenous they also became corrupt throughout and permits and licenses were sold to the highest bidders and international poachers came in like terrorists to harvest tusks for ivory, it all became uncontrolled and corrupt. The take over department heads, completely inexperienced, were warned about all of this and those moving on were told that they were racists. Not true of course, these white rangers had dedicated their lives to protecting these areas and animals for a low salary but they believed in what they were doing, they loved that life and the wild animals. We moved into this animal densely populated area right off the bat, every type of wild animal you could identify, almost not bothering to move away from us. We noticed this first with the elephant; they were everywhere tearing down the tree vegetation for food, they eat the tender branches and leaves that is what they do. We had to drive carefully through them and they were not unduly perturbed, obviously, very little hunting had been done in this area. It is not an area easily accessible and this had been a sort of protection for these wild animals. To see them like this in all their glory with little concern for a group of Land Rovers weaving quietly through them was remarkable and a precious gift from the Almighty. He gave us these creatures to look after and care about and we did, these park rangers whom we came to know were completely dedicated to their perseverance. A Park Ranger is not high up on the government pay scale as our payments were rated and although we were on contract we adhered to the pay scale of a comparable position consequently, we did better than the rangers. However, the surrounding land of this park area was so devoid of indigenous people due to its hard living conditions and only suitable for wild animals. Consequently, the Kafue National Park was in effect at least 20 times bigger than shown on the map. And it doesn't stop there, Ngamiland to the south of the Caprivi Strip along the Zambezi River west of Livingstone; the huge Makgadigadi Soda Lake Pans in Botswana are all no go areas from the point of view they are too difficult and unknown to the average traveler. Only those with business, so to speak, in these areas are probably the only ones able to survive and even with these experienced travelers there is considerable risk. I knew and worked in all of these areas and had a tremendous respect for them and the animals that lived there in their terrain. Then also to the south and further to the west is the great Kalahari Desert, another magnificent area where game survived virtually unbothered right up to my time of passing through and working there. Unfortunately, later even these areas were opened by rogue government members for a paltry sum allowing ivory hunter's uncontrolled access to murder Rhino and Elephant and shoot and kill other game simply for their skins. They used automatic military type weapons and just wiped out wild animals by the thousands. The white men who had been managing these reserves for the benefit of all mankind were taken off the job and it was given over to un-trained ex terrorist locals to take care of and they abused it and used it as if it were their own ranchland. When the white rangers took care of it they held it in posterity for all mankind as bidden by the Almighty Creator of these wonderful creatures.

Having all agreed as to where we were now we once again split up into these same two groups to look for the ideal campsite bearing in mind these features: a) nearby good water supply remembering that within a few weeks some ponds would begin to dry up and we needed a four months replenishment source b) a dry easy move about clearing, this area was rife with lion. We needed to be able to see if lion were approaching, how many and what they may be up to, yet at the same time have some trees for tent sun-shade, and at night we wanted to spot them if necessary with our flashlights.. c) Sufficient old dry wood to keep fires burning in the labor camp and, our own cook fires and camp fires. This was our main criteria, but it is also good to keep look out for a pleasant site as we would be there for several months.

Many of these areas have a small escarpment and these are always good sites with water filtering in the sands at the base. We discovered an excellent attractive site with all the features we wanted and move on to begin unpacking and setting up our tents. Most of us had two Indian Pattern Tents so called because they were designed after an expensive Indian style tent and, we still purchased direct from India whenever we could. The tent was 10′ X 12′ and had bamboo main frame poles at either end supporting a bamboo ridge-pole with end rings that slipped over the spiked top main-frame pole, The tent had a white cotton exterior with a yellow lined interior, all cotton for cool-ness. Over this fitted a fly sheet also white cotton exterior with blue lined underside. These tents were the best one could get and very desirable by the hunter safari crews for their, at that time, $300 per day American clientele. We set up two tents in line and then suspended a temporary existential 12′ long ridge pole between the tents providing good accommodation. One or two of the younger Rhodesian's were content too have just one tent and then, of course, we had a common work (calculations) area and another gathering area close to the main kitchen and this was where the one tent guys hung out. We also had a vehicle/garage area where we dug an inspection trench for on the spot repair work to vehicles of the hard riders. Also, we invariably found one or two good mechanics in our labor gangs who were only too happy to take over this work. Most of our guys were fair mechanics and together they were capable of good maintenance. It usually took two or three days to establish a camp like this and then someone would go out and look for a clean source of water in an area not puddled by animals and we could drink it direct if they had to dig down in the sands for it otherwise it had to go through our charcoal filters. (There were emergency times when we just had to drink water from where we could find it but our routine was to be careful and practice sanitation. Speaking of sanitation we dug deep holes a distance from camp, down wind and these had little log and branch-wood seats built over them by our clever works crew with a pile of sand beside each one

Finally, work had to commence and we would have a day teaming off into working partners and groups as required. A couple of our surveyors were content to work alone and these were the same ones who always brought back meat for the pot. Small game, wild pig and or birds like wild guinea fowl. They operated alone by providing and setting up the targets needed for observing onto. They had a couple of boys that they took along with them but they didn't need a technical partner. It required knowledge of whereabouts to find the proposed site only yet seen on the map contours and be able to identify the position the observers were in at another location. It was experienced work not undertaken lightly because any false location could cost us a lot of time. In my whole career in doing this I can't remember more than two or three occasions when someone miss-identified his location. These guys loved hunting and shooting and never failed to bring back enough meat for us and for all the labor gangs, they were great guys. If the game rangers were in the area then they would skin and cut up the animal where the shot it and bring back only the meat in 10 gallon milk cans just to be safe. At this site too, Louise had big kaffir pots cooking on three fires with buck meat (veal we never called it veal), wild pig and a pot of birds all simmering and bubbling. The game rangers came by too often to be just looking for poachers they wanted a bowl of stew. Louise entertained them and told them they were welcome they were young men and they loved being with us and partaking of Louise's dinner menus. All our bread was cooked in hole dug into the dirt, some hot ashes placed in the bottom with a tin cover and then another top cover and dirt, the bread was excellent.

The rangers told her when they stopped by that sometimes they hadn't tasted bread for a week or more.

Some weekends when things were a bit slack and we had made good progress we would go out on a hunting trip not just shooting whatever we saw but being preferential and selecting buck we knew was good tasting meat and made the best biltong (jerky). Some of these like Roan and Eland, especially Eland (Royal Game) were not on game pot license provided by the Director of the Dept of Wild Game so we had to skin fast and burn the meat and horns. If we had already started to move into the dry season traveling was becoming problematical in the vlei's, (open light wooded areas). Elephant had been everywhere and their feet go into the soils at least, in some cases 12" or more deep and now the Land rovers had to clonk – clonk- clonk through these holes alerting everything in that area. Louise usually had to drive our L/Rover and someone in the back had to flat hand the cab roof for her to make an easy halt. This was virtually impossible but she got cursed out anyway. She was terrific and handled it all so well and she was a good shot in her own right. Some times I didn't go but Louise would. I am not a hunter and I never liked shooting and killing but I enjoyed the meat. One Saturday morning I thought we were at war all the shots being fired, I grabbed a Land Rover and went off to find them. There was a small herd of Kudu and they had not hit nary a one. I stopped all the craziness, sent Louise and one other to go by foot and get one and one only, it took them about 20 mins. and Taff came back and said Louise was sitting on the Kudu waiting for us because it was hers. We were allowed Kudu Antelope and we were not concerned about the Ranger's catching us with a carcass. We had fresh meat that night like almost all days and the laborers got a good feed and some biltong was cut and put up to dry, we kept it under mosquito netting while it was wet to keep the blow flies off. We also kept the rack close in camp or the hyenas would take it. I would find sticks of biltong lying around in the bottom of most Land Rovers and guys would just pick them up and chew on them when they were hungry. I envied them the ability to do that, my teeth were not so good but not the desire to pick them up and chew on them.

One day from this camp I took Singano, one of our best trackers, and a couple of other reliable black souls and went off to look for a far distant point the other observers said was a big hill or a small mountain beyond where they had extended but should be investigated. I got as much information on it that I could, including their compass bearings and departed camp knowing I wouldn't get there the same day. As it gets dark early because it was winter time and very cold at nights, even freezing. The days however were beautiful and comfortably warm unless one was up a hill in those cold winds. There was a very good trail in the direction we were heading and we were making good time because of the easy going. I said to Singano, Ndjovu? (elephant) and he affirmed. That night, I decided to get off the main trail slightly up on a small rocky mound. They laughed at me but, of course, helped me set up my bed area, we were not using tents. They placed a quick temporary bush screen across the trail and pegged it down in case a wind got up in the night. We had our meal and then all turned into our sleeping bags. I awakened to cold bright moonlight, something had disturbed me and I knew not what, I checked that my rifle and flashlight (torch in Brit language) were handy and then layback and listened and there it was again Cha-cha....Cha-cha....Cha-cha like an old Puffing Billy railroad locomotive it took a while for it to sink in and then I knew what it was, the elephant's legs swooshing through the heavy long grass off of the trail. Being off the trail meant he was alerted to us and going carefully, I cocked my rifle and waited, I had no desire whatsoever to shoot but my *intelligent* boys were down on the trail fast asleep. This loan elephant came out warily onto the trail and moved stealthily up to the little wimpy barrier and there he stopped for a long while looking down at those peacefully sleeping Bushmen. I kept at the ready knowing it would be useless if it decided to trample them but by now I was sure he wasn't going to do that. After a while he turned gracefully and carefully around and went off back along the trail. He sensed no danger and yet he knew I was there as well and that is when I realized that he had accepted us sleeping peacefully in his domain — incredible! I told my gallant Bushmen when we were fixing coffee next morning, we had a visitor last night and they said, Ha! Ha! Mr. Frank until I said, come take a look and there was the spoor in the fine dust with the under-foot fine ridges of their feet marked clearly—Uh! Uh! They exclaimed and studied those prints for a long while looking at their flimsy barrier while I was drinking my coffee. We moved on and discovered the hill easily in time for me to take readings that day and set out back to base on the following, an uneventful side trip. Meanwhile back in camp Louise and the only other girl belonging to another Welshman Taff Vaughan had also had a visit from elephant in the night. Our main camp had an extensive kitchen area used several of our cooks, most of us had our own cook-boy and they were there along with us so the kitchen was a big active area. Every night it was re-brushed with tree branches and sprinkled with saved washing-up water to keep it firm and clean therefore, even if a mouse moved across it the evidence was left behind. However, on the morning of that day I returned to base two elephant had paid the kitchen area a visit. Very little damage was done by them because the area was so open and large, they were able to walk in and investigate freely. Some big pots standing on the ground had their lids pushed off and other pots up on the home made tables were lifted off and inspected and that was about the extent of it. No one heard a sound. Louise, Kathy and the cooks, the rest of the guys were out by day and in late at night and fast asleep. Elephant, like most wild creatures, are curious but not aggressive unless attacked or something is amiss. Lion are also curious, unfortunately, and we had an experience that sometimes can turn out not so good.

One has to know, that knowledge has to be gleaned when living out with wild game. How to live and survive there amongst them requires time, knowledge and experience. To rush off into these far away places without experienced members in the group is asking for disaster. Of course one has to go there to get this experience but it is a roll of the dice if you intend to go in ignorant and expect to know how to respond until you gain your own insight and intuition and gut feelings start to work for you. Another time I was out on my own up the Kafue River, it feeds into the mighty Zambezi River about 50 miles south of where we were camped. I had completed my survey tasks but stayed over another night to do some fishing. The Kafue at this time of year was not too fast flowing and was rich in good sized Pike and fishing was plentiful. A strange phenomenon is, although the Kafue joins the Zambezi there are no Pike in the Zambezi River and no Bream in the Kafue, strange! Pike is a sweet white meat fish but has a lot of small sharp bones and one needs to be very careful when eating them. I made a good catch and decided to return to base the next morning with a bag full of fish which would be a change from wild buck. I pegged the bag onto the bank just trailing in the shallow water to keep them fresh and that was not a smart thing to do because a crocodile took the whole bagful, I was so disheartened. We were temporarily sleeping there on the river bank, my two boys and I, close to the water and I thought wow! Those damned adult crocs which are on average 12 feet long could easily walk off with one of us too. I fished again the next morning until noon and made another good catch of average 20 inch long pike and was back at base camp that night as it got dark in time for a fish dinner for all the white guys and the cooks.

Shortly before we left that Kafue Camp-site we had a Lion encounter. It was a bright moonlight freezing cold night and we had all gone to bed, the fires had smoldered down and the Tilley (pressure) Lamps were out. I heard grunting which had awakened me and instantly knew we had lion in camp. I went outside of our tent and in the moonlight saw about six half grown ones with a couple of big adults hanging back but watching carefully. I assessed the situation and saw that it was not a very good one. These curious young ones were not going to leave. Louise came stumbling out half asleep and I said, come here quickly, look at these young Lion, we have a problem with them all running around our tents, it is most dangerous. I am going over to the tents of a couple of our guys to awaken them and get them to start up their jeeps and run these kids out of camp. Then I heard a vehicle horn being sounded from one of the guys who had pitched his tent out on the periphery of our camp area and one lion was already tearing down his lean-to fly sheet. I jumped in my jeep, drove over and chased it off, he got out of his vehicle where he had gone for safety and jumped in with me shivering either from cold or fright, I didn't ask him, and we came back to Louise. Then I went out again to rouse the two guys that I wanted to patrol the camp and one young lion was almost in his open flap tent. I said, get up! There are lion in camp and he sleepily said, leave them alone and they will go away. He was a young Rhodesian born kid off of a ranch but I got him up and told him to take a look outside he got into his jeep immediately and set out with the horn blaring rounding them up and chasing them out, his Buddy got the other land rover fired up and they moved them all off. We all moved back to my camp fire, kicked up the coals, put on a pot of coffee and sat around it trying to keep warm. Very quietly Taffy, sitting opposite from me said, turn around quickly Frank one old bugger is moving in on you and it was, in the last crouch before a jump and I shot it dead, I had thrown the flashlight to Taff, he caught its eyes and I fired. He said, for a non hunter you are the one I want around Frank, I want you around when lion are in camp. I said, get the boys to burn and bury that carcass when it's light, skin and all, the game department will have no mercy on me except for a $2000 fine. I would have preferred to have collaborated along with them but it never worked with the current director we had, all he knew is that I had shot it for fun!

Another time Louise and I were coming back from a survey point and she said, we need fresh meat I said, it's too dark already when she said, Stop! Look over there to your right and there were two beautiful Hartebeest at about 400 yards, a long shot for this time of night. She said, shoot one! Shoot them both! She knew I could do it. I said, No! it's too dark, I can't afford a flubbed shot at this time of night and it goes off wounded, She said, I know you are by far the best shot of all but you just don't talk about it but I have your old khaki army shirt with the crossed marksman rifle decal on the sleeve you don't get that for fun, I said, all the more reason not to shoot. She said; give me your rifle knowing that would make me take the shot. I opened the Land Rover door quietly and rested on it then carefully aimed and squeezed and they both leaped and she cried you missed! I said no, it's a heart shot and it dropped dead and I felt terrible over it, the other one ran off a way and then looked confused. Louise said move over, I'll drive and the two boys and I will load it in, she knew I was hurting. A Hartebeest weighs about 500 to 600 pound weight and they could do it okay with Louise singing along. She was tough and the right girl in that place and the right one for me, she knew me inside out and how I ticked. I really didn't like killing them, it was killing to me and not hunting and shooting, killing! However, it was a joyous camp that night our cooks took off what they wanted for us then passed the rest on to the Boys everyone was happy but me I kept seeing those magnificent creatures and we were not allowed to shoot them either, they were not permissible on our hunting license. Shooting Hartebeest (protected game) — that damned game director could confiscate our rifles. Hardly likely, because we needed them for protection but they could seal the triggers with a light wire easily broken in emergency but showing the Rangers that we had broken the seals for some purpose.

This Primary Survey Control in the Kafue National Park was one of the best and most enjoyable of my 10 year long career as a Bushman

Surveyor in the Rhodesia's. It was a very nice area as far as Game Areas go with plenty of vegetation and water keeping it almost as a year round locale for game of all kinds. These preservations were valuable assets as well as great places to tour and visit and the preservation of these wild animals is part of the heritage of some African Nations. Should the terrorists, who were pushing for so called independence by killing and frightening local inhabitants, ever succeed in gaining power all these peripheral agencies will not be funded and the game will be killed for gain (as it turned out this was a proven fact) Mugabe and his terrorist group did take over in what is today known as Zimbabwe and they destroyed the economy by simply emptying the lucrative coffers filled by the previous responsible government good management of the Colonial settlers. The Mugabe Regime began by killing farmers who had lived out in the rural areas for several generations and then took over their lands but they did not know how to farm these big ranches and they just receded into scrub desert. The economy slumped simply because they did not know how to govern and it only took a few years for them to party off what was left of the tax revenues with now no income. All of this had been warned of when American academia and college students were clamoring to get the whites out of Rhodesia and then when starvation began for the people and aid was being shipped in the professors and their students were silent. However, the aid never went to the indigenous people it all it went to the government and their supporters and these academic professors, to this day, brag about getting the white people out of Africa but they forget to add, and causing thousands of deaths amongst the poor by starvation, the poor people were no longer cared for as they had been with clinics, hospitals and al kinds of aid. This aid was generated by the Southern Rhodesian economy

Many of these African countries can be productive especially agriculturally, as was shown prior to these murderers taking over, which is so important but it takes scientific farming and money to irrigate and provide the machinery. The science is also of a practical nature and the money was built up over the years by these white farmers and was used for the benefit of all involved, workers, bankers and manufactures and government. This is big machinery that has to all fit together like hand and glove and can not be emulated overnight by murderers. Nevertheless aid in the way of food and funds are still being poured in and it is abused and used as fast as it arrives there by the in-power groups. My plan would be to put these professors and students in that country to start up these remunerative farms again and manage the government. This is not a political discourse but having spent so many years in Africa especially Southern Rhodesia where my home was I had a stake in it, and saw it come apart egged on by so called intellectuals (academia) from another country whose own educational system is in tatters, the USA.

We completed that work successfully in five months and returned to Salisbury before the rains commenced in the Kafue. If we do not get out of most of these remote areas before the onset of the rains our vehicles, although 4-wheel drive would not make it out and possibly neither would we. As I look back on the areas in which we worked with so little protection and guarantee of any kind whatsoever I am amazed that we could do that work for ten years and come out virtually unscathed. It is of note that the Survey Bushmen who survived their first survey safari were also the same who were with me a decade later when we were told our work was done and, job well done…Thank you!

This is just an add-on maybe. There was one individual who should have received recognition for all she did out there with us and that is, of course, Louise (Cunningham) O'Hare. She did all that was asked of her and maybe expected of her with delight and pleasure. She was a rare find for me and loved by all who knew her.

8

Victoria Falls Road
Survey 1962

Following the completion in the Kafue Game Park we returned to our new home in Borrowdale and wallowed in the joy of being in our own home. It was adequate for Taff, Louise and I with a spare room for guests. We had many friends and when we decided to build a complete stand alone add-on, ostensibly for Louise's mom who wanted to come out to Africa for an extended visit, they all got busy helping us on building the extension. We separated "her place" with what is known as a breeze way in Rhodesia. There is a connecting roof attaching both buildings and enclosed with only a low wall around it, thus allowing the breeze to pass through under the shade of the connecting roofs. It is also a useful semi outdoor party Braaivleis (Barbecue) area where friends may gather. As soon as this was finished Louise's mom came out and commenced her extended stay. She had her own place with kitchenette and her own servant and was totally self contained if she wished or if we desired and it seemed to work okay. The only slight annoyance was, we had over two acres of garden with fruit trees and all kinds of nice rare bushes. Because we were so often away she considered that her domain and as we also had a garden boy she directed his activities. It wasn't always what I wanted but then I was never there so she took over by default.

This particular rainy season in 1962 I took on a group of African HS students as survey leveling technicians, and taught them the art of precise leveling, a very accurate leveling technique that can be carried forward for miles forming a traverse network throughout the country. We got started early back in head quarters in Salisbury and it must have been difficult for them initially to understand the accuracy required and the techniques to achieve that standard. Finally, after six weeks of training I decided we were ready to go out and begin our stretch from Bulawayo to Victoria Falls. We had two teams and I hoped to increase it to three before we were through. These student learners were going to be the nucleus of not bringing in ex patriots to do this kind of work which is a matter of learning the job piece by piece and having a good standard of education to begin with. I am not sure how it came to me but I got the job of putting it together and being the instructor for these students. I had two black technicians and this was a tremendous help although we all spoke adequate English. I noticed however, my two black technicians often reverted to their own language to get a point across.

We got off to a slow start and I wasn't surprised, once out on the road all kinds of things come in to play to be encountered and dealt with. This kind of leveling can only be done during the early morning period before it becomes too hot causing too much shimmer on the staff readings and again in the evening hours similar. The work is broken down into lengths of approximately one mile per part of day. However, if the stretch is on a sharp gradient many more set ups are required to cover the same distance, and on steep grades I cut down the distance otherwise they would never have completed a leg. After we had covered some 20 miles their capability improved and we could creep back up to the one mile steep or flat. When the terrain is flat only a few set ups are required to cover the same distance. Shortly after getting away from Bulawayo and those hills we hit a long flat stretch and the guys got their techniques and drills honed up before we hit the many hills coming in to the Zambezi area at Victoria Falls. I never doubted that they could do it but several of our surveyors said, the work would be unreliable. I said, that is nonsense the leveling procedures are self checking, surely you know that, but some guys didn't like it and criticized me for training them to do the work and maybe giving away something special that only we knew how to do. However, I realized it was only a matter of time and the people at the top had seen this as well and thought it best we teach them the precise leveling techniques. I enjoyed it and was so pleased that they could pull it off, eventually when we got closer to Victoria Falls I kind of left them to it and went down into the gorge to do some survey work that had been long in the waiting. Unfortunately the river was beginning to run strong in a back water I had hoped would be low but I got a lot done by setting my instruments up well into the bank side, that gorge is very deep and the work was tricky but I had lots of time as my guys were going along well on their own with only the two senior black technicians doing the supervising. We started the leveling about 20 miles north of Bulawayo picking up on work done previously and completed about 70 miles in four months which was extremely good by any standard for the work. I would imagine these now technicians, who did this initial work with me, had already made a place for themselves in any future independent government, I hope so.

Louise did not come with me on this boring routine and it was an opportunity for her to have some time with her mother and help in the interior setting up in her new place and her new country. I was also able to go home every two or three weeks once the teams got going and understood what they were doing so it was an easy period for me for a change. However we knew our life as it had been was coming to an end and we had nothing yet planned for our own future. We did not want to leave Africa especially Southern Rhodesia which was now very much our home, where would we go? But with the hope and expectancy of younger people we always expected things to turn out well and for the best.

9

The Northern Rhodesian Safari Survey

Go to Wikipedia for a complete history report on "Northern Rhodesia" as it was known from about 1924 until 1963 when it obtained independence. Prior to 1924 it had been managed and governed, so to speak, by the BSAC British South Africa Company (Police) — interchangeable. Cecil John Rhodes had a commitment from the British to establish these countries as British territory and had a pretty much free hand in doing so. They were not to be any cost to the British tax payer and he recruited mostly from the English universities known as public schools in England, (the opposite nomenclature of the American system). Rhodes had big ambition and attempted to spread in all directions but, after 1924 Northern Rhodesia became a British Protectorate and remained as such until Independence. The Federation of Southern Rhodesia, Northern Rhodesia and Malawi was formed in 1953 mostly for the benefit and development of Northern Rhodesia and Malawi because Southern Rhodesia was already a developing power house.

Following the successful enjoyable trigonometric survey in the Kafue

National Park we returned to Salisbury and cleaned, tested and turned in our delicate surveying equipment. Then we took some local leave to work on our new house and grounds, we had already moved in and there were lots to do. All our survey group guys turned up to see what they could do to help and it was great fun.

Francois returned from his small local survey job and he got together with us in our big plotting-room to go over where we were so far in our preparation work. This took several days because he had many questions to put to us and we made notes for a final check of our planning work. Then we told him the status on transport and equipment, we also told him what arms we had purchased (in Southern Rhodesia in those days good hunting rifles were not expensive and no one yet was using automatic rifles). We also had a number of hand held pistols and lots of ammunition. Francois was also very familiar with guns, rifles and short arms and gave us all a run down, in the circumstances as to what would be suitable arms to have along with us. He said, Frank and I will go through the survey equipment one more time just to be absolutely certain we have got it all, there were a few smart rejoinders to that but they were taken without malice. Everything was being refined down to almost nut ready to go. The following week we would receive our Land Rovers, six in all, and those not receiving one would be driving and riding in 2 big 7 ton Bedford 4-wheel drive vehicles equipped with water tanks and winches. These big specially equipped vehicles were essential on a remote job like this one, the changes and add-ons being designed especially for our purpose. Within reason we were given much leeway in what we asked for, it was a most unpopular project because of the pending Independence to be under Kwami (Kenneth) Kaunda, no one in the department wanting to go there now other than our group who did not have the concerns voiced by the other guys, but we had our quota. We also had our regular black workers who always went with us on these big survey safaris, they were experienced and so much more valuable to us than any casual laborers being also technical and good reliable drivers and any and all work that was needed on these surveys jobs. They were most essential to the project and we truly appreciated them and I doubt we would have been a success without them in so many ways. I have given this particular group of about eight regular Black employees ("boys") a lot of praise here and they have earned it and were amongst the best technical support gang I have ever known. They were truly honest and devoted to us and their job – what a great versatile group to have along on a safari of this kind.

We had checked and double checked and we had given the Land Rovers a good workout to ensure they were reliable and operational for the long haul. We were all familiar with these incredibly suitable vehicles which were also relatively easy to maintain by their drivers and our Black Gang some who could virtually take any vehicle apart and put it back together again. We took along some spares but they were all new vehicles and all we should have to do was good maintenance. Once in a main camp we would locate a bit of gravelly ground so as not to have a cave in collapse and dig a maintenance pit. These pits paid off because the vehicles were in rough raw ground and being able to easily check them out underneath was essential. There was nothing else we could do here now in Salisbury so we had a final long weekend to wrap everything up at home and say a temporary (we hoped) good bye to family and friends. One of our team for that project was an Afrikaner by the name of Jacques Kricke. He was a happy soul and like me he liked a drink or two so he and I got together, unfortunately, the night before leaving and had a little party. He was ex South African Air Force and a qualified Land Surveyor, He had been seconded to an USAAF group in Viet Naam and had some tales to tell of that and I being ex military with the occupation forces in Germany and in Africa we had plenty of drinking time to share. It was a very bad idea having to arise very early and follow up with a full days driving feeling most unwell. I, of course, had my co pilot, Louise, and she drove the full day while I busied myself feeling sick. At one stop for coffee, Kricke and I drank half a joe-sack (a canvass water bag tied to the front of the radiator sucking air through itself as you traveled that kept it cool). We drank that with some kind of stomach settling soda to try and feel better, which we didn't of course, we didn't make it all the way in one day's journey; we stopped off at the border crossing into Northern Rhodesia. That night we made two small bonfires and had a meager meal and then François opened a bottle of brandy and we all had one or two drinks apiece. I needed that drink and I made sure that I only had two hoping for a brighter tomorrow, Kricker, likewise restricted his intake, François suggested that Kricke and I take it easy from now onwards, I had no argument.

We all passed through the Congo Pedicle without too much of a problem, however, there was much delay scrutinizing all of our passports. Kricker had kept his South African passport and that really was a problem, of course and Louise's American passport also got extra scrutiny and special attention for some unknown reason. Eventually, we got underway again and made a temporary stop that night within the area we wanted to make permanent campsite later, we had done very well that day and for two days. We remained at this temporary site whilst we got ourselves better oriented; however, this was not a suitable position for a permanent site. It was too close to the main road, we needed to be out of sight and not too obvious to all passers by. We did not know where our water sources were going to be although it was plentiful in this location but were we close enough and would it be a clean safe supply. We had to have dried old wood for our cooking fires and it was not here so, we needed a day or two to locate a good site with the requirements and consequently on the following day we began to scout around. We didn't have cell phones in those days so we scheduled meeting back at base every three hours. De Wet and I searching together finally came up with what we believed was the place; however, we decided to allow the others to check it out if they did not have something they believed to be good enough. Everyone liked the site except Taff, my Buddy whom I had been on the leveling job with during the rainy season and he had an ideal site beside a fast moving small river, one of the many tributaries in this area to the fast flowing big Luapula River which was about 500 yards across in this area and there was a ferry raft big enough to take a truck pulled on a pulley rope to stop it drifting away down stream. It was a very good site but noisy from the water falling across the rocks and I asked them if they would be happy at nights being only able to hear the fast running water, I was thinking of terrorists possibly creeping around. The turn down of this good site was unanimous so, we all opted for the De Wet/O'Hare location. The next day was a detailed planning session prior to going out in our teams to survey for suitable triangulating sites. We had to survey, first then adopt and proceed with the observing. It is normal and ideal practice to first carry out a survey and when that is confirmed continue with the observing. This has the advantage of not having to carry equipment for two procedures. There was heavy vegetation and we had two towers dropped off for us in the area to use reconnaissance and observing platforms. However, because of the urgency of this project and probably a one time visit we were combining reconnaissance and observing where possible. Once again, I don't want to drag this procedural work out but we were surveyors and that is why we were there and what we were doing. Anything else was additional and often interesting but I am and was a surveyor that was my whole life consequently, this story is written from a surveyor's life experience in the African Bush, we were "Surveyor Bushmen"

These towers were in two bundles one for each tower which could be erected to 75 feet high. They were three legged and access was by tiny clip-on steps up one leg, no security loops and we didn't tie off, it was just a tower to climb to facilitate see over the tops of the trees and observing angles from that same platform at the top. Some people found it scary but not many in my experience with them, it required a certain strength and agility and, of course, no fear of heights. There was an inner tower and this was for the instrument to sit on, it was free standing in that it was not connected to the outer tower and even the foundations could not be interconnected or vibrations would pass from the main standing tower to the instrument tower thereby not allowing the delicate observing equipment to stay on level. The life was hard, we dug our own foundations either mixing concrete or, if available, using rail-road sleepers sawn to size. On one occasion we were getting poor triangular closure and the tower point was being occupied by one of our new guys. We asked him to check that the foundations were not touching and he was adamant that they were not. Taff and I spent half a night looking and checking all the observing readings for the three points and we were sure the tower point was faulty. The observer there became most annoyed, I told him to stop it and get busy with us exposing each leg to confirm separation of inner and outer tower legs. On the second leg we discovered a big rock wedged in between the two foundations. He said you got to be kidding me, that can't do it. I told him to re observe everything and see the outcome and the outcome was a very good closure of that triangle. Another primary surveyor lesson learned and he apologized profusely. We lost a few days because we could not leave the other stations until these readings were corrected.

The occupying of the towers and ground level stations meant we had to get well ahead with the reconnaissance because some stations could not be finished until all other stations related to it were completed observing to and from. We also had to pass over into Katanga on the other side of the Luapula River which at that time was not Congo although fighting and negotiating was going on between these two countries. Meanwhile evolutionary fighting was happening in Northern Rhodesia, currently mostly around the Copper Belt area. This Copper Belt was discovered in1950 and it had been known that copper was evident since late 1940 when exploration drilling confirmed it and expanded the areas to start mining. It was a massive high percentage lode and the country should have become wealthy as a result of it which it did while the white man was there and managing the proceeds to everyone's benefit, however, following independence it all went into the big pockets of the new government. Northern Rhodesia was a British Protectorate and, of course, Britain was accused by certain Black African Independent groups of stealing the copper profits. This was not true, and they knew it, but it was a typical ploy for an independence rally and believed by many in the American Liberal academia who happily helped spread the poisonous slander for their own political progressive reasons that they only knew. However, the mining was a huge success and carried out by white English imported emigrant miners who were there for about 30 years and their children growing up and schooling there before going on for higher education in the good colleges in Southern Rhodesia or South Africa, I believe one or two went back to England for higher education. Unfortunately, the huge revenues derived from these Copper Belt Mines, was never invested wisely by that Black Government. The transportation systems, railways and roads were barely adequate and as we went through there around Bancroft (one of the first copper mines) and Kitwe there was only a short stretch of paved road, about 50 miles total. All the remainder of our traveling, hundreds of miles, was on dirt roads that were not always maintained. Maintenance on dirt roads (gravel roads) was done by motor bladed scrapers which should be stationed at 50 mile intervals, with a few tip trucks and a loader's to repair washed out sections. None of this was done by the independent group aspiring to be, *we will run our own country drama*. There is so much that must be managed and although, American Liberal academia does not like to hear it, these "people" were not yet ready to manage their own country on the scale and manner required. (Many of them soon came to believe this as poverty now took hold and spread rampantly) after independence was achieved. I was there, working before and after independence and the condition of the roads and other services severely deteriorated. The copper belt lost more than half of its output because most of the miners moved to South Africa and as far as I know, conditions in Zambia are worse now than before independence, certainly no better from what they once were, especially for the local people. This is most unfortunate because had there been a phased handover and learning period of government department management, the production and outputs would have increased and the indigenous people would be the beneficiaries as previously. As it was, and is now, the indigenous are kept poor, at a standstill and now possibly poorer than they were years ago, if that is at all possible. While there was overview by a white minority, success was being made in the advancement of, schooling, jobs and other achievements for all of the people. It is all very well to say it is their country, give it to them, however, having once been managed to a certain standard that standard had to be maintained and completed otherwise chaos takes over and it has. Nevertheless, it is even now superior to Nairobi which has had billions of dollars poured into since 1958 after (I left in 1952) and we are still donating billions, I see ads asking private Americans to donate funds to drill wells for the African villages in and around Nairobi. Yet the governments in and around Nairobi receives millions of Dollars in aid for this very purpose, and more to run their government unfortunately the government takes all the contributions for their own nefarious purposes such as mansions, palaces, traveling, expensive automobiles ordered from Germany . Our government is fully aware of this but say, East Africa has strategic value, what a croc! It is a bottomless pit now like it never was.

Meanwhile back to surveying: Normally, to occupy any trigonometric station in a bordering country it is always essential to inform both government departments. However in this situation we could not find anyone to liaise with, previous attempts only upset the individuals we approached so, we gave up on them and proceeded without any approvals from either side of the border. Kricke, van Jastian, two more of our team and several Southern Rhodesian Black "Boys" went over to the Katanga side to occupy and observe from those points being part of the network along the river section which is the defining border. These points in Katanga were set up previously by our surveyor's, we had established them several years back for this very purpose of extending a network along the river route to build a road. (Roads, of course, can be built without knowing exactly where they are in relation to all other added features. However, in an advanced country such as Southern Rhodesia was at that time we followed the custom of establishing global control. Today, of course, this is easily done by GPS. When we left Salisbury to do this work we acquired some new short range radios for communication that worked reasonably well but not always and Kricke and his group took one unit with them across the river and agreed to make contact daily at a given time. This was a success for two or three days and then all went quiet, De Wet and I discussed going across to look for them and he said, as our leader he would go. I countered, as our leader he should not go and it was my place to do that. Eventually he gave in and we went in our Land Rovers down to the ferry and I asked the ferry man did he know where our people were but he shook his head. I drove on board and waved to Francois as I moved off. We agreed that when I found them I would communicate, alternatively I would come back within five days and he must not cross just get everyone together and return to Salisbury, Southern Rhodesia and try the diplomatic angle. However, if it was a terrorist group the diplomatic approach would not be much use. Of course, I had a good idea as to where they should be and I carefully kept map recognition of my search rather than just drive around willy-nilly. I knew the points that they were to occupy and figured that they ought to be on the second and camped somewhere in that area. I also watched the side of the road for vehicle access and eventually saw some. I followed these new treks and could see that a narrow gauged wheeled vehicle (a la Land Rovers) had been in there so I continued to follow. I eventually came to a camp but no one around so I stopped and waited. If they were in hiding because of an approaching vehicle I wanted them to carefully see me and check it out and, out from the bushes they came. I asked why they were not observing and they told me that too much checking up on them was going on and they didn't want to get separated. We talked about it but I could see every one was jittery and I wasn't going to second guess these guys I knew so well. We held a little war counsel and I said, we will pull out tonight.

All was apparently well and everyone was safe but there was a lot of nervousness and finding stations (points), concentrating on the observing work and keeping it all together was not worth it. We were able to establish our triangular network without occupying some of these points in Katanga so our consensus was to pull out. When I came across the river I gave the ferryman a very healthy tip, his eyes almost fell out of his head. I told him to watch out for us over the next few days and make sure we got across quickly when our jeeps showed up. We broke camp leisurely in this location the next day and made all cleared and ship shape as usual leaving in the early afternoon time. There was army border control point before going down to the river where we boarded the ferry and we hoped that these guys were not going to be a problem.

We had been across a few weeks earlier doing some reconnaissance and later that evening had a bit of a party in the pub without problems. Louise's uncle Hale, a circuit court judge in California was out visiting

Louise's mom and all of us for that matter. I had been down on a visit back home to our home in Southern Rhodesia and he came back with me to our main camp in Northern Rhodesia. Louise gave me a few bottles of his whiskey she had been able to get in Salisbury (now Soweto) and off he and I went on that long trip back up there. He was 76 years of age at that time and was a remarkable man with never a complaint about anything. The first night as we were sitting around the camp fire, nights were cold up there in July, and having drinks before dinner Uncle hale asked what the South African guys were drinking and it was brandy and coke or brandy and ginger ale. He said he would try a brandy and coke and that became his drink, I ended up with the bourbon which was fine by me, I was an active drinker in those days, maybe too active. Uncle Hale was with us at that party we had to cross the Luapula River and we were drinking beer. Beer there came only in liter bottles and the local government officials, who evidently drank a lot at any time of day, kept sending beer to our table and we didn't want to refuse their hospitality so onwards the party went. Later some girls joined in and it was a grand night and Uncle Hale held up unbelievably well. The following morning I found a women's shoe in the back of my jeep and said, where did this come from and Hale said, if you don't remember maybe you better leave it at that. A few weeks later when I took him back to Louise and her mom they were quizzing him to find out all that had happened, mother evidently asked him had there been any good parties but he was not forthcoming Louise told me and never spilt the beans on us but he had a wonderful time he said and those guys are the best.

As we got down towards the river, all loaded up for crossing, the barrier was down, I was in second place with Kriger and I had previously said, if it looks like these guys are going to be difficult the lead vehicle pull aside and ours will crash the barrier down. They were armed with rifles and usually drunk and not very good shots. These were not the guys we were concerned about it was the terrorist movement that knew how to shoot and how to move quickly and quietly across the country. The army guys were drunk and being a real pain in the ass and would not lift the barrier for us. I honked my horn one sharp beep and the lead vehicle pulled over and we drove right through it. It was just a flimsy pole on a bolt at the base and did no damage to my vehicle. We all drove on, it was about 5 miles down to the river, they had no vehicle there and I knew they were too drunk to run after us so I didn't feel too alarmed but I didn't want a shooting war. We were more than capable of handling them and we were all good shots, however, it would be a very dangerous and sticky situation. Fortunately the ferryman was there and we were able to drive the 3 jeeps right on, the big 4X4 had to wait with two of our Rhodesian blacks. There was a canoe and I told them, if the army come down leave the vehicle which was mostly camping-gear and a tower and come over. They never came and we had time to get the 7-ton vehicle back across and that ended Katanga for us. De Wet said we had done right to abandon the project as far as Katanga went and we must now finish up at this side and get out of here.

I think this side had become more dangerous for us than Katanga was now. I was driving back as far as Fort Rosebury one day to pick up some equipment that had been sent there to the pub for us and going down a long run into that area, hundreds of women ran out onto the road from a big village shrieking Kwatcha! Kwatcha! (Meaning; Beware! Beware!) I just drove on fast right through them if I had had to stop I know that I would have been torn to pieces. Their currency was called the Kwatcha as opposed to the Dollar but they were not meaning for us to, "give us some money". Northern Rhodesia became a very hostile place for whites during this period of gaining their independence and, like all political campaigns; many vicious lies were spread around about whites by the terrorist party moving into power. Their hatred for white people had become very problematic, especially for ones like us living in remote areas with no protection whatsoever. While I was there in Fort Rosebury I managed to get through by phone to our office in Salisbury, Southern Rhodesia, and talked with the senior managing surveyor, a man called Oggie Rates, a South African (Afrikaaner). I told him things were not good for us, in fact dangerous, and we had pulled out of Katanga. He wouldn't give me a straight answer. Of course, he wanted the work completed almost at any cost, ours of course, but he did say, you are the man on the spot Frank and the decision is yours. We went ahead and completed it which in retrospect was, to put it mildly, silly, we didn't need that information now the way things were going in that country or all of them for that matter, we should have pulled out there and then. One morning in that Fort Rosebury area I went out to start observing angles and I was going up the leg of the tower and saw missing bolts, at first I thought they must have fallen out but then saw too many missing ones and upon testing slackened off ones this was definitely interference to try and have the towers collapse after we got up them. There afterwards we had to check carefully before going up or on our way up and that wasn't the only time it happened. However, we got through the observing without any collapsing of the towers and the time finally came to pack it all up, do our final book checking of observations and plotting of the triangle completion and accuracy and that was the finish of Northern Rhodesia for us.

Some time later when we were closer to Fort Rosebury, our black crew, the Rhodesians, had gone to town for some supplies and a bit of a party maybe although they were not drunks at all. But, coming back they drove off the road at an old wooden bridge river crossing and three were killed. My buddy Taff Jones was there in charge and he reported in and told Oggie that things were getting ugly and the local political party were making a big issue out of it and we had better give them a good burial. Oggie said, they get a pauper's burial, that's all that is in their agreement. These were guys that had been with us for years and were virtually our friends in a way, especially with guys like us who worked along side of them. Taff said to Oggie, I don't have anyone here to support me I think someone had better come up but when Oggie put the word out there were no volunteers. Taff called again a couple of days later and said it was getting worse, very bad and he was uneasy about it. I took the phone and said, I will leave in the morning Taff and be with you tomorrow night, He said thank God Frank, see you soon, have a safe trip I need you. We were letting one of our black guys doing most of the negotiations and we provided the transport and, of course, better coffins than what Oggie said they get, out of our pockets. This funeral was the worst sacrilegious debacle and devilish performance one could imagine. There was only Taff and I and what seemed like thousands of others. Two of our own, " boys" were standing close to us and said, in our own broken Ndebele language not understood by these local blacks, this is not good boss, you shouldn't be here, they are going to use you. Before the burial ceremony was final held prior to placing the coffins in the ground a lot of in fighting and scuffling was happening on top of the new coffins which were on top of our big trucks and two fell off on end down onto the ground – it was bad! They got them back up again and one business suited government man got on top of the coffins and made a big speech evidently some of it against us. We had a couple of reliable local guys who kept us informed about the proceedings and we were the whipping boys. Speaking of which, there were tribal party men dressed up in leopard skins and head caps going around with huge cat of nine tails keeping everyone in line. A hush was called: paganism, quasi Christian religion and politics were all rolled into one and everyone was told to kneel and worship this big leader and they all went down one in numbers and finally one by one. Taff whispered, are you going to kneel and I said, no and he said, okay, we could feel the sweat running down our spines but it wasn't the climate. One of the leopards came forth and motioned us to kneel, we shook our heads. He looked back up at the leader-chief, up on the coffins and everything froze in that stinking heat, it was like the world stood still and then the leader waved his guy on and we survived. Taff was very upset over the way the department and Oggie Rates, our chief, had handled everything and rightly so but we were different then. Now, as an American, I would have torn those guys a different place in society but we were mostly accepting of our circumstances.

But, this was about the end of colonialism as well. Our department knew it was here for quite some time but never told any of us about what was happening and what would be happening to us. The bottom line was, when it all came down to it we didn't have a job. The Federation of Rhodesia's and Nyasaland was now dissolved and we didn't have an employer. We were and always had been Federal Government contract employees and it was now non existent. A few of us were offered a position in the now Southern Rhodesian Government although its prospects were not looking far into the future either so the majority of we old Bushmen accepted the inevitable and I think I got 300 Rhodesian Dollars which at that time were about the equivalent of a US$ but not for long. I was also offered a free train ticket to Cape Town, which I declined. I had about four weeks left in the office and we had yet to sell our home.

10

Bechuanaland – Mineral Exploration

After the break up of two Rhodesia's & Nyasaland in 1963 these three countries soon attained their independence and became known as Zimbabwe (Southern Rhodesia); Zambia (Northern Rhodesia) and Malawi (Nyasaland). Southern Rhodesia was named after Cecil John Rhodes and understandable that having once obtained independence would adopt a more appropriate typical tribal African type name. Northern Rhodesia was, of course, an adjunct of Southern Rhodesia and it was now independent of Southern Rhodesia and needed an African name hence, Zambia. Nyasaland, however, changed simply to disassociate itself from that colonial type era.

I am not sure where this brief paragraph belongs yet but suffice it to say here, it has taken me some time to see the break up and independence of these countries in a different light to how I had for many years following this independence, take over and the ousting of the white man

*There are still some white men living and working in these coun-
tries but their status and positions are not the same and, those
of my age are now passed on or certainly retired. My difficulty
in accepting what happened in Southern Rhodesia is for several
reasons: a) The country should never have been handed over to
terrorists, they were gangsters feathering their own nests at the expense of a strong economical self contained country – they simply
robbed the coffers just like gangsters (terrorists) do.*

*b) There was no one in their quasi military rabble who could man-
age a sophisticated country which is what Southern Rhodesia was.
It was the bread basket for all the surrounding starving nations; c)
I was emotionally attached to the country, its incredible progress
and development under a very fair and judicious rule of law. It was
my country, my home and my life.*

When I showed up at Rhodesian Selection Trust's office in Francistown
in Botswana a town on the rail line coming from the north through the
edge of Bechuanaland on down into South Africa. Although Rhodesian
Selection Trust (RST) was exploring inland westward it had established
itself at the railhead to facilitate, in those early days, the receiving of
heavy exploration equipment by rail and there really was no other
convenient place to be then for connection to the "outside" world.
Land line Telephone service in those days was most difficult and from
any of the inland towns was non existent or impossible. We had a
radio link between Francistown and the main base camp, Matsitama,
but even that was unreliable, (I doubt that anyone today under the
age of 70 years realizes what communication was like in Africa once
upon a time..) Upon independence the company name was changed
to Roan Selection Trust but was still (RST) a roan was one of the protected buck (deer) a very lovely one. There were two motels one at
either end of the one partially paved road running parallel with the

rail track through town and we had some marvelous drinking parties on the weekends in those pubs. I am amazed I am still alive as I think back on some of them, but it was a routine we kept up with the geologists and related engineers and mining types, I was classed with the geologists and learned a lot about their field of work. It is also true to say that any geologist when coming to a new area has also to learn to recognize the local rocks and their identification By Sunday, the guys in from the main camp would be lying quietly on their beds reading novels and not drinking, trying to mend their hangover's and recover before heading out to camp before sun up on Monday morning. The desert where we sampled along the scrub lines was unbearably hot at around 110 degrees after the noon time hour and doing that with a 48 hour hangover is not fun,

One of the geologists, John Reid, the Rhodesian born guy, was extremely brotherly friendly with a local Botswana born Caucasian guy who managed one of the pubs and when John was in from the field these two were as close as twins and I don't imply anything to the contrary because they were simply the greatest of buddy's. This was an amazing friendship because they just didn't match up educationally or professionally but somehow that was not a hindrance to this fantastic friendship, they were like glue. John had a girlfriend up in Salisbury, Rhodesia but she had to be long suffering because he rarely went up home there was too much party drinking going on in Francistown. Eventually John did go up and spend some time with his girl the outcome of which they got married, and his Francistown friend was Best Man, but it was all very sad from there onwards. John then got a transfer back to Salisbury and that left his pal desolate. I use the word desolate purposely because very soon he hanged himself, all so awful and tragic. It hit John like a sledge hammer and he blamed his wife for being too possessive, unbelievable! but that friendship was one of the tightest I ever saw and I am an old soldier and have seen some good friendships. I too had one as a young soldier when I was first up in Nairobi, Kenya and they are very strong relationships that don't fall apart easily. John Reid, the Rhodesian, was never happy after he left Francistown and the tragedy of his buddy. Louise and I knew John and his wife and they sometimes came to dinner at our home in Salisbury when we were in from the Bush and we could see that they were not in love. I don't know how it ended up because we eventually lost touch as well.

I checked in to the Tati Hotel (Tati, a local tribal name and also given to a river) as a drinker, it did not take me long to get to know the explorers: the engineers and geologists two Canadians, one English, one Belgian and two Rhodesians, and a South African Doctor Geophysicist . There was an engineering crew for managing all the equipment used on a sophisticated investigation such as this one and me the surveyor. They had never had a surveyor but began to realize that as they discovered rich soil samples everything needed to be on a map and some kind of quick reference for areas of interest as drilling log results began to be assessed. It wasn't that they didn't know what they had done or discovered but not to have this mapped and high lighted was delinquent. When senior geologists arrived at the camp there was no map to spread out and say here's where these good results are which is x miles from so and so etc. My job was to catch up on all of this, contribute ideas and try to manage a drafting office in Francistown as well.

Once again, I didn't want to make you a surveyor and I don't want to make you a mineral exploring surveyor or geologist. Our jobs and tasks overlapped and we provided each other with all we knew without becoming possessive, it was really remarkable. The geologists would say to me, stop by the shed Frank there are a couple of good logs there you might like to see and then they would show me and explain why they were good logs. (A log – core of rock brought up by a diamond drill and laid in viewing trays so that you know the depths and can see the strata) Simplified here's how it goes: I am not certain how one knows initially that it is an area or land worth the time and money involved on a big mineral exploration investigation such as this one other than big companies had huge tax write offs for investigating mineral rich areas. There were some pointers and I will get to that description later. The dirt and sand roads just to and from the main camp to Francistown were vehicle wreckers let alone the areas we covered with only desert scrub terrain The best trucks for handling the equipment, materials and samples in and out were the Mercedes 7 ton trucks and these were a very expensive vehicle to purchase but they lasted. The smaller more personal type vehicles we had a variety. The American pick-ups were the easiest on the spine but not as reliable as a Land Rover, because of the kind of work I did on the move through rough cut lines I had a new Land Rover, I was used to them and quite happy with it but if I got a ride into Francistown with one of the guys in a big Ford F250 I took that gratefully as well.

Louise and I initially rented a house in town close to the RST Office, very convenient and sensible but my personality was not compatible to living in this manner and I was able to rent some land about 12 Kilometers out of town on the road out to the Maxwell's, we were back nearby our old friends and able to make visits to them on weekends. Because I was going to be out of town on and off Louise somehow got herself a job with the one and only big mostly dry goods store in town but they handled just about anything and every thing. She was always very capable and conscientious and became popular with them, The Haskin's and an associate of theirs, a drinking man probably an alcoholic and a real grouch, it was one of his farm lands that I rented. I built up a small herd of cattle, some in milk and one bull who I allowed to roam and graze with the herd. There was an old dipping tank on the farm and every 3 or 4 months I would swim the cattle through the dip to keep them free of ticks and other disease bearing insects. John Walsingham, the associate of Haskins, first objected to that, I can't remember what his excuse was but if he could stop me dipping the animals they would become infected and then he could condemn me and them over that. This is the kind of individual that he was and there was no way for me ever getting along with him because he didn't want to get along with me or anyone for that matter. At night when he was well into his whiskey he would call me and accuse me of all kinds of idiotic things and at first I was so upset and worried I didn't know what to do. Then Louise said, you have to stop worrying about him, just do what you have to do with the cattle work and if he calls put down the phone and that worked for a time. Then we had very bad drought, my watering well dried up and I had no grazing this, of course, delighted Walsingham and he sent some one to take away my cattle. I naturally ran them off. I found a good watering place down in the river bed that ran past the bottom of the land, no running water but the sand was full in lower places. I encamped the herd there and allowed them to graze the banks and bought and hauled in fodder for them. Louise now knew that I had lost my mind but she unlike John Wallsingham, held her peace.

Following a long that bitter struggle with Walsingham and trying to keep my herd healthy and alive I got the opportunity of a big Rondavel house (round house) on the other side of town on a good section of the river where I was free of Walsingham. It was a big house, old but we liked it and I was free of rental problems. I sold off some of my herd but kept the younger good ones and we were now having calves. Louise became happier and helped me and we also got chicks which were railed up from South Africa and we reared and sold them for cooking purposes. We also had egg laying hens and when I was away doing my mineral exploration in the hot desert Louise was one busy girl. She had farm boys and herd boys but it was still a lot of work for her making sure everything was cared for properly. I got one of the geologists to take a look at the river bed in my stretch and tell me where the water was underground. He huffed and puffed and finally showed me where he thought it was. I thanked him and let him go then did it myself by seeing where the natural rock strike dams were and some diving then we hired the well digging equipment to come in as they were in the area doing government work and gave me a terrific low price. Unfortunately, like so many in that life in that area the drillers were usually drunks and when it was time to drill mine they were in the Tati Bar. The guy who owned the rig told me not to worry he would round them up and get them sobered. Well he got them into a hotel room and then sat out in front of the door so that they couldn't leave. However, he forgot the window and we lost another day but finally started drilling. We were down about 25 feet, no water and the operator said; he had a bad tooth and would have to go up to Bulawayo in Rhodesia. The rig owner said, he's got a hangover and wants to get back into the Bar, have you got any beer, I gave the boss a dozen bottles that he could control. The driller said his tooth was still bad so the boss took a look in his mouth, asked the other one to pass him his small pliers and pulled the damned thing out on the spot just like that. The driller spit out blood for a while, I gave them a half bottle of brandy and the drilling re commenced. Suddenly, at about 37 feet deep we hit artesian well water was gushing up and all over. Every one said, they had never hit such a good water-well as this. Did the geologist divine the site but the rig owner said no, it was Frank himself who sited it. I could have started a business right there and then, everyone wanted me to mark them a drilling hole.

Out in the desert in the exploration sites a lot of ground had already been covered and there were poor maintained files of areas soil sampled but only people who had been involved knew where these locations were on the ground, I was horrified and said so but all I got was well you are here now, fix it! If anyone had moved out away from what was known as the soils exploration team then no one knew where that document filed information location was. I told the chief field geologist I needed to fly over the whole area starting from the beginning to where we were now operating. He couldn't see the point of that. I could have gotten in touch with a higher authority and I would have been given the OK but I didn't want to do that so, I explained it to one of the Rhodesian geologists and he could see why I needed to do it. He said; leave it with me Frank I'll get the okay the rest will be up to you. I hate to say this but the chief geologist was an alcoholic and felt so bad during the days it wasn't possible to talk to or get through to him but John Reid, the Rhodesian who had known him for many years managed somehow and the chief leaned on John a lot even down to ladling out the soup otherwise he poured it on the wrong side of the soup dish. It was a shame but no one wanted to do anything about it, we were bush-men, of course. The big boss was also a Rhodesian and whenever he came out to camp he would ask John, how's Ewing, is he getting by yet! and John always said, he'll be fine, John covered for him and the top guys knew that but as long as John wanted to do that they kept hands off. It was a rich copper field area and we knew we had massive sulphides but we had yet to expand it, zoom in on it and especially get it surveyed, there was no way we could go to the financial backers without a proper location map indexed to all the high light finds and discoveries. The information was so sadly lacking in this manner, if I wished to see one of the good areas I could only do so by getting one of the soil sampling technicians to take me there, the knowledge of its whereabouts was in his head only. This again was because of Ewing being debilitated through excessive drinking. I too discussed thus with John Reid, the Rhodesian born geologist , we had become drinking buddies too and, he said, just leave it Frank, don't try and take over just do us a good job and put it all together so that we know where we are and what we have. Anything you need talk to me and I will get it for you. Now, do a good job of surveying because there is wealth here. One night out there in the camp known as Matsitama before dinner, we had cooks and lived pretty well while out there but no air conditioning. We had powerful generating capacity but we just didn't live with air conditioning in those days in Rhodesia. Our huts were all well screened and no mosquito nets were required, the boys (servants) went around each hut about 5 p.m. and sprayed some deadly DDT fumes for you to breath throughout the night but, no bites to itch you all day.

The next place of any note or notoriety down along the rail line was about 100 miles south and it was called Palapye. It had a motel on the road that always ran parallel with the railway line through town and of most importance a pub. The owner of the hotel was a South African ex Bechuanaland government employee, discharged for suspicion of diamond broking. (If you don't know, illicit diamond broking is receiving diamond from some employee and selling them on a black market yourself) It was never proven so he got his pension, for what it was worth, but he got a clearance and grant from the Chief of Bechuanaland and built his hotel alongside the main road, he also discovered an underground water gusher and even sold water to the railway line steam engines. The government tried to buy him out but so far when I was there they had not yet succeeded because he was friendly with the Bechuanaland Chief from way back. Everything went at a snails pace and the drinking and alcoholic rate was very high consequently not much work was done and no follow through on anything like it. However, Jack also had an aircraft, I forget now what it was but it was a single engine high wing slow "wobbler" but, I hired him to fly the exploration field for me. I had no comprehension of its extent and would only get an appreciation from seeing the cut open scrub lines from the air. These lines cut through the scrub in this delicate desert land last for a lifetime and the international environmentalists today no longer allow it if they can stop it. When we finally got airborne I figured, with Jacks help the extension of exploration lines was about 150 miles wide westwards south of the Makgadigadi Salt Pans and maybe 100 miles southwards. This was a massive area to cover and to allow it to happen without knowing where it was is to me unbelievable. The procedure is initially soil sampling along lines spaced about 3 miles apart parallel at intervals along the lines of 500 feet intervals. This is just to get a view of what is natural in the area and what is of interest. However, it is necessary to have at least three lines to see if there is maybe any anomaly but the main reason for the apartness of the lines initially is to find (ppm) parts per million, defining the area and what might be high. If a high reading comes in along one of these base lines a more dense-like grid is then set out over the high reading areas, sometimes nothing and sometimes interesting. If, interesting more soil samples are taken and sent in to the lab in Francistown for analyses. Now there may be an area of interest and light drilling is now required to see what is down there. The Wagon Drills are brought in which consists of diesel driven drills mounted on a truck bed which can go at an angle into the dip of the rock along the strike and can get to a depth of 40 feet deep. Samples of the powdered rock are bagged every 24 inches and marked for its position on the grid set up. The powdered rock is set out in a pattern so that the sampler/driller can return to the area and take further samples if required at any depths from the piles set out. I could ramble on but will cut it short. The last phase of exploration of this type is to use the diamond drill rigs and go down to one thousand feet if necessary. The cost of putting a rig on an area is expensive and the decision belongs to the chief field geologist only he wasn't capable and at this camp my friend John called the shots. After I had been there for six months and had good mapping of hot areas he and I did it together along with an engineer who had never been included prior to this and we were beginning to function. George Swift was this engineer, a South African, and he was pleased to be part of it, as he should be, and he said it was beginning to look professional. On the other hand, the old South African Physicist did not like it because he was not automatically included in the final decision making whether to drill or not, but we made some great finds and we now knew where we were and how the deep bed rock was laying (striking), and we began to see a pattern. When the chief geologists came down from the copper belt in Zambia (Northern Rhodesia) they were extremely pleased that we could lay out maps of the area with all the information referenced and they began to look at our results and ability in a different way. John told them our progress in this area was due to me and I was a necessary member of the team. I know that they wanted to put John in charge and they had high regard for me because of the mapping and the reports from the other geologists who all now had copies of the maps of the area. There was still a lot of mapping to do and I had suggested bringing in an aerial photography group. They agreed and said that they would but to hold off for the season. We did run some short length infra red negative flights which were excellent in confirming areas of interest. Our main location for doing these infra red flights was to see what was happening in "old ancient mine diggings"

These old copper digging areas belonged to a tribe of people dating back around 500 years as best we could ascertain. We brought in University types who love to be involved in these kinds of finds. They were able to tie it in with similar diggings in other adjacent country spots where they already had come across relics, they believed, of these same peoples. We don't know what it was that identified the copper discovery to these ancients but they found it and took out enough to rudely smelt and work into tools etc. The infra red photo's of these old mine areas did not help us a lot except for Dr, Bozzaza, the physicist, who poured over them for months and held forth upon it night after night but we moved on around them with our exploration methods. The Northern Rhodesian miners and geologists claimed that it was only by discovering the old mine shafts we were able to find this high grade copper. They did not want to give us the glory. However, now that we had the maps showing soil and light drill rock samples plotted on a topographical map we were beginning to see where the main copper finds were and start thinking along our own exploratory mine shaft locations. The exploratory shafts along with diamond drill recordings, is what finalizes the decision to mine the ore. Of course, it is not only the scientific hard discovery that counts, especially in this part of the world however, Bechuanaland has always been a very peaceful nation and it would be mainly the logistics of transportation that would be the final decision. Seretse Khama, the Chief and President of Bechuanaland soon to be named Botswana was more than ready for us to proceed with mining so we did not have a political problem as so many other emerging nations had. Seretse was still very much supreme and generally supported by the people. He was a western civilized educated man first in South Africa at an English speaking university and then Oxford in England. I was also one of his many close friends and we partied together often at a hotel and pub that he owned along with his white wife from England. The Brits initially debarred her from returning to Bechuanaland along with him but this caused such a furor in the country power structure they had to back off and allow her to return. I met her too and also had a few drinks with her but the main drinking was held like the old Oxford Club boys do with Seretse singing bawdily away in the group.

Finally, it was decided and agreed to put down three deep exploratory mine shafts where we knew we had high copper lodes and of course they came out tops. Mining was finally to start after all that wonderful mineral exploration. Ewing, the alcohol troubled chief of party was first to go, pushed out and he returned to Canada, the two younger Canadians followed and the Rhodesian, John Reid was offered the position to remain as an exploration figure head. He turned it down and went home to run the family business of stores (kind of early day supermarkets) in the rural indigenous areas and of course, to drink. Dr. Bozzaza and his second wife, ex secretary, bought a huge yacht, retired and went off to Europe to sail the Aegean Sea. Obviously, the old exploratory team that found that copper was breaking up if not already broken. One day, over in Serowe which was the Capitol of Bechuanaland I was having a whole day party with Seretse and I told him about the dissolving of that great team that discovered his copper and, I was now out of a job. While we were still sober enough he wrote down a note that he had to contact Ray Renew, the Chief Surveyor of Bechuanaland to tell him I would be joining the government as the senior surveyor. He was furious, Renew that is, and told me he did not like the underhand way this had been done. I told him in reply, it was not underhand at all and it was not my suggestion. I was an honored friend of Seretse Khama who was rewarding me for helping find all that copper. Also, I am a personal friend of Seretse and if he so desired we could go along to where he could voice his opinion because my appointment was by Seretse himself, Do you want to do that Ray? He scowled at me and told me to fill out the application forms and they would be passed along and I would be informed. I believe, from a good source, he tried to have my appointment squashed by down playing me in government bureaucratic circles, but there were too many knew me and that I was a close friend of Seretse. They were afraid to go against his appointment of me no matter where it supposedly originated, it did not have to have originated in Seretse's Pub we could have done it anywhere I only had to ask, because it was that simple. However, it was a genuine reward for services rendered to his country

We had been with RST now (Roan Selection Trust) about 18 months when we experienced a tragedy. We were immediately south of a confluence of two rivers which are dry for the most part of the year.

However, when they do get rains the downpours are monsoonal and the rivers are in flood for relatively short periods of time. Unfortunately, the flood burst the river banks on the upside of us and the whole area where we were situated went under water. I watched the water come up over our river bank at an alarming rate and then started making deals with myself:....if it gets to the first rung on the fence wire I will pull out, get all the livestock out remove the kerosene trays from the bottom of our big freezers for poultry meat and milk. Get the vehicles and animals up on to a dry high island etc. Then I made another deal.....the next wire rung on the fence and eventually I had to accept we were going to drown. It was night time and the engines that we ran on the river bank also pumped our water to the house from the sands where we had sunk well points and supplied power for the lights. I told Louise we had to get out and we needed to do it now and get whatever we could to salvage and save as much as possible then get out ourselves. We went to a neighbor's house that was higher than ours and they were flooded to some extent but not their house. The next morning we returned to our place to view the damage and the mess and what a mess it was. We had lost so much of our developing hard work on the land and property and I had no idea if I could salvage the engines which were still under water. We had about 100 Cornish Hens that roosted in a big tree away from the Jackals but the silly hens came down to see what was happening and they all drowned. Louise cried for the first time living a life such as ours. Later after it was all over and we were salvaging whatever we could, most of our soft furnishings were lost including beds. I was all set to start over when she sat down beside me on the high bank watching the water whorls tumbling past and said, I can't do it again please Frank so I decided it was time to move on once more

(RST) Roan Selection Trust, just fell short of begging me to stay with them, they knew I was a very close friend of Seretse and they valued that friendship within the company but I told them not to worry they would always have the Chief's ear via me. There are still a few stories to be told and I hope to add them in later to my Bechuanaland RST Story. That remaining massive mineral exploration work data lies dormant to this day as do the guys who achieved it and most of these have passed on to their next job, some on high or maybe low.

11

Botswana Government Work

We went almost straight from work with RST based in Francistown, on the main rail link, to our new position as a Surveyor with the Department of Lands and Mines, in the Botswana Government. In those days, most of the Botswana (Bechuanaland) Government Offices were in Mafeking, over the border in South Africa which was the Capital of the Protectorate of Bechuanaland from around 1896 (the siege of Mafeking) until 1965 when Gaberones, in southern Botswana, a newly built township, became the Capital of Botswana. We still lived in the old fortress in Mafeking, South Africa where Lord Baden Powell directed the defense against the Boers; he also created the Scouts to become, "The Boy Scouts" which eventually spread throughout the whole world

Our Director of surveys was Ray Renew, a South African (not a Boer – Dutch) whom I mention in my chapter with the Rhodesian Selection Trust mineral exploration paragraph before getting my job with the Survey Department through Seretse Khama, Chief and President of Botswana and, of course, upsetting Ray, he felt he had been sand bagged, by-passed, and I guess, in a sense he was. I did not really need the position, I was well established with the exploration and mining group that were going to mine the copper there in Botswana that we had discovered in Bechuanaland. However, a survey was needed of what was known and called the Okovanga Swamps – a misnomer. It is a magnificent huge natural wetland named as a swamp because it is fed by the run-off of mountains and rivers in Angola. It fills up the Okovanga Delta until it too runs over feeding the rivers going south in Botswana and west from there. Today, it is a great tourist attraction with many wild life photographic camps in the area. I knew the area when it only had a couple of hunter's huts and no safari camps. However, I am pleased that it now has photo safaris and virtually no hunting, it is a fabulous delta and those swamp area tracks are kept open only by elephant, hippopotamus and buffalo that one is sure to meet along the way through the "swamps".

That was how it was when I knew it and worked in that area. It was not even known as a tourist area, there was only the dilapidated Maun Hotel. Maun being a "town" on the edge of the delta where the Botletle River flowed south west into Lake Ngami and then sometimes back again depending on the season and the rains up in Angola. The hotel was there mainly for Bechuanaland Government employees: Cattle people, game wardens, surveyors on works safaris, well and borehole rig diggers for water and other employees of that ilk. The remuneration was very poor but the life for those of us who appreciated these wildernesses it was the only way to live and the best. It was in Maun in that old hotel that I met Bobby Wilmot during his crocodile hunting glory days, I had already read his dads book, (Always Lightly Tread) Croc hunting was how Bobby made his living and, of course, the "swamps" were full of crocs, only the belly skin is useable and that is cut out and the remainder thrown back for the crocs who are surrounding the boat in hundreds. He cured the skin and sent it in bundles to his source in South Africa where some of it was used but most of it was shipped to America and the Far East. Bobby said, get in with the pike and pull some big ones close for me to shoot. At first I wouldn't do it but eventually I too became even crazier and jumped in waist deep sorting them through -- CRAZY!! I have been in Maun, at the hotel when by coincidence a number of government fellows all showed up in the same night or weekend. It was practice, if in the area, to come in to Maun for a weekend party and there were some good ones I can recall or, barely recall, I think there were about half a dozen residents in Maun in government housing, there was the inevitable government garage where one could get repairs made for a few Dollars. That was a remarkable life and we that lived it never thought that for many of us that one day it would end but it did, times change and we never know how, when or where. The Wilmot family lives on and Bobby's photographic camps were finally built and became very successful as they are today. The Wilmot family of 3 daughters and a son, now all still living in Maun, descendents of old Kronje from about the year 1900 and involved in various ways with the Safari's. My first task with the department was to go off solo and reconnoiter the areas proposed for finding and taking water to pipe and pump to the new mines yet to be established. I was sent out alone I think as a punishment for getting my job with the department from the top down. That territory, and the work involved was not a job that could be done by one man and Renew knew that better than most. I was aware of that and he was hoping to get rid of me in that way because he had no other avenue open to do it. I decided to let it ride and actually be on the move in those areas that I knew and familiarize myself with as much of the rest of it as I could, locating possible water take-off sources. I was out about four months and discovered it was also full of lion and one needed to be very careful especially at nights sleeping beside my Land Rover as I did when moving through those desert areas. I picked up a lone black guy named Chang? That area too, once had Germans in it prior to WWI and he was a hangover descended from that period, I gave him one of my rifles and felt better with another pair of eyes and a shooter on the job He had worked with white men on many safaris and in permanent camps and was a real handy man of many talents for the dessert. I told him I would employ him when this safari was finished and he was okay with that. He acted as my cook, my vehicle man, night watchman and many other useful tasks that these guys did for we white-men. Nothing was stopping him from doing away with me at nights if he wished but he was a man of his word. He knew the area and was a wealth of local lore and I needed help along the way. It was a terrible thing that Renew did sending me out alone like that, I could have been killed in one of several ways and he probably would have been delighted and no one would know what happened to me but, I decided to play the game and with Chang it was not a problem except that we had only one vehicle in that far out god forsaken land.

With a lot of traveling, I was able to refuel in Maun with my government ID, and with names of rivers, areas and sketches I returned to Mafeking and set about formalizing my discoveries and recommendations. Finally, Renew asked me into his office, he asked me had I seen Seretse and I replied, yes, of course, he is my friend. He asked what I thought about the territory I had reconnoitered and I told him only the rivers I have listed have sufficient water to feed an extensive mine and the distances are too far to invest in pipelines and pumps for initial mining. I was a lightweight mining engineer as well and was the only guy available to do this kind of work in the department but it needed a team and at least two jeeps with a big support vehicle as we were always self contained and no contact with our base. And then he said, are we to work together or do you work for Seretse? I told him he knew better than that if I had wanted to be with Seretse I would have stayed with RST. He then said, you are one of the best bush and desert men I know and a most knowledgeable surveyor but I can't have divided loyalties if you are going to do this work which you know I have been instructed to do I need you, but we have to be open and honest with one another. I asked right there if he was going to try and get me killed off again and he laughed, stood up and offered his hand and said, you are a hard man O'Hare and that is what I need. Keep your friendship with Seretse but work for me and we will get along. He was a very shrewd and conniving man himself.

I left to go back into the Kalahari Desert again with two fairly new jeeps and a two-ton 4-wheel drive pick-up heading out to Serowe again, Seretse Khama's desert town home and stayed a few days there whilst he and I caught up with our news. This time, our safari had 2 young white South African surveyors, four experienced black survey crew and my man Chang. Seretse asked me if I was spying for Ray and I replied, I am in between you and Ray, Seretse, and you know that I am not in the spying business but we might as well understand up front that I will share some of what I know naturally, both ways, and I will be the arbiter of what I pass along. I had had my disagreement with Renew and made up, now I was forthright with Seretse, my friend, and he was satisfied with my answer so we drank to that. Upon leaving Mafeking again I headed north about 40 miles to Lobatsi where the paved road ended and from there onwards all the way up to Francistown was red dirt road. In the rainy season this dirt road was like a 2 foot deep River and often vehicles would be stranded for days on end waiting for the waters to subside. I was familiar with every inch of it, where it would be impassible and where I could circumnavigate and also how long it would take to open again. Lobatsi was a big cattle center with an abattoir (slaughter-house) and meat packing plant and literally thousands of cattle were slaughtered and the meat sent in both railroad directions but mostly south to South Africa.

On this safari we were also going to survey part of the southern area of the Okovango Swamp territory in the event of taking water from that source. It was unwise to mention this to anyone because all were so protective of "The Swamps" and rightly so but; it was on the books as a supply source. Seretse asked me for my opinion on it and I told him he would lose a lot of respect and support if he was for it. He asked, will you find water without the Swamps and I assured him that we could so he agreed he was not be in favor of pulling it out of the swamps (wetlands) However, I did not tell him that the amount of water we needed for the mine would probably have no effect on the level of the swamp, I too simply didn't want filters, generators, pumps and all that paraphernalia in that natural setting there either. Unfortunately, at that time there was virtually no mapping in that area, the aerial photography that we had done with RAF Lancaster Bombers in 1949/52 did not extend to that territory so whatever we did now was from the beginning and this, of course, needs an astronomical fix which requires a team of at least 3 experienced surveyors and I did not have that. So, I established a solid concrete beacon in a safe locale and gave it a locally adapted coordinate value before going out on this Okovango Safari. Some future survey work in that area would hopefully work on this same coordinated original value until such times that a geographical grid value could be provided by an astro fix of this beacon and the coordinate values adjusted to main meridian origins. Ray promised me that one day he would come up there with me and we would do an astro fix, it never happened in my time

The survey had to be very selective because the area was so extensive, time was limited and my aides were relatively inexperienced yet in this kind of survey work. They had joined Botswana surveys they told me in the hope of becoming bush surveyors and they had heard about the activities of the Rhodesian Bush guys, they were exited and delighted to have this opportunity of learning with a real professional in their field. I carefully selected an area to cover near Maun in the Ngami River outflow section which ran south west into Lake Ngami.

However, I confined our activity to what would most likely be the pump station site and covered about 50 acres in that vicinity. This may not seem like very much land and yet under the circumstances, moving around in the swamp water and that high vegetation was quite an achievement and there were crocs around us. I also was aware that this survey would be important and an essential document for any future activity in that area. Once again, without going into the technicalities of the job in hand, our only method of progress was to traverse in the hippo and elephant cleared trails along with the crocodiles and this was a scary task at the best of times regardless of what I had learned with Bobby Wilmot. The progress was slow but my guys were willing and once they understood what we were doing we were able to observe and measure enough data for us to do a sketch compilation on the site. We were there for about two months carrying out this work and it was the only mapping available in this area for a long time to come. Later, when the copper mining activity began in earnest a number of aerial strips were flown of this area too and, much better plans and maps were produced. Nevertheless, we were proud of what we did under the circumstances and Renew thought we had produced a good working plan for any activity to commence in that area.

Once again we returned via the Magaddi-gadi Pan, this is a massive section of desert that has a high percentage of salt in the surface sand. The sand and the salt are so fine that they will penetrate anything and everything that you have in your vehicle loads as you travel across it. Once into this Pan one can set the hand-throttle and sit back and relax for hours on end, it is level and never ending. The instrument boxes that are especially well sealed were not exempt from this fine penetrating sand and we would find a little even there. As for our bed rolls and other camping gear well, they were just full of this fine sand that ran down the vehicle wind shields like dirty water. We often had to camp overnight there especially on the way into Maun; we would simply overnight by sleeping in our canvas bags beside the jeeps and we always had a tuck-box available containing a few cooking utensils and items to prepare a meal before climbing into the bags. We were now familiar with this area that was always occupied by large groups of lion and one had to sleep with only one eye open preferably one ear. At first they could be heard in the distance growling and grunting and then we would hear them grunting around closer to our encampment. If one wanted to sleep soundly someone had to be on duty and now with several members in the party this was possible. Blowing sand would make minor drifts covering our tracks and it is not always possible to backtrack along the incoming trail and if the sun was high a compass bearing was always necessary. If traveling East to Francistown one would have to travel the length of the salt-pan or alternatively go south on compass bearing constantly checking again after ground interruptions and then out into typical scrub desert bearing East again to hit the main Francistown/Gaberones south trail. Once again it is interesting to note that no one ever knew our whereabouts or location, no one knew that huge area other than we that used it – two vehicles are essential in those conditions.

Upon contemplation of the survey of the Okovango Swamp territory I somehow got into selecting local high school graduates to be trained as survey technicians. It was a political decision to have locals trained as surveyors and I am still uncertain as to why Renew gave me this task, he new that it was not part of my resume and I was better employed elsewhere, however, he insisted I get started. I did all the usual by advertising and visiting the high schools and inviting applications. Reviewing the applications and then interviewing about 100 likely candidates, and with this information I reduced the candidates again to about 50 and interviewed them again bringing the number down to 25 class size. All this work had used up about two months time including one week off for me, and Louise, my wife, and I went down to South

Africa and met with the friends in the construction and surveying business, I didn't know what Renew was up to but I was not very happy with what was taking place. However, I started the class and with help and assistance of two local survey technicians who had been working with me we got started. As a matter of fact I thoroughly enjoyed the teaching and my class was a huge success coming in something like 90% passed the final exam. My exam papers had been previously submitted and results were very high for new technicians but I then redesigned and used them for the final exams. Nothing like this had ever been done before in Botswana and I became a celebrity overnight. Many high-ranking government officials insisted on meeting with me and some of my students, it was unbelievable. Seretse called me up to his headquarters and thanked me formally in front of many dignitaries and officials. Somehow, all the kudos I was receiving completely upset Renew and he canceled all future technical training activity. I was not concerned because I was unable to go forward with the training agenda as planned because of Renews underhand and secretive way of canceling it and because of my notoriety I then decided my time with the Botswana government (Renew) was over.

I did not want to do any more work with Ray Renew. Surveying in Africa at that time under those conditions required the total commitment and dedication of an individual. It also required the confidence and support of the senior staff dedication, especially from the one in charge and Renew was too far removed from the work and his professional employees (few in number) to have a close enough relationship. We would meet occasionally at some party but not friendly enough to discuss anything in regard to the job or in a more intimate way. He was a quiet man and kept pretty much to himself, his passion was what we called surf fishing. He had a boat which could ride the surf and he did deep sea fishing off the East Coast like Durban in Natal. He had been in private practice as a township land surveyor in South Africa but the partnership dissolved and then he got this Chief Surveyor's role. His marriage was not good, she was not a looker in any sense of the word and he was a handsome athletic individual and I think had a girlfriend or two. She realized this and drank too much and bad mouthed him to whoever would listen -- no one would. She was a wonderful artist and I saw many of her clever paintings. She was also well educated and was a researcher of sorts, an academic and was a bad match for Renew, it was all very sad and had this dampening effect on him. For some reason he saw me as a challenge, maybe from the way I came in and my association with Seretse, the mining company and all the copper discovery that was happening so, Louise and I moved on and went down to South Africa for another new life.

12

Living in South Africa

Following winding up our affairs and business in Botswana we returned to our home in Southern Rhodesia to assess the housing market and our possibility of selling it. Much had changed, the country had been at war for two years now, many reservists and regulars had been called up and terrorist groups were infiltrating the country in the remoter farming areas and even some of the urban areas. The outer farming areas were the most vulnerable and it was the plan of these terrorists, whose leaders were Moscow trained, not only to terrify the local tribal people but also to scare the white farmers from their land as it had been done when I was in Kenya all those years ago. The white farmers were not only the bread basket of the whole country and even for the survival of the indigenous in neighboring countries but their agricultural products were the main revenue of Southern Rhodesia. These farms were big, intensive and very scientifically managed. If ever those farmers left then the country would go back at least 100 years and that is exactly what happened when Britain and America condemned the white population of Southern Rhodesia who had been settled there for over 300 years they destroyed the countries revenue sources.

Rhodesia protecting and defending itself was also condemned and a naval blockade was put on the Mozambique port of Beira so as to stop material and equipment including military requirements going through to Rhodesia. Of course, the supply route and supplies were obtained through South Africa but this was slower, longer and more costly. Britain and the USA did all in their power to break the backs of the white population of Southern Rhodesia by several means, particularly ginning up public world opinion. American educational professors commenced propaganda school programs and demonstrations with students who did not even know where Rhodesia was or what the history of the white settlers were. However, they demonstrated in the streets screaming, "Whites out of Africa!!!" if it wasn't so tragic it would have been a laugh, we had not killed or exterminated anyone The difference between British and American settlers is that the Rhodesian whites did not exterminate the black populace who at that time were not so plentiful but instead provided good healthcare for all, managed by a white group of people increasing the livelihood and life of the black Rhodesians by a hundredfold. It would have been better had they left us alone to deal with our own terrorist invasion from neighboring communist controlled countries, Angola to the east and Mozambique to the west. We were already pretty much in control when they began their blockades and bringing in regiments of the British army into Botswana. (America is never in sympathy with anyone else protecting themselves, only America is allowed to kill peoples in the hundreds of thousands to protect themselves no matter where it may be).The Southern Rhodesian army was made up of a mixed population who shared everything in the way of housing and mess facilities 80% black and 20% young white-men whose great grand fathers had come to Rhodesia to work hard, teach the locals and find opportunity for a better life, kind of like America?

Our home was on the outskirts of Salisbury (Soweto) in an unincorporated area of small ranches and people were beginning to be uncomfortable (scared) there too but nothing like what those farming families were experiencing. Many of the heads of these families were away in the military already hunting down these bands of terrorists who were not necessarily tribal Rhodesians at all but from other surrounding countries and in many exerts from far a field.

While we were putting our affairs in order, so to speak, we advertised and placed our house up for sale but no one even came to look at it and it was a give away, we knew that we couldn't get what it was worth any more. I had been dropping in on the offices of Muir Wilson and Associates, international consulting engineers, offices in Africa and they have their head office in Jersey, Channel Islands. Peter Muir, one of the partners, had told me to check in periodically and see what was happening and this time he offered me a job in Bulawayo, south again in Rhodesia not too far from where we were married many years previously in Gwanda. Louise said if we are going to South Africa then let's not hang around here in Rhodesia but get down there and find a job. However, I wanted to be on staff with Peter for future work if necessary so we took the Bulawayo job. We got rid of most of our possessions and left the house better than basically furnished and gave it to an agent to try and sell, we still owed on the mortgage which was already under water after having paid off half of the loan. The realtor asked, are you going to walk away from it and I said, maybe. I think he had it in mind for himself it was a sweet deal. This new job in Bulawayo required someone who could keep their mouth shut. I was taken into the confidence not only of Peter, my friend and boss but also government officials. It was a "slaughter house for cattle and a meat packing plant. I found that a bit odd as we were right in the city and able to regulate the slaughter and distribution easily without having to cold store. Also we had an aircraft runway we were building not too far away and it stuck out like a dog's hind leg. Bulawayo had all the runways it needed at the regular international field and this was so extra. It was to be used for flying out beef to Europe, Greece and some other participating countries in the middle of the night. This method of export continued for more than 12 months while we progressed with the new abattoir and the runway airstrip. My position was an on-site resident engineer monitoring the contractors work, progress and quality. This was good for me as I phased through from surveying to construction engineering and management. We were a success with this project and when it was completed I told Peter, my boss, that I was going down to South Africa for a position with a quasi government agency, not government but initially supported by large subsidies. Once the project was up and running it became registered as ALUSAF Aluminum South Africa.

We moved down to South Africa in May1968 to that big project on the Natal coast in a town called Empangeni in Zululand where we were building an aluminum smelter plant right on the coast subject to incoming tides i.e. loading docks etc capable of meeting low and high tides, there was an oceanographer checking the tide levels as we did the massive earth works, removing all the swamp material and soils down to a predestined clay level. When the foundations were laid for the docks the oceanographer would then give us a final tide level. We removed millions of cubic yards of top soils to reduce the site level to this designed level (all top soils removed) clay level for all the pile driving that was required for future housing such as, the furnaces and the potting sheds etc (the potting shed was ¾ of a mile long) and many ancillary buildings, many of these piles were what is called raked piles, driven in at an angle to a predestined level. The two furnaces were mounted on deep vertical cylinder 48″ diam. piles down to a minus level from finished site of 50′ we went down inside of these to determine centering of the hydraulic rams over the founding pads. All of this layout and then leveling was my domain and as control engineer I had a very busy and active life. We were provided with a newly built large home which was a novel for Louise following how we had lived for so many years. Empangeni was on the ocean and that was where one wanted to be, in the sea because the temperature was in the high 90's and total saturation, not a good town to be in. We were friendly with the Resident Engineer, a South African, and quite a bit of entertaining and excessive drinking went on. My work here was through in May 1970 and I had obtained another project to move on to which was, chief field engineer for the location and establishment of the centerlines for future roads scheduled for construction of national roads and freeways. Following the marking of the centerlines by hidden and visible bench marks I was asked to stay on and be resident engineer for construction but I didn't want to remain in that sand dune desert any longer The company was, Jeffares and Green of Johannesburg just outside of Johannesburg and our first road was from Cape Town on up the West Coast to Port Nolloth a distance of about 200 miles.

The terrain was incredibly difficult to maneuver and even a four-wheel drive vehicle had great difficulty getting through. Locating a road route under these conditions was a laborious task, however, this is what I signed up for and we moved on with it. The strong whippy vegetation was known as Port Jackson Willow and the ground was mostly sand, these trees had been planted years previously to control the moving sand dunes. This road had international and military connotations and periodically had to be viewed by the provincial engineering with whom we had to notify and liaise when necessary. Locating the route was done from our design plans and aerial photographic strips flown for this purpose. However, there were occasions when it was essential to detour from the plan and proceed on experience alone but if this was a big detour the provincial engineer had to be notified and mostly he would show up to look at it. On one occasion where the access was very difficult and now literally far off any beaten track we had to call him and he was frustrated because of this difficult access but we proceeded and my leg went through some old dry brush and I was bitten by a cobra through my jeans with enough venom received to sicken me. I told him I needed to rest because I could feel my heart racing and he could go forward because my team were out there in the area working but he was afraid of being lost so I told him to make his way back to his Jeep and go home and we would do it later but he was afraid he would not be able to find his way back to his vehicle, now I was frustrated, he kept saying, What is going to happen to me (him) not me who was probably dying. He should have been saying, hang in there Frank I will gat the jeep and take you to a hospital – brave callous man. I was feeling the effects of the venom and this man was worried about finding his Jeep I just gave up and lay back against the tree and he waited. I eventually got him back to our vehicles and I said goodbye to him and good riddance under my breath then made my way back to our main camp and told my guys I was suffering from snake bite. They managed to get through by phone eventually to the University in Cape Town and gave them the story and the professor said, if he is not dead now he will be okay. I was okay in about a couple of days and moved back to the road alignment survey area route location and got on with our work. I decided not to call that engineer again unless the access was more accessible, we had plenty of calculations and visibility on the aerial photographs to show what we had done and my company approved. In all my years in Africa I had never had a close call with a snake bite until now and I had seen many snakes in the course of my work, I thank God for my escape from what could've been fatal.

Luderitz and Windthook

My final project and job for Jeffares & Green was to locate and align a new road route from Swakopmund to Windhoek the capital city of Namibia. A road location survey at that time in countries where previously there were no roads as we think of a road today. Roads were only paved through and in the immediate vicinity of big towns and cities.

Connecting routes between these towns was usually what we call a dirt road (gravel road) except in the case of Southern Rhodesia, where we had roads known as strip roads. "Strip Roads" were two parallel paved strips each strip 18" wide and placed apart to fit the width of the car tracks. Landover's of that era had a narrower gauge by about 4" consequently barely straddling the strips causing driving and riding to be most uncomfortable. The existing road from Windhoek to Luderitz was one of the regular dirt roads built in many places on sand. Moving dunes often cut these roads off completely for weeks or more.

The government of South Africa who administered South West Africa, as it was know also knew a nuclear mine was to be built 40 miles outside of Luderitz and naturally wanted to have a reliable road on which to travel to the railhead and International Airport in Windhoek.

Usually the consulting engineers who get the contract also receive the states road building standards along with any maps and plans and a detailed description of what is required. Jeffares & Green got this contract and I got the job of placing the future center-line of this road to be on the ground. We flew aerial strips along the route and with maps made from these low level strips and the route description I went out with a team to locate it and identify it by many beacons and steel pegs locating it's position when being built. The construction goes out to bid after the alignment survey is completed. This final position of the road center line has to be measured in the field when the survey is being done. Even at that time we had mostly graduated from measuring with a steel tape. The tape has to be suspended and taut with weights the temperatures read at the time of measuring for the coefficient expansion of steel. It is a laborious and time consuming work. With the advent of radar this work was speeded up but distance between points was limited until along came the tellurometer enabling measuring distances by sound waves. The equipment is bulky and very expensive however, I was able to get the use of the one from Witwaterstrand

University in Johannesburg. It had never been used on an actual job and the university was glad to make an arrangement with me. They supplied the equipment, use of, for also submitting to them our results. They had to agree, of course, the measurements could not be released until some time after awarding of the contract.

A road alignment survey is a complex and difficult job and that is why we have road surveyors and I am one of these as well. The road straights are located, and then measured several times for accuracy. With the tellurometer it does the several measurements on different band waves enabling an on the spot check. However, roads have curves and the beginning and end of a curve has to be identified and calculated in the field – all the small straights on the curve. Many things happen once in the field doing the job and decisions have to be made by the Field Engineer at the time. Holding up a job just to get someone else's opinion is not a good idea.

Our first stretch coming out of Luderitz was very tricky and difficult because we were in dune sand and these dunes can travel quite a distance in a short period of time. This area around Luderitz was well occupied and administered by the Germans prior to WWI and everything had a German flavor to it including the town of Luderitz (German) but especially the diamonds that they discovered during the time of their occupation. These diamonds were still being mined and recovered during the time we were doing the survey. Mining in that area was not developed at that period. The old Germans made the local natives make small heaps of sand which covered hundreds of acres and were quite a sight when flying in to Luderitz. These heaps had only been hand sieved and not all of them so access was forbidden by the Diomont Gerbidt...... Diamond Restricted Area. We were not even permitted to locate the new road within 300 meters of the fence which we ran parallel with our new road center line

I could see that these heaps were not sand and I needed to know what the material was so I asked permission to go in, inspect the ground around the heaps and qualify the heaps for sub base road material which was very scarce in all that sand. I was told by the diamond police that I could not take samples away or use heap material at road surface. I identified the material as suitable but the contractor had to make arrangements to do tests on site supervised by the police.

Diamond Recovery in Swakopmund

DeBeers used mostly two methods of extraction (collection): deep plowing up and turning over the sand along the shore stretch then sieving – also forbidden entry and sluicing up from huge barges out in the shallow water section off shore in the Atlantic ocean. Some deep drilling had been done but not enough survey sampling had yet been carried out to make drilling a proposition against the other two methods, before incurring the costs of diamond drilling a soil sampling grid is required to high-light the anomalies. There were 3 helicopter pilots in the pub where I too was staying and I often went out with one of them to change the crews on the barge. The crews did eleven days on and 4 days off which kept 3 pilots busy. One pilot could only land his 'copter when he was lubricated with beer. That Atlantic Ocean has big swells and I have to say, landing a 'copter on those heaving decks had to be fearsome. I even made sure I too was lubricated when I went out with him, he never had an accident! I got to know many "locals" while in that area and attended some great parties. The bank manager and his wife gave fantastic well catered parties with booze flowing like the Atlantic, I wondered how they could do it.....they couldn't, one day he just wasn't there any more. He was a Brit but he disappeared, as far as we know to somewhere in Gabon. He was never captured as far as I know.

We worked (measured) our way through this heavy sand dune moving area with great difficulty and eventually came out into more typical desert locale. No special cross sectional road type will allow moving sand to pass over the road in areas such as this. These average 30 foot high dunes are constantly on the move and bury anything in front of them we just have to let them move. In the more typical exposed hardpan desert sections sand still moved although often, unless you were doing similar work like ours, you wouldn't know it. Until I realized this I was becoming frustrated and annoyed by the fact that I was getting poor comparable distance readings. Our road had long straight sections which was easy to achieve in such conditions. The longer the straight sections the quicker and easier it is to complete the survey. However, identification concrete beacons had to be offset at regular distances and any other feature of interest noted and described. Especially gravel lodes this material is of great importance when building new rods. The less distance you have to haul it the lower the costs will be and it was part of our survey to provide this information to the bid documents.

I worried about these poor results in measuring and taking many more readings than was necessary until one morning we were making a measurement in what appeared to be a very calm peaceful and happy day. I was standing behind the unit which has a reflector and everything was apparently still and quiet. I said to myself we should get excellent results in these conditions but it hadn't always turned out that way. I was still looking down then realized I couldn't see part of my boots, only the upper portion. I put down my hand but the "mirage" disappeared. Standing up again and looking down no lower boot visible. I started walking along the path of the ray between the two units (both units measure and receive) It was obvious that very fine almost transparent sand was moving along close to the ground but it was so hot one just didn't notice it and you certainly couldn't feel it. Nevertheless, this small, fine moving was sufficient to bend the tellerometer ray causing those discrepancies in the readings, I was so happy I danced, it wasn't the equipment and it wasn't me that was faulty it was simply a natural phenomenon that normally one would not encounter. Following this enlightenment we moved along at a much faster pace northwards towards Windhoek

We were reading to an accuracy of .01 centimeters I changed this to .05 and we hardly had any more problems. My company took big exception to my being so bold has to decide on my own to change the allowable error which they had arrived at theoretically sitting behind a desk. Had I written or tried to call in they would have poured over this "problem" for weeks while we sat in the desert. There has to be more trust and faith between office types and the cowboys in the field. The university worked on it and said, not only does this lower accuracy make no difference on this project we will make similar recommendations to that taken by the engineer in the field (me). I wrote quite a report on this to be made available to anyone making measurements in desert areas with equipment susceptible to these conditions and another report for the University of Witwatersrand. They received it with great interest and asked further questions about it.

The road alignment design and survey included a 10 mile curve encircling Windhoek; this was quite an undertaking to be "on-curve" and having to adjust the cords in relation to obstructing objects. It had been assumed by the design group that this road curve would be unobstructed and enclose the city. Not so, we had a lot of recalculation to do out there in the field to make this curve feature appear like what their assumption in attention was....Which was to enclose the city within this grand curve, we worked hard at it day and night. I sent copies of our new layout and calculations back to our office in Johannesburg and to another consulting company who were doing similar work with a road coming down from further north to meet on a common curve. I twice contacted this company to remind them to make sure their field engineering crew had copies of the changes in location of the curve which had to meet and marry with ours.

We finished a couple of weeks ahead of them but I hung around to meet with them and see how our lines merged. – they didn't wait. I asked the engineer if he received the changes to the curve, he said, No! Your work is in error. I told him an emphatic, no but I was willing to stay by and go over the calculations again with him, he said again, no! I did get a copy of his layout document which included the curve data he worked to. We set it out again, a lot of work, and his ground work locating was incorrect. I showed him this and he said, go to hell! I told him that was probably where he would be going. Their head office was in Windhoek and I went along and introduced myself and explained our miss meet-up. Their Chief Engineer told me to go and he would find out what was amiss in their work. I asked if I should delay my team, he said, no. I went over your work and accept it we will straighten out ours now. I told him it was no big deal at this stage and we can change to accommodate a match but he declined and said, you have been very professional thank you now it's our turn.

..thus ended the drama of the new road location and design. I am basically a geodetic trigonometric surveyor and construction project manager but these titles cover a broad swath of work in locations and conditions such as these ones in Africa.

We went back to Luderitz, an old German town on that rugged isolated west coast and once again checked through all our calculations and put them in a presentable manner before returning to Johannesburg. We checked through all of our equipment cleaned it up and packed it away for the trip and eventually headed out for our head office in

Braamfontein. There does not exist any east to west roads across the Namib Desert because of terrain so we had to drive to Windhoek once more then south for 400 miles, then east for 350 and north again for another 350 miles. It was a long two day journey and I was ever so relieved when I saw the Johannesburg skyline looming up over the horizon. During that trip I had made up my mind that I would leave, Jeffares and Green, a good company to work for and a good bunch of guys to work with but I did not want this kind of life for much longer, I was not sure what I was seeking but it was not this and I decided to talk about it with Louise after I got home.

I think what I was looking for now was something more settled, not only for Louise but for also for me as well. It was like we had done our share of a rambling safari style life of 10 years and living rough then moving on again. I wanted to have my own permanent home but where and how could I find that in my line of work

13
Rhodesia and SW Africa Again

It was good to be back home and with my wife and I told her that I was leaving this company because of the away from home kind of work. She was very happy about that but asked what I we going to do I said I am not sure. However, I went to a club where I knew many of the old Rhodesian's hung out and of course I was asked what I was doing, I told them and I also said I was looking for a different job and I left my card at the desk. A few days later Nevitt Thornilly, an old Rhodesian surveyor colleague of mine, asked me if I would join their new aerial survey company and they had work starting up in Rhodesia. The political and terrorist situation in Southern Rhodesia was getting worse and I don't blame Louise for thinking this is maybe not a smart move but we went back up there and got a house which we rented in Salisbury (Soweto). Meanwhile I was back doing survey work in the Bush setting out control for aerial photographic work except this time I was coming home most weekends. At first I was the only one there for our company and our first contract was expired already. Nevitt came up and asked me to develop computer forms for submission to the Surveyor General. The Surveyor General, Clem Bouic, was an old colleague from my Rhodesian survey days but now moved up in the world he said he would give no special favors for me with these designing computer forms. Up to this time all surveys had to be submitted handwritten and a computerized notion of survey work had not yet been accepted by the surveyor general's office. The computers were still very large, cumbersome and slow but we wanted to do it and I did. I locked my office, set off the phones and kept at it and after two tries Clem Worrall the SG accepted them and that was a first computerized approved survey . Nevitt finally told me that he felt we had another contract which would mean my being away from home up in the North in the Chambesi Game Reserve. It was very dangerous and things were just not working out for us and I had brought this all down upon my own head. I was considering what my next move ought to be when a couple of Americans and a South African showed up at my office. They introduced themselves and asked me out to lunch to make me a proposition.

Over lunch they explained to me who they were and why they wanted me in a hurry. It was all providential and I had no qualms about leaving Thornilly with short notice and anyway, he understood as we were all in flux. They were a Uranium Mining Project Management Company, (Rio Tinto) Rossing Uranium about to build a uranium mine and processing plant in South West Africa but they needed someone who could understand the South African 2 degree belt meridian system based on south around. Part of their commitment to the Cape Provincial Engineers was to base the entire established survey framework on this system. The location was out in the desert and they were completely at a loss regardless of their engineer's crash course studies prior to leaving the USA. One cannot learn geodetic survey in this manner it was a complete mystery to their engineers who had been schooled on it again prior to leaving the Bay Area. I sympathized with these two head-hunters and they explained they were not the engineers involved. One was with the American Consulate in Johannesburg and another with a mining group in now Zimbabwe (S. Rhodesia) and a CPA with Rossing Uranium. We lingered over lunch and they eventually asked me how soon I could leave my current job and when would I be ready to fly over to Swakopmund back in South West Africa again. We would have a new house on the coast and there would be daily transport to and from the site 40 miles away into the desert. They insisted I do all I could to get away quickly, they told me they were at a stand still and this was not good at all. I asked how had they traced me and they told me it was not too difficult after they discovered the ex Rhodesian surveyor's club in Johannesburg. They said, not many surveyors have your kind of experience and when we told a few what we needed your name came up with only two others who did not want to leave their current employment but it was suggested we could get you so we flew up here. As soon as you are ready we will charter and take you right over there. I was shocked and wondered what the problem was. I said, I haven't accepted I need to discuss the terms and all and they said that will not be an obstacle just tell us what you want and it's yours. I knew something big had to be askew to have this kind of special treatment so I told them I was available at short notice and would be in touch as soon as possible. I eventually contacted Nevitt and told him what had come up and that I wanted to leave at short notice. He said that was okay because he should really do this next job himself to keep the costs down and I could leave whenever I wanted so, Louise and I sorted out all our stuff again and I told the Rossing Uranium office in Johannesburg when I was available within a couple of days. Poor Louise had to drive all that distance over 1200 miles to bring our car through and settle all other matters here in Southern Rhodesia.

As promised, Rossing Uranium charted a flight from Johannesburg and came up to get me in Salisbury and we flew off to Swakopmund. Before landing on the airstrip in Swakopmund we flew low several passes over the site and I could see lines of new yellow colored construction equipment standing idle. Amazed! I asked why is all that equipment just standing idle and the embarrassing response was, we don't know where to start, I almost fell out of the plane laughing. They were offended and asked me why it was so funny and I said you don't need me to start but they could not understand my remark so I said no more and we landed in Swakopmund and I was shown to a hotel and checked in there. They told me your furnished house will be ready soon until then you can stay here in this hotel at company expense, I was still the popular man and they did not want to upset me. The following day we went to the site to meet with the project manager, Danny O'Brien, and he said, for God's sake Frank get us moving we've been standing like this for five weeks and no one knows what to do and it's not looking good for me how long will it take you to get us started? I said it all depends on what data and information you have, already. Show me what plans of the area and any coordinate systems you have and they brought me what they had. The South African government had shown them the grid coordinates of the mine area and told them that is what they had to work from but on a conversion to the Longitude system he said sadly. A grid coordinate is usually temporary and arbitrary and may have its origin anywhere convenient. However, a graticule system is based on longitude and latitude and much more complex to manage. The management group should have insisted on working on a closed grid system which would have been more suitable to the project. He asked me how long it would take to set out and show the contractor's where to start. I looked at what they had and realized it was of no immediate use to me and I told them I could get them moving within an hour and he thought I was joking or gone crazy. There was enough information for me to know we were roughly within the area and that was all I needed. I studied that earthwork plans told them to bring in the earthwork supervisor and I showed him where to start right then and there and what to do for the next few days without any survey establishment control. They asked me how is it possible to start when you have not yet laid out any survey control points at all. I told them it doesn't matter I will catch up with it later and accurately fix the whereabouts of it all we have to do now is get this equipment rolling. They looked at me and said, Oh My God is that all it is I said that's all it takes to get it rolling immediately. I will find out exactly where you are within a few weeks and they all laughed and sat down and we had tea and I could see the relief on the Project Managers face. He said, it's not what you know but to know how, where and when to use it, thank god you are here Frank However, I spent the next few days with the contractors filling them in on how to do it and where to work and what to watch for and that I would come in behind them with this surveying work which would give them control points and levels and there would be no corrections for them to make so keep moving, It was that easy if you knew how. Controlling a mining construction project like that on a complex geodetic system was very unnecessary.

However, there was a way too much surveying work for one man including the paperwork and calculations, and keeping up with the work in progress. I had to find out how much that O'Brien's engineer's were capable of in this field and see if I could train any of them to help with the survey or even to direct the contractors, I couldn't do it all. Unfortunately, they were out of their own environments and not able to understand the South African contractors, mostly Afrikaners and, whenever new sand dunes were formed they couldn't find their way back to camp. We had to put searches out for a couple of them every time we had a new landscape form. Eventually, I asked Danny O'Brien if I could get one of my own surveyors to help with this work because his engineers were not able to come up to speed and I left it at that, he said go get your man Frank you're doing a remarkable job and we need you. He was happy and relaxed as he had not been for several months and didn't want to go back into that bad situation again. Stateside big-wigs had been out in the earlier days before they hi-jacked me and Danny felt completely embarrassed and frustrated as did the senior management, Danny had approved these engineers and assumed they had the experience and would know what to do but I think it was the enchantment of the location that tempted them to say they were experienced surveyors, they were not even field supervisors. I eventually got an old South African buddy along with us and we had no difficulty keeping up with contractors. In other areas for the oversight and supervision of the project the American superintendents were very good and capable of all that was required of them. I must comment that for first-time field engineering in a desert environment like this one, which was one of the toughest, it was not the place to take on any immediate responsibility.

The working drawings from the architect's and engineers was coming in abroad ("in time" is a jargon amongst contractors meaning you will get it in time when you need it) known as "in time" as the work progressed, and were supposed to be checked prior to being shipped out. Not having all the architectural and a complete engineering set of drawings before commencing is always a problem. Part of it was being done in Foster City, Bay Area, USA and another part in London but I discovered that neither of these two groups talked to each other or knew the South African coordinate system and the drawings didn't fit together. We learned later, they were so hard up for draftsmen that they were simply pulling them in off the street When I discovered all this I realized we had a problem and a lot of checking to do but once again the engineers let me down and it was up to we onsite surveyors to do it all. I told Danny had I known this you wouldn't have gotten me so low balled. He replied, how much more Frank? And he made up my salary. I did not ask for much, and I was still only getting 75% of an American engineer's salary with the increase.

Poor Louise arrived eventually after her long journey and I told Danny I wanted her in the hotel for at least a week he said, no problem Frank I agree so, Louise was back amongst her American compatriots after all these years and she thoroughly enjoyed being with her compatriots and I was so glad to see her having fun that way and making lots of new friends. We moved to our new home in Swakopmund there right on the last sand dune on the Atlantic coast and we were invited out to lots of dinners while we settled in and got to know the town. It was really a most enjoyable old German style environment with good shops, especially pastries and the town was booming now with all the new housing and mining construction activity. It was also a different kind of life to what I had been accustomed to but it was good for me now and I was happy with it. The temperature difference between Swakop on the Atlantic coast where we lived for the duration and the mine establishment in the desert was about 50°F so I was always happy to get home and cool off. The desert was an area of constantly moving sand dunes commencing about 10 miles into the desert from out of town and over one night a power-line could be buried not to mention the roads. The site stretched from the main course ore crushing shaft to the secondary crushers 8 km of huge conveyor belting and another 5 km to the tertiary crushers. Then the layout and waste pits for all ancillary buildings and other works was acres and acres and my surveyor buddy and I were responsible for all the initial setting out along with so much more work supervisory added as time progressed. We were never free and in demand of all contractors. Such is the life of a construction surveyor who is usually grossly underpaid.

The main hill(s) where the rich Uranium ore was discovered was where the main crushing plant was located, huge jaws each one the size of a house.(We worked there without any special protection in that rich ore body which would never have been permitted today, neither were we ever tested for our own level of radiation) We had already started blasting and hauling rock to the conveyors loading the main ore crushing plant but open cast peeling down of hills was not the expertise of the mining contractor we had so, Rossing brought out miners from Arizona to lead the way and they were very popular, got along with every body and knew how to do this work so, the Americans did have something to offer and it was a boost to all the "Yanks" which they deserved.

Danny O'Brien finally sent back most of his so-called field engineers and then any work that they had been doing, which was not a lot fell to me, he said, he could not justify keeping them here as they were not doing what they came out to do so we were then very busy. He said if it's too much for you just say so and tell me what kind of replacements you want to fill in the gap and he knew I could find someone but we left it at that for the time being. The preliminary management group was beginning to send there guys in and they were local South Africans and Rhodesians and knew the contractor's and their work methods better than the American engineers so they were placed on lone to us surveyors and that lightened my load a lot. They, of course, asked me why had the engineers gone back home to the States and I suggested they talk to Danny O'Brien. I was not going to get into that I had enough to do.

It was a hard life working out in an extremely hot climate day after day. We worked 11 days on and 3 off, the 3 off being very nice, of course. After 14 months I could see I had almost worked myself out of a job and would have to go on permanent staff. The incoming management team had their own surveyor and all the beacons had been established and coordinated on the South African system which met the SA Provincial and trigonometric geographical requirements of the original contract especially as it is a uranium mine and processing plant on the earths surface recorded globally. Danny O'Brien said, don't leave me in a bind Frank, hand everything over to the management group surveyor and make sure he understands it. He was a South African from Pretoria and I knew him, I didn't have to teach him anything just show him where all the identifying beacons and the calculation data was filed. When I went back to South Africa after this project in Namibia Peter Muir, of Muir Wilson & Associates said, we have sugar work coming up in Malawi Frank and it's yours, keep in touch. I had advised him two months previously of my finishing date here and he said, come on over to Durban, South Africa when you finish and I will bring you up to speed on what is happening. Don't commit to any housing accommodation we will put you and Louise in a hotel until you go up to Blantyre in Malawi. We had old friends in Durban, Taffy Jones and his wife Libby. They had lived with us previously in Southern Rhodesia when we purchased that property together in Borrowdale, Salisbury. And so here we were preparing to go back north again close to Southern Rhodesia. This time in Malawi once named Nyasaland only now as the senior engineer for the feasibility, location and construction of a huge sugar estate to be known as Dwanga Sugar. It was close to the old lake town of Nkota-Nkota mostly a fishing village spread along a portion of this huge Lake Malawi. We obviously had a lot of catching up to do in the Durban, South Africa office of Muir Wilson Assoc. South Africa.

14

Malawi and Sugar 1975

(MWA) Muir Wilson & Associates, Consulting Engineers had a great friend of Rene Le Clasier (known as Mr. Sugar) from the Mauritius Islands in the Indian Ocean. It once was a big sugar cane producer but the economy of shipping out of this remote area in huge quantities does not pay now. Mauritius has no natural resources and has to import all its energy fuel generating requirements so, other than their recent developments in the area of wind power transformers and solar systems they have to utilize energy carefully. However, the country is developing and has improved its standing against similar country island nations of this kind. Many developing nations invest in sugar production because it is a useful development crop especially in countries where land is plentiful and has good top soils, available water and labor for intensive growing management systems. This brings us to Malawi which was only "colonized" in 1953 by the British Government into a semi independency with the two Rhodesia's. Prior to this time it was colonized at the turn of the century by Bantu races moving out of the Congo Areas. The British became involved with Nyasaland, as it was previously known, to help this country which was in dire straits because of its poverty. There was nothing to take away from it in the way of exports; any progress that has been made is as a result initially, of British funds provided for relief of the people and development of mostly agricultural crops: Tobacco, Tea and Sugar being the dominant three export crops. However, by this time of writing May, 2012 more exports are being added. It is unfortunate that any nation, in this case Britain, is accused of theft for being generous enough to lift a nation from out of its poverty. Even the schools and teachers were budgeted for by the British during the time I was sent up there from South Africa and lived there in 1977/78. Most of the tea and tobacco crop development was due to private company investments under very strict government control monitoring (Nyasaland's) Malawi's interests in developing these crops for export.

There are many factors to initially consider: First and foremost long term loans or grants from wealthy countries preferably the latter. In North Africa some of the wealthy Arab countries are willing to help if the country being assisted is Muslim or has a Muslim majority. This was the case in Somalia which is ninety nine percent Islamic. Secondly: A feasibility study including all development costs is essential not only to the country going into the sugar growing business but also to the lenders. Obviously, they are not going to lend on a blind hope. A budget has to be prepared covering all costs which has to include, first the land suitability and water availability; an experienced design-build and management consulting engineers like the group to which I was a field engineer with. This consulting engineering group or the sugar growing management group is usually responsible in deciding into which team this individual sugar growing consultant will be attached. In the two estates we built from scratch including bush clearing and initial land plowing and leveling we brought in Le Clasier under our wing as a specialist consultant for sugar and we were responsible for his remuneration. This was preferable for us then he could not be used against us and we had his backing and expertise. Muir Wilson also had experience with sugar growing and processing in South Africa; I am also agriculturally experienced, educated and qualified so we were well represented in this field to be appointed as managing consultants. In the early phases of development following the feasibility study and acceptance by owner and farm managers; in this case owner is government and cane growing and processing managers were to be the London-Rhodesian Group (LonRho). They were dependent initially on engineering groups like ours, a big existing sugar plantation down in the Shiree Valley managed by a Mauritian and Rene himself intended to switch as growing consultant. We are talking about huge sums of money borrowed and the application and initial management of a 100,000 acre estate like this is critical in getting up and off the ground, everything has to go like clockwork and management has to know how. LonRho were not big in sugar experience and had to depend on us, Muir Wilson and Associates and the Mauritian and they didn't like it but they liked the risk even less but, wanted all that went with being managers.

The first big sugarcane estate we built consisting of about 300,000 arable acres of land including a river flowing annually through the proposed estate and a long lake shore frontage and this area was called Dwangwa with its local fishing village named Nkota-Nkota. This country is Malawi and Lake Malawi makes up almost half of the country and the land that was set aside by the government was in this remote area along the lake shore on the East and the only road north/south on the west. It is an idyllic and lovely setting albeit somewhat on the hot humid side. I was there for two years as we literally carved this wonderful sugar estate from out of the bush to become the most popular site in the country. I did not want to leave when I had to and there was still much work to do but, we had a similar but somewhat troubled site in Somalia and I was left no choice but to get up there and sort it out. I was told, you can come back to Dwangwa, but I knew I would never get back again. Correcting the problems we had in Somalia was going to take me at least another twelve months up there in that dangerous terrorist territory.

We fast tracked Dwangwa and commenced work on several fronts at once which included, locating material locally for concrete mixes to be provided to the building contractor yet to be selected, and awarded a contract. This had to be an international contractor for all building works: excavations ,concrete foundations, wall structure, dams and irrigation canals and much more The expertise was required mainly because of the remoteness of the estate, it had to be a company familiar with specific conditions and know how to work in them. The mill, where the cane is hauled in to and squeezed through massive rollers, a complex process and all the ancillary structures including canals, balancing dams, bifurcaters and in this case a weir across the river and off-take structure for an irrigation water supply feed. We had field contractors already on board but they, as yet, had neither maps nor plans and everybody needed my attention and the fun was only just beginning. There was little or no accommodation available for anyone although we planned to establish a township for some 500 field workers and some better housing accommodation for more senior staff type housing to go for management and administrators. I brought forward the housing plan so as to initially house the construction people. We designed the labor houses on site, I asked Peter Muir, my boss, for a resident design engineer until we got the work on them started but he wasn't very responsive. I hired an out of work engineer locally in Blantyre, the then capital city, and was able to start getting plans off the drawing board. (I asked a colleague in Blantyre did anyone know this guy and yes, he was an alcoholic but so far so good). I did the township survey and layout including utility runs and roads. This was really all too much for me and so much more was not being attended to. I managed to steal a surveyor from a local company of surveyors a Portuguese/Black local guy and he was one of the best men I ever

had he could do anything, and I sure needed people that were willing to do anything. We had to mold and burn our own bricks for the
housing works all to be dug, molded and burnt on site. This meant
having enough wood cut to kiln the bricks. My wife, Louise, was with
me and I gave her all the minor early contracts in the budget to control
and manage. We brought brick builders in from Lilongwe 400 miles
away and a couple of old worn out alcoholic white men to commence
a program of gathering rocks to crush for concrete aggregate (There
was so much to be done in preparation for the contract to begin that
this initial work was major in itself). The procedure for gathering piles
of rocks was to get a huge gang of women with head loading pans
which they filled with rocks that they gathered and carried in to the
stock-pile. These wonderful girls walked miles and miles many with at
least one child on their side all day long, in bare feet of course with
these heavy loads upon there heads. However, to have had to hauled
in crushed aggregate rock would have cost a small fortune; the trucks
were not available and would have been wrecked on the one terrible
so called access road before we got a tenth of the requirements. I purchased an old quarry rock crusher in Lilongwe through my East Indian
accomplice and our two old white men, great guys, who started the re-
assembly, they had to work through Louise for funding but they knew
her and respected her. She did a fabulous job with the brick making
teams and they had all the confidence in her that kept the brick kilns
popping up like mushrooms, we needed millions of bricks, and we did
all this budgeting and cost estimating for it on site through Louise

An Important Comment:

*I want you to see here that no one is trained for this kind of work,
It is not something one can learn as part of a diploma course, it is
a lifetime of experience living in these hardly yet commenced developing places in remote areas in countries like Africa. There were*

white people who spent their lives this way for whatever reason under a quasi colonial type era to the benefit of the emerging peoples. These nations and projects could never have gotten off the ground without the help and teaching of these white people that no one knew existed. When the time came for the brass band and the accolades no one knew who they were or what it had taken in the doubtful early stages to make these miracles happen. I am one that does know and I wish I had a medal for them, then there was one or two more who knew how it came about but they were too busy being congratulated to think back on how it all happened initially and by whom before they ever came to the area.

My wife's sister, Frances back in the USA was ill with cancer of the lung at a time when Louise was such an incredible help to me with the huge work load that I had which I could safely trust in her most capable hands. Nevertheless, I had to tell her to leave and I had to reorganize my group to pick up the slack. By this time I had been befriended by an East Indian, Rashid Jakhura, a long time resident himself of the Rhodesia's and Malawi. He had come to Africa from India as a small child and went to the then private schools in Southern Rhodesia, he, a Muslim, went to a Catholic private boarding school to be taught by the Catholic Brothers. What a remarkable and wonderful friend he became to me and Louise. There was also a little Catholic Mission Church out in the lowland adjacent to the lake shore (Lake Malawi) I went down there to meet with the old French priest and the two sisters to introduce myself and ask them to visit us at the project and maybe say mass from our house. I had a tricky time getting through due to a very bad section of road and a small bridge wash out. Soon afterwards, I was in Lilongwe visiting Rashid who also hired out building equipment along with many other enterprises he was involved with and I told him about the mission road. He remarked, when you are done with it Frank, take it down to the mission and let them have it as long as they need it to fix the road and the bridge. We did the same with labor and trucks and got them opened up again pronto. He was a generous man and I suppose remembered his schooling in Salisbury, Southern Rhodesia, whatever it was it was a nice gesture.

After Louise flew out to Nairobi in the contractor's small plane and got a flight to the US; my weekend indulgence in alcohol increased. I worked an average of 14 – 16 hours per day mostly 7 days a week but this began to slow down on weekends now. Rashid had a house on the Lake and I sometimes would meet him there with the family which was then he and his wife, Maimoona, and two children, a boy and a girl. In the course of these meetings I met up with other Malawi business people, some friends of his and some not. One evening I was swimming in the cool deep depth of the lake and something slid up tight against my body like a huge eel, I was petrified and then *she* surfaced and said Hi! You scared! I said yes, you idiot and she laughed so gorgeously the same way she looked. We swam around and I think she was naked which didn't seem to embarrass her. She said I have been watching you for some time now and thought we should meet and this seemed like a good way to do it, Yeah! Afterwards, we met on the weekends as often as we could and we became pretty much an item. The people at the Dwangwa Project became divided about what I was doing but I had by this time, thrown caution to the winds and was numb towards those I was offending. They were friends and ad-mirers of Louise and didn't like what they were seeing evolve between Khadija and me, Louise's husband and the project manager on site. I was concerned over it myself but was also completely in her power, I know that sounds weak and I was weak I just had to have her and be with her as much as I could arrange it. She was from a wealthy family that owned property along the shore with some big mansions rather than big homes. We had the choice of two or three with servants and all. Her dad was a politician as well as a businessman and most of his colleagues new about Dwangwa and the supposedly dedicated engineer who managed the start phase of it, made it and brought it up out of the bush. He told us to keep our heads down and behave ourselves. There was all the liquor to kill off an already well on his way alcoholic and our partying and nights belonged only to the devil. At the home property were two big fast speed boats and Khadija and I would some times go way out and just float and drink and gaze at each other. One day out there she said, sit up! There is a fast boat coming and I think it is ours and we may be in some kind of trouble. It was her two brothers, dedicated Muslims, she was only dedicated to one thing and that was me for now. They drew alongside and one jumped in and they argued in Arabic. Then he turned to me and said, I don't think you know what you are doing, she is our family and a Muslim, you can't live like this and if you persist then you will have to marry her. On the other hand if you two continue like this something bad may happen to our sister and you too Frank so now you have been told. This is not a joke or just being annoyed, you can't do this, understand? I said, yes! Then they went off and we sat and looked at one another wondering what to do about it. She could no more give me up than I could leave her.

There was another big sugar plantation down in the lowlands north of Blantyre, an awful hot humid place in the Shiree Valley. it was managed also, by another French-Mauritian from the same Island as Rene LeClasier, both good sugar men. This manager, Clem Bouic I knew well enough and one night he had stopped off at "our" mansion where some kind of a party was in full swing, as usual, and when he saw his opportunity he said, Frank You have to stop this, you are one of the best thought of engineers in the sugar business as well as in this whole country but this behavior is going to get out and your name will be mud. Rumors are going around already so let people see that these are a pack of envious lies, come with me now and get cleaned up at our place so we left and went down into the valley at his place where

I stayed for 3 days. He sent word out that he had asked for me in an emergency and yes, it certainly was an emergency. I pulled myself together after that because I had such a hard time sobering up as I went cold turkey to recover. He wanted me to just ease off but I so much wanted to get sobered up I said no. I'll just go through it and both he and his wife looked after me as I got well. Then I went back over to Dwangwa and got on with things as if it had never happened. I was on top of it all and feeling good again. I kept mostly away from the club and the parties which I knew were not good for me and everybody waited and wondered how long it would last secretly hoping it would not be long, there was a lot of enviousness about my position and yet there was no one could replace me and my boss, Peter Muir and others knew that. They wanted my downfall because they were envious of the position and reputation I had and the gifted ability to manage every phase and part of the project. They wanted the standard routine of a company general manager with section managers. That is okay once a project is up and running but you can't do a design build on the spot construct project in that manner it will all unravel.

A lot of the estate survey was still outstanding and I had to get it done so as to get the bid packages out for the main contract. Lawrence, my do anything surveyor, and I went around the High Schools in Blantyre and Lilongwe and told them we would like to Interview a few of their best students to teach them some survey work on the job and we would pay them a wage. Of course the schools went crazy trying to give us their best students but we took our time and finally selected 12. We gave them the rudimentary of traversing and leveling with Lawrence's help and in less than one month we had them out doing some site work, they were exceptionally capable and good at it and I was so pleased about it. They were much more than I had anticipated, we got to know them well, where to use their particular talents and they were a great asset and the surveys progressed and I went on with the layout of lands (fields), contours for irrigating and canal locating with balancing dams. (A balancing dam is a smaller dam capable of holding a quantity of water to irrigate a certain section. It would be impossible to irrigate such a huge area with water being only constantly supplied from one source) Lawrence took them under his wing and we were able to get the surveys going for the contractor bid packages. We had three South African contractors interested and they had already visited the site to see it and ask questions. I would have preferred confining the bids to Rhodesia and South Africa but Peter said we had to include Europe, I don't know why it was only a lot more work for me. He said he would take care of all the bidding, you just do the packages and get them out, and that was all the work, of course. Anyway, he had to have me there for the pre bid conferences and the adjudicating in Salisbury, Southern Rhodesia he was a menace that way.

I was supposed to receive some sugar supervisors wanting to get out of Southern Rhodesia to help me design and set up the irrigation layout but they had no idea or experience for this stage of work. They were area managers once the estate and lands were built and laid out. We had received a lot of the farming equipment which included several D9 CAT Bulldozers but once again even though my guys, by this time, had demarked the lands the area manager's idea of leveling was to push dirt around from the higher areas and fill up the lower sections. One just can't do that because you are removing good topsoil and burying just anywhere. I took the time to show them what had to be done it has to be a mean tilted plane with as little disturbance of topsoil as possible. I had them come to my offices and with a white board explained what was required, simple leveling and profiles deducted then set up these cross sectional values on stakes in the lands and level accordingly but, they could not understand. The guy who brought them up was a very good private sugar farmer in the Southern Rhodesian lowlands himself. I got a hold of him; he too was acting as a sugar growing consultant but just went around interfering and annoying people. I explained to him the situation and he said, of course they know how to do it so, I got them together again in my office with him and went through it one more time and asked them, can you do it, their answer was no. I told Ronnie to find them work until I could get the lands all staked and marked for minimal cut and fill. I sent Lawrence to get four more HS leavers and it did not take very long to show them how to do this task. And we brought these expensive bulldozer operators back in again. They were upset that black people were doing the level staking and wanted them gone out of the way before they came in to doze, I said no, they have to be there for checking, don't forget this area is to be furrow irrigation, water wont run up hill. They didn't like me and made no bones about it and I didn't particularly care for them either I could have gotten local operators at one third of their remuneration but they would come into their own later when the growing started. Land surveying is a very important task in the starting, design and setting out of all building works of all and any description and these white Rhodesians should have known and learned it. These indigenous local Malawians were going to be streets ahead of these guys in a very short time. I think they realized that and it upset them and they placed all their disappointment and anger at my door so if they could disparage me in any way whatsoever they did it. However, I had so much work with so many balls in the air I couldn't stop to worry about it.

My total budget needed watching carefully to keep it up to date and available weekly in the event that they should pull the rug out then we would not have spent too much. Peter knew what I was doing and approved, the future estate management group had an office in Lilongwe and they received a copy of the budget expenditures and also approved. The management group (LonRho), London Rhodesian, tobacco growers in the North of the country, but were expanding to take over sugar growing at Dwangwa. They were also very upset that

Muir Wilson had funding consultancy because they felt that they were capable of doing it themselves and this would have been an absolute disaster if I had to go to them for every decision I needed to make in a hurry. They were very government like and bureaucratic with the dust gathering on letters waiting to be answered. This was not a good situation for me as they were skeptical about everything I did and they did not want Muir Wilson's name or credit on any document whatsoever. And any opportunity to discredit me, Muir Wilson, they made a big thing out of it and spread it far and wide. They were not stupid and knew that they had no one capable of doing what I was doing but they didn't care, they would willingly have lost time and money to take it away from us but that was not likely going to happen

We, the involved, were all fairly sure this was a go and that is why we were doing so much in advance already. We had prepared and submitted a document of work and costs to the Europeans, in fact, I had finally flown over to London with it from Blantyre, the old Colonial City, at an elevation of 4000 Ft AMSL. It had been a very lovely city in times past and was the summer capital for the old colonial senior white administrators. It had become much more commercialized now and was the head offices of most industries in Malawi and subsequently had developed a big industrial township attached to one side of the city. My old Southern Rhodesian colleague lived there with his black Malawian wife and seven children. When I first met him in 1957 in Salisbury, Southern Rhodesia when we worked for the Survey Department he was married to a beautiful Cape Colored girl, to all intents and purposes white. However, like so many guys who marry these lovely Cape Colored girls they become embarrassed and feel that they are not part of the real society. Nonsense, of course, but I have seen it in so many of these marriages. In South Africa, in that era it was that way but in the Rhodesia's no, not ever. Nevertheless, John Gilmore an intelligent educated Englishman and a Sandhurst graduate had himself a problem with it and they were finally divorced. I did have the opportunity of asking what happened and she said John couldn't live with her; how sad, they had a beautiful white son in school and I was just baffled by it. After their separation he fell apart and hung around in a bad area of town hanging out with black prostitutes.

John (Taff) Jones and I, his friends, tried talking to him but when some-one goes "loony" it takes time or something to bring him back to sanity, (yeah!) The sad part is that he married one of these hookers and Taffy and I attended his wedding in the town hall offices. He invited Louise as well, they were the best of friends, but she just was not able to go and watch him marry a girl of this profession. As can be expected, it didn't last very long, he got a position with the American Aid in Malawi and one morning he just left her and home and flew up to Malawi. However, she was not giving up her bread winner too easily and fol-lowed on up there, got a lawyer and sued him in a Malawi court. However, by this time he had married a respectable black Malawian girl, we met her and got to know her well. He had to make a settlement with the Rhodesian girl which wasn't a lot compared to his salary and also refund her airfares. They had seven children, John and his Malawi wife and lived in a home just outside of Blantyre city. Because Malawi was a British Protectorate the Malawians were able to immigrate into Britain as some kind of colonialists. Then there came a time in 1976 when this arrangement was to be annulled because too many Africans were going there to live in Britain. All Malawians were warned that there was a time limit and then the window would soon close perma-nently, no more easy immigration. John's wife took the kids and they all immigrated to England and left John alone in Blantyre. He told me that he could not return to England and he had some kind of a job in Malawi, the Americans had gone back to Washington, DC. He made several attempts to live again in England but he couldn't do it and she would not come back as they were so well provided for with British aid and entitlements she had never had it so good. The kids were all educated there, grew up there and got jobs. I think the two elder ones came back to John in the old home in Malawi. As I write this in the year 2012 John and I still correspond and other than a few old mans illnesses he is alive and well with a couple of girlfriends living with him.

Well, I fell off the girl wagon again and subsequently the drinking wagon too to the gleeful delight of so many. Khadija just showed up one day at the site and we picked up where we left off only this time in the house Louise and me. I will be forever mortified and ashamed and suffer over it daily these 30 years or more after that eventful period. I knew I didn't have the strength of character to resist and it was not right to blame her, I was the one to have put it right by saying, No! This relationship is over now but I couldn't, she was so exciting and I was totally into it. Somehow she knew a back road out of camp, we were situated upon an escarpment in an old house that once belonged to a sugar man back when some trials were being carried out in the area but it was abandoned. The house was away from the main new camp area and that was fortunate to some extent but I was in a mess of guilt. The back road went down a hairy track in the escarpment, I had a good Range Rover but it took skill to get down there in one piece, we did this regularly say every two weeks so that we could get back to one of our mansions on the lake shore our departure undetected by the watchers. At this time, she kept a pretty good report as to where her brothers were hanging out and so far we did not collide. Talk about being crazy, I finally decided I would marry her and divorce Louise, a terrible thing but that is the solution I came to in my sickness. And I loathed myself that I was willing to throw aside a lovely person, my wife then of 20 years but, it's no good saying, I hate myself and doing what was wrong, the right way was to say goodbye to Khadija and throw myself on the mercy of Louise. Every time I took leave of Khadija I was sickened with myself and my weakness and told myself, this was the last visit with her but I just didn't have the character and fortitude to carry it through.

I would be waiting in a hotel for Khadija when suddenly my East Indian friend Rashid would show up and ask me what I was doing there. I didn't try to hide it any more and just told him I was waiting for Khadija. He asked me how long I was going to keep up this affair and when I told him I was thinking of divorcing Louise and marrying Khadija he was severely saddened and tried to talk sense into me but it was no good, I had handed myself over to the devil and Khadija, it was a monstrous obsession with me and I simply couldn't let go. My work was now suffering from the aspect that my mind was constantly on the wrong thing. Previously the very big challenge of this project was all mine and I gave it everything I had and fought against all odds including the politics involved and, of course, being grossly profession-ally understaffed. To deal with a situation like this one has to have all their faculties oriented and divided up where they are needed and to see and know what is happening moment by moment. Like it or not one has to have a small network of "spies" that will keep you informed about the rumors in regard to what may be coming down the pike. Prior to Khadija's coming into my life I had been obsessed with get-ting this project going under the most trying of circumstances which included the management group LonRho willing to jeopardize or slow their own project.

Meanwhile, the brick making and kiln enterprise was a fabulous suc-cess, it was a tribute to the greatness of private enterprise. Those local contractors consisting of groups ranging from one team up to three managed themselves other than for purchasing payments of completed kilns. Kilns are left where they are burned until hauled away for actual building thus avoiding double handling. Our house building bricklayers were also small private contractors that with the help of Louise we got started in the same manor as the brick makers. A team of brick makers (molders) consists of two diggers in the clay pit where the bricks are made. A waist deep hole is made and one man, the molder stands in it all day, he has wooden molds shaped the standard brick size (9"x4-1/2"x3") these forms are usually in doubles, a digger roughly fills his mold with a shovel and the molder shapes it up with a special trowel and tips them out onto a flat board holding about four doubles. There are young boy carrier/runners who take the bricks to the kiln where they are stacked by two more guys and built with a tunnel in the bottom center to kiln the bricks consisting of 5 plus two boy runners, and of course, the boss who supervises. Any place where it is not convenient or economical to purchase and haul bricks this is the way we do it in Africa. The other related contract is a group collecting and chopping wood with women carrying to the kiln wood in bundles on their heads. All this has to be tallied at the time of delivery and Louise had set it up very well and all involved were pleased with it and with Louise. They held their breaths when they learned she was going to be away but her trainees managed well with one of the old white men standing in for Louise.

Now, whether LonRho were trying another trick to discredit me or whether it was simply stupidity and ignorance I don't know but I suspect the latter. One day, they told me that they had shut down their big brickyard in Lilongwe and this guy Edgar was an expert on bricks, in fact he said they had many loads of bricks he would first haul in and he would take over and manage the brick making because these people must be ripping me off. I pointed out, they were certainly not ripping me off because I only paid for bricks kilned but the top men said, Frank, you are an engineer and you certainly don't know what Edgar does, he knows "these people" and will do a much better job of it. I told them, for the record I don't agree we are producing top quality bricks cost per 1,000 better than anywhere in the country but,

I was told to turn it over to Edgar and here's what happened. First: he wrecked 3 20-ton trucks supposedly hauling bricks from Lilongwe 200 miles away, not one load reached its destination — that's why I didn't haul. Next: He fired the boss brick makers – what kind of an idiot does that — his kind. They were not paid because he said they were not turning out enough – he knew absolutely nothing about "those people" my people. Two weeks later they all closed up their sites and left, of course they came to me first and I begged them to stay close because we have to have bricks and we will start again. They wanted to know when Louise was returning I said, soon now with a catch in my throat and I'll swear the old brick boss looked at me carefully. I didn't say anything and my brick men went further on up the lake to a village called Bandwe about 50 miles north on the lake where they had a small job but this job here, for them was wonderful, 10 hours a day and purchased on the spot when Louise ran it. It wasn't long before a LonRho man and Edgar came to tell me that there was so much fraud going on in the brick making that it just couldn't work. I anticipated this and had all my costs available, the quantity of bricks made and their quality which you discover when using the kilns, we had an 85% usage which is exceptional anywhere. They ignored that and said, well under the circumstances that we know Edgar doesn't want to have anything to do with it it's too liable so, make your bricks how you like. I asked who was covering the cost of the wrecked trucks and I was told to mind my own business. I told them we could have used those vehicles on the site to great advantage but they were already walking out of my office. He had also messed up the wood gathering for the brick burning and I had to get it all going again from top to bottom without Louise and I knew they wouldn't work for Khadija, I didn't try, even my house boys wouldn't work for Khadija because of Louise

We got it all started again and everyone was chanting and singing once more. They do that in their jobs whenever they are happy in the circumstances and they were all pleased with this task. I won't drag this particular brick enterprise story out but back they came once more, after it was all up and successful again, LonRho to put Edgar in charge of it again. I insisted on meeting with someone high in LonRho and told him, if we don't deliver bricks this job goes down, the country will not allow us to start any big employment work without a labor township you know that and, Edgar does not know how to work with contractors. He knows how to make a big noise in the old big bossy manner way but these brick makers are specialists and we need their help and support and they need our respect, he can't do it and they will leave again. They said, that's your problem you want the job, I said, you mean you want me out and then there will be no Dwangwa Sugar Project and you know that, I don't know what your game is but I don't like it. They told me that they were contacting Peter Muir to have me replaced, I said, good luck with that and left their office.

Of course I wasn't replaced regardless of my affair, (life), with Khadija much to the upsetting of the wives of some white guys now working on site for Lonrho. Most of the current available work they were not experienced in, and what was started in the land leveling fields work again, they could not do without help from my Malawi survey technicians and they claimed I set it up this way purposely to intimidate and embarrass them. They told this tale to anyone who would listen to them but it was beginning to wear thin. I too kept describing why we had to have the survey technicians out there and the real story was beginning to get through. These white guys from Rhodesia should never have been given work here but Ronnie Yateman, the big sugar Farmer from Rhodesia now a consultant to LonRho/Dwangwa had told them that they could come up to Malawi and have a job. They brought Ronnie along to my office with their complaints and I described the difference to setting up the initial land tilt plane to simply doing a shallow leveling crop level after reaping. Ronnie knew the difference and asked, why can't they take over doing the initial level and I simply told him in front of them, because they don't know how and wont learn and yet the local HS graduates already know how and are staking it out so that these guys can simply drive the bulldozers. Ronnie said, let Frank show you how to do it and they replied yes, Frank, but not these kids. I said, sorry I'm busy and take it or leave it I don't care. One was genuinely disappointed but the other two were simply furious and said they would get me, I asked what that meant and they walked out of my office. Ronnie hung back and asked if I wouldn't help them and save face for them but I told him no, you go and peg it out for them but he claimed to be busy I said, you got it Ronnie!

All the contract small building supply work came back to us after Edgar's 3rd attempt at managing it flopped and he went on down to the lake shore as I suggested and built some wood framed cabins where we could go to on weekends for relaxation and partying – I never went. This job kept him out of my way and occupied for the rest of my time there before going on up to Somalia. By this time our own guys put together a rock crusher which was operating and the two white men were busy with that. We had provided them with a small dozer, a front end loader and other equipment and they just kept their noses to their own grindstone. I had them on contract as well and was accused of crony favoritism by the disgruntled white men because I provided plant operating equipment. I was weary with explaining to all and sundry the difference and how it all works. This was the equipment for that job purchased early to have enough concrete aggregates on hand for whomever the contractor was going to be when he came on site. No one will ever really know just how valuable these two guys were in establishing the early initial work on the site. The head pan girls had increased in numbers to almost 100 and the wood gatherers too were a big group to keep the kilns burning. I must repeat here, had this work been left to LonRho or similar organizations it would never have started, they would have planned themselves out of existence. When doing a job of this nature in the back of beyond you simply have to do it and make it work and few there are who will give it a try.

The contract called for the contractor to set up, on site, his own means of providing and crushing sand and aggregates. We already had one site walk and visit with invited contractor's and they said, they would haul aggregates from Lilongwe, I said, then you better bring a fleet of trucks, you will wreck half a dozen per month. When they saw how we were doing it they laughed but after they got the contract they kept on the same 100 head pan girls and they haul-washed sand from the lake just as we had been doing. However they told me that neither the sand from the lake or the onsite crushed rock would meet international standards for concrete. I was fully aware of that and had hoped they would have had the sense not to broach it. Fine aggregate (known as sand) has to meet certain grade standards, it must not be mono sized so as to mix well and rock for coarse aggregates has to be from a clean quarry and not be sandy or limey etc. I had discussed this at the walk thru but never openly said we would give anyone a waver although I was fully prepared to do so but I didn't want the word to get around. The type of concrete work we had on the site was predominantly heavy foundation work (only 3,000 psi crushing/breaking stress) and both the rock and the sand when mixed and poured as concrete would meet all the test crushing standards – I know, I used to design concrete mixes. Most of our concrete work was under ground and only for static heavy machinery bases in the processing plant. The contractor who got the job was from South Africa and a friend of mine but shortly after being awarded the contract, he was up at the site making lots of notes and spending much time with me. He said, he wanted it written into the contract that I would permit them to use materials found in the vicinity and if they failed cube testing it would not mean breaking out any sections of the work to re do them. I was more than prepared to give them the benefit of the doubt in any concrete work anomalies and told him so but he wanted it as an addendum to the contract. I told him no, and I wanted his reply immediately to allow me to bring in another contractor. He said he would take it up with Peter Muir. I told him that would not help him as I was the engineer of record and any contractor that would not play along reasonably (both sides) under these circumstances was not the contractor I needed anyway. They left and went up to Durban to talk with Peter and, of course, brought up the concrete problem. Peter who claimed to be a great concrete man really wasn't and he asked, what did Frank say and they told him exactly, they had written it all down carefully, verbatim and Peter's only reply was, then I guess that's it. He also told them he would get me to write some kind of blurb to add to the documents. What he said to me was, you have to help these contractors out Frank, you need to learn how to work with people, and write something innocuous so that we can all be happy. However, I believe that it was Peter that needed to learn how to work with extremely clever contractors. I knew I was going to have to cover them eventually but not at their beck and call but we all managed through it somehow.

In the very early stages of the investigation – following the feasibility study, I commissioned two Portuguese builders to build some temporary housing and a club/bar which for many months was the main attraction around for hundreds of miles – they came. We built cabins (chalets) and everything was decorated in the old Portuguese Spanish style, we did not import any expensive materials and yet the "club" as it became known was something very distinct and different, for instance, the bar front was faced with little pebbles gathered locally and behind the bar the bottle alcoves and shelved had a similar decoration, it was all so clever and attractive. During the course of the project lots of cabins and rooms were added to cope with the never ending flow of visitors. I had to employ a couple of the wives when they moved on site with their husbands as managers and hostesses with several local people in various functions. They had their own jeeps and one just constantly fetched booze from Lilongwe and I finally had to get a liquor license which I was told I wouldn't get under 12 months but I got it same day, all it took was an invitation and a promise to the issuer. I turned it all over to Ronnie Yateman and his wife and she more or less managed the whole thing. Ronnie was constantly commended and thanked by all visitors on the terrific bar and accommodation and yet never once said, it is Frank's baby. I once said, you are a popular guy because of your fantastic club and he said, Frank, I know you are the builder but LonRho have forbidden me to let that out, I smiled but it was a great place in a spot like that as was the one Edgar built down on the lake shore and that was a big weekend attraction as well. I had earlier in the survey work sank three wells up on the escarpment where our temporary housing and club was situated with the help of tradesmen from Lilongwe hoping later to do business with us and they surely earned it. We piped one borehole into the club and it was a good thing because those cabins were never empty. I awarded work naturally to the tradesmen who helped set us up there on a whim but once again LonRho came and canceled their contracts, it was so difficult having to put up with that nonsense and keep it all moving and progressing as well. That club was popular far and wide they did not want my name in any way involved because visitors came from England, Canada, and South Africa, they went back and told their tales and more came and LonRho wanted the glory. Finally, Ronnie could not take any more of the duplicity and started to introduce me as the man with the ideas. Everyone does not have to know how it all came about for him to be honest about our club and accommodations but they were interested and asked questions which left Ronnie in the unenviable position of piling one falsehood on top of another and he simply could not continue with it. When we built that club, sank those deep wells etc we were only a handful of people trying to discover if we had a project and then for them to try to hide the real facts on small stuff like this was insane and that's how Ronnie felt about it finally.

We were now concentrating on the work at hand such as making sure we had captured and surveyed lands to be planted in the first phase and the survey traversing for this aspect of the mapping was carried out by our local graduating technicians under the experienced eye of Lawrence Dias. These traverses always closed back upon themselves in a series of loops catching any possible errors before they could be extended. Lawrence and I were both very experienced in this kind of survey work and our local new guys had caught on fast. They were good and wanted to learn as much as possible about surveying knowing that a couple of surveyors are always needed full time even after the estate would be established. So, I left Lawrence doing that work without which we would not be able to distribute the network of irrigation canals, we had to find the natural fall routes down to the lake at the same time covering as much secondary loops as possible. At nights, Lawrence and I and his team would plot the traverses that had been surveyed and plan the canal routes. Normally this would be done with the help of existing contour maps and often added aerial surveys we had none of these essentials but did a great job as we progressed.

One day, when my boss was on site, Peter Muir, of Muir Wilson and Assoc he said to me, I believe you are allowing black guys to do survey work and they are not certificated nor are they surveyors. Who is going to be responsible for this when it doesn't work and the water wants to run uphill. I said, either Lawrence or I, probably both he said, Lawrence is black and I am not going to approve any work done by him or these school kids, I reminded him that he wasn't approving any of it, I was, and I said, then we better pull out of here because this is the only way we are going to get the data we need to design the canal routes. Peter said, have you any idea of the cost of building these canals and I replied, of course, I am he who budgeted for them. You Peter have done nothing and yet look at all the progress we have made. I have asked you for field engineers, design engineers for here on the site or allocated to me back in Durban, South Africa. He said, you always get out of line Frank this could have all been done differently and I genuinely asked how? But, he went off to the bar for a drink with Ronnie who also would have preferred it done by his white guys who didn't know how to and refused to learn from the black guys.

Of course, I could have slowed down the work and done all land surveying myself but then all other work we had done and were doing would come to a stand still. I had a huge spreadsheet on the wall of my office that showed all the dead lines that had to be met by dates for us to have bid packages ready for the contractors invited to bid by a certain date, then all the other enterprises which had to be completed to dovetail into the final package. Peter had no idea just how much had to be accomplished with barely any staff to do it. He always went off on a tangent and got himself sidetracked on an itsy-biddy item that didn't add up to a row of beans in all the work on hand to be done. Mostly, I ignored him but when he was on site making accusations and idiotic suggestions to me in front of others who should not be hearing these differences he was way out of line. I thought about slowing everything down and just doing as he seemed to think I should be doing but then it would have become a difficult situation and we probably would have been replaced. I decided just to listen and as soon as he had gone get on with it just as I was doing.

I did sign for and approve all the work done by Lawrence Dias and the local Malawian survey technicians and Peter kept his mouth shut but opined I was finished. Yeah! Yeah! One other big job we had to get into quickly while it was the beginning of the dry season was a cross sectional survey of the river bed where the weir was to be constructed. A weir is a kind of dam that elevates the river level at a given section backing up the water and making it plentiful to gravitate off into a structure and on into the main feed canal. Earlier, as soon as it was low enough, I had rerouted the river out of its existing stream bed and into a path we had prepared for it with the bulldozers. Once again, this became a bone of contention with Peter saying I had gone off on my own without discussing it with anyone. Wrong, I had discussed it with him when we first moved on the site. I told him, if we had to meet the scheduled dates as he gave them to me I would have to re-route the river and he said, yes! But, later decided we should have a big Pow-Wow over it with LonRho and others. That would have been a complete disaster and no one would ever have agreed to reroute the river. It is a dangerous and tricky job and decision and it can easily be lost for good and then one may have a weir sitting on dry land as a memorial to some hapless engineer. My plan was to reroute it and do the river crossing survey and let the design guys working on in Ireland finish it as quickly as possible so that we could have the plans and drawings as soon as possible. The weir was in the total package contract but I decided we couldn't wait that long. I had already got-ten the Irish engineers to design as much as possible with what I was able to give them before the water level went down enough for us to complete the face depth and one or two other details. *I told Peter*, we must bring this forward for construction and start right away now and he agreed. I more or less knew who was going to get the contract a South African contractor and I negotiated the contract extract with him for the weir at a good price for us because it was a foot in the door for him. At the last minute Peter wanted to have a major meeting and discussion over it but I told him we don't have that kind of time, we have about an eight or nine month window to get it all done. He was furious and ranted on like a mad man but I could not dispute losing at least twelve months doing it his way, he succumbed and we gave a weir contract to the contractor who finally was low bidder for the project. We were able to get dozers down into the dry river bed and prepare and build the foundations and leap slabs on the down side and actually commence the work ahead of the availability of the drawings. The Associate in charge of the Dublin office was a friend of mine and he constantly released incomplete plans to me to keep us going, Peter knew nothing about that.

I will jump now to near completion of the weir and close to the time for the initial cleansing flood to come barreling down the river. The contractor had a small plane and initially we were using it once a week, now that the time was near, to check for the tidal wave on its way down the river. Then we stepped it up to twice a week and finally a daily visual run as the time came very close for the river to come down from the distant mountain range, it was costly on flying time but the alternative would be disaster. We would see it from way upstream giving us maybe 48 hrs to 72 hrs at the most. We had made good progress and were not now afraid of any damage to the weir structure and off-take structure from the initial debris sweep, such as trees etc but we had to get the river back into its original course and one day the pilot came back and said a tidal wave is on its way. I called in all equipment on the site to the weir bank closure. All bulldozer's , loaders, scrapers etc and told them to dump fill where the new course was leaving its old course and to get as many rocks as possible at the bottom of the fill we had to close to force the river back into its old course and over the weir. Unfortunately, Peter was onsite again and looking down from the old road bridge across the river. I saw him begin to wave his arms madly and yell but we couldn't hear him for all the plant equipment noise and didn't want to, I did not have time to listen to one of his philosophical ideas of what should have been done. We were proceeding as I had planned, I had anticipated this event and it was working out good. He sent someone down to tell me to go up there but I sent the messenger back with, I can't leave here now. Finally he came down and acted like a crazy man and a fool, I told him the river was coming with a tidal wave and we will lose it forever, maybe never be a river again just a swamp ground and what about growing sugar then. He was frothing by now and said we would have a serious talk later and I may have to get off the site, I shrugged and got on with the dangerous task in hand with some resentment towards Peter, I was not appreciated, of course.

However, we successfully closed the gap and cut off the river reroute and I could breathe again, I didn't give a damn about Peter, carrying out work like this was completely draining. I could not allow the river to scour out that temporary new deviation and become permanent no matter what Peter was thinking, he didn't even know what was going on and maybe I was to blame for that but we were completely isolated and most of the time the telephones didn't work because of the inadequate exchanges. He left a message for me to get cleaned up and meet with him in the club house. When I got there they were drinking beer, of course, but I only had soft drink, I wanted to keep my wits about me for what I had to say. He introduced me to two guys from the British/ European foreign aid group and said, tell us about this afternoon, what was happening and why the panic. I replied, there was no panic, that fast closure of the river temporary reroute was planned and is a floater on my schedule contingent upon the river coming down which we were monitoring by plane flights daily now, we knew that is how it was going to happen but not when within a couple of days and needed to be constantly alert to it. It was essential to complete that weir structure to a safe phase and then rebuild the banks around it and dress them with baskets of rock as much as possible before the flood. The aid guys were impressed and remarked that it was an excellent maneuver now that it was explained but looked panicked like from what they knew about it and what they saw from the bridge but I wasn't sure about Peter. Peter went and got a hold of Ronnie Yeatman to entertain the aid people while he and I took care of some business. We went into the storeroom and Peter said, Frank as you know I think you are one of the best field engineers I have ever known but you play everything too close to the breast, I looked like a damned fool there up on the bridge. I told him, Peter, you have a copy of my timeline schedule and I am pretty much on it, there are asterisks and pages of notes explaining everything with alternate activities, I worked many nights into the late hours on that so that all involved will realize the number of critical points involved and when to anticipate them. He said, one thing you don't have on there is to meet with me prior to all the critical major activities so as to keep me informed ahead of time and allow me the opportunity to object or change the timing of it. I said, I suppose you are right Peter but sometimes I can't contact you for weeks and I just can't let things go that long, I have no one here who can take over for me, imagine leaving someone to carry out an activity like today and the contractors people had to react immediately to my request, they would not have done it for anyone else. Peter said, we are friends Frank and I appreciate all what you do but from now on if I am not here you get out and fly down to the Durban office and explain to me what is about to happen. I know you think I will not understand and you want a free hand to do it your way and you have to admit you have my absolute faith and I don't get in your way, and I added except when you are here. He said, okay! and that was a magnificent procedure you pulled off this afternoon I only wish I had known what it was that was happening and then I wouldn't have felt so foolish in front of some of our project funding visitors so, okay let's go and drink now. We went back in arms over each others shoulders and everyone was smiling as we returned, they all knew I had been taken to the woodshed whether fair or not. Ronnie as soon as he got a chance sidled up and asked me what is going to change now, will you still be here, I parried with, why not? So he smiled and went back to the group.

All of our earlier ancillary enterprises kept going at full steam ahead, we still needed millions of bricks, the women's teams, wood and rock gatherers were increased because the weir and the river bank training baskets had used up so much rock, the wood collectors had to keep going to kiln the bricks and it was a lot of activity now. The land surveys were in full swing to enable us to capture as much field land as possible to be under the irrigation canals and balancing dams. The area was divided up into area manager's sections we did this with Ronnie's input for sections through studying our survey plans and proposed canals and balancing dams. A dam usually provides for a section to have enough water to irrigate daily if necessary and then the dam are replenished from the river by night, hence balancing dam, particularly after the cane is just planted. We selected sections and provisionally drew them onto the plans and then Ronnie with his Rhodesian's went out to the area and confirmed the plan or adjusted it, His guys said, they had to admit that the local technicians had done an incredible job, the kudos' belonged to Lawrence and I but we wanted Ronnie's team to have their part in it as well but they were not surveyors and Ronnie was at fault to bring them with that understanding. Peter, of course, said I should be using them for the traversing around the sections but he never told me how I was supposed to educate them overnight with trigonometry, geometry and mathematics in general alternatively the local Malawian schoolboys now technicians already had that learning fresh in mind from high school

After the total contract was awarded the contractor brought on new rock crushing equipment for making rock aggregates for concrete he also brought in two big skip drag cranes to pull sand out of the lake bed. The contractor's CEO visiting asked me to accompany him up to Blantyre as his guest and we checked in to the best hotel available. He thanked me for the contract saying, I know we got it because of you but I need you to do something so that we can support you and give it our all. I knew what was coming, he didn't want to be in the hot seat if extensive crazing — surface cracking formed in the concrete as a result of using a monolithic sand from the lake and a non suitable rock type (non suitable only because it was not indicated as one of the typical in the General Section of the contract bid documents). I had no concern whatsoever using any of these aggregates for the concrete we needed on this job, we had nothing greater than 3000 psi concrete gravity placed and I gave them a waver on the condition he filed it and not attached it to the documents in use, I didn't want snoopers checking stuff out and there were plenty of them trying to get something on me and I was not vulnerable. I never told Peter about this deal he would not have gone along with it and I asked the contractor to also not reveal any special conditions we made like this and he agreed. He just wanted to be covered for the concrete because that was the bulk of his contract work and he worried about it in the weir and the off-take structures and the balancing dams, I was not the least perturbed having worked under these conditions for years. South Africa was a very advanced country and all their standards, laws and building codes were as good as US or British

Very soon we had housing built and the utilities connected and now available to various groups who wanted to be on site including the contractor's supervisors and men, of course. We were building and had available three grades of houses down on the flat, the sugar growing area and lake level, therefore it was hot and humid. I also had a much better quality of housing under construction up on the plateau where I lived in an old house. Ronnie asked me how soon I could have a house ready for him on the plateau and I told him a week or two if he wanted it now. He wanted to bring up his wife and family from Southern Rhodesia because the terrorist situation there was getting very bad and dangerous especially there where his huge sugar farm was in the low veld. I put it on fast-track with Tom the Irishman and it was done in less than two weeks. We, my guys and I, designed and located these houses very carefully taking advantage of the suns trajectory and yet maintaining a view of the distant lake across what was going to be waving fields of cane. The houses did not have air conditioning, we were on our own limited generated power which was expensive and there was not enough for air conditioning at this stage. The contractor who was running his own generators did install some kind of temporary AC in his housing down in the flats and he helped wherever he could. We designed special roof type ventilation up on the escarpment which was a success and the windows were louver type and also designed particularly for the individual house and its location and prevailing breezes ....every one who occupied these houses on the plateau liked them immensely. We furnished several which were not yet allocated and used them during times of influxes of visitors. They all preferred these unique housing up on the plateau to the contractors AC down in the flats.

Ronnie was so relieved and asked what could he do for me? I said all I ask is that you keep an open mind and truly see without bias what is going on here. Ascertain how much has been done already and who did it, and give credit where it is due. After that he was a very fair man and often went to bat for me over bureaucratic matters mostly out of LonRho, Malawi that they considered their domain and did not want intruders such as Muir Wilson Assoc. moving in They were in no way set up experientially or qualified in any way to commence and build a huge estate of this nature and capacity, it was simply asinine for them to take the approach towards me that they had been doing simply because they feared MWA being in their territory, so to speak.

Muir Wilson had a small design office in Blantyre and did small design jobs around the town such as office buildings, warehouses and such. They also had a nucleus of a small construction company and Ken McAvoy, the office manager and design engineer asked me to find them some work because he had nothing going on for them and didn't want to lay them off. I got them started with a contract for some of the housing down in the flats, we had several small contractors in there already, and we had yet hundreds of houses to be built. I made a bad start with these guys, we had a big party on site the night before and I got involved and it went on nearly all night, I was useless the nest day when these guys had driven out over 400 miles for a site walk of the area where they were going to build housing and to discuss it after-wards at a meeting and they would stay overnight at the club. I feigned illness and remained in bed but, my darling wife, Louise, brought them to my bedside chairs and all for the meeting. I was mortified but she wasn't giving me any leeway and said, these guys have come 400 miles to see you and talk business. Ken had said, he didn't want to give them any favors other than to negotiate a bid price that was agreeable to me and give them that contract. I never got over the embarrassment of that meeting and it even followed me to Dublin, Ireland after we had come to America and later went over to Dublin to build a microchip facility for Intel. I was not a part of the Dublin Jacobs Engineering office, it was simply a clearing house for me but I did work for Jacobs Engineering at that time, one of the biggest multi contract engineering companies in the world. We had several bids in for some of the work from Irish com-panies around the south of Ireland and one company was from Cork, way south of Dublin. I got a call from the Dublin Office to come in from the site to meet the contractor and discuss the work that was out to bid. When I walked up to the big conference room on the 3rd floor everyone was standing around in the main hallway and who should be there for the bidding contractor but Tom, the guy who met me at my bedside for a meeting at Dwangwa Sugar — was I embarrassed. He looked me in the eye and said, never expected to see you here Frank and construction manager as well, how things work out eh? How is Louise, looking after you I hope. I said, cut the crap now Tom and lets go inside I want to discuss the work and he grinned broadly, whether he kept silent or not I will never know I guess.

Important Note of Admiration:

I must repeat again here, that to achieve what was done and get the project producing cane in the second year, growing under irrigation and milling and processing in the third year was a wonderful achievement. However, it could not have been done without using the indigenous tribal people. To have purchased fleets of trucks and hauled in bricks and aggregates for building purposes in the first two years would have been a huge mistake and a disaster and I had to fight and object to this with all my wiles and expertise. That Nkota-Nkota road to Lilongwe would have had to have been ripped up with mechanical equipment and re built as a dirt road with gravel having to be located, dug out and spread over the surface continually while the hauling was in progress. I had put the upgrading of the road in the contract to be built at the contractor's decision. He would have to build it to complete the contract at his disposal.

Using the locals as we did and when we did was not just to give them work although if advantageous to the beginning of the project then, of course, it was a good and wise thing to do. Having weighed up my options I decided this was the way to go but, again, I had everyone against me, unbelievable! The real cost savings could have been derived by using the women and the contract brick makers costs although after Louise and I departed I doubt there was anyone who cared. Nevertheless, those women should have been awarded a huge bonus and those HS students also guaranteed a position with Dwangwa sugar for as long as they wanted. Strangely, most of them wanted to come to Somalia with me. The whole idea of building a sugar estate in that location was to provide work for thee local villages and why not when it was so useful do it right away.

15

Somalia – A White
Africans Last Round-Up

1977 - 1979

..Then we flew up to Nairobi, we had a MWA office there too but the office manager, a design engineer claimed he had no involvement with the Kismayo Sugar Project. Kismayo is a port on the south east coast of Somalia, isolated with only a bad sandy desert road through the Abyssinian frontier. We never used that route as it was far and away too dangerous from terrorists and bandits, bandits had ruled it even when I was first in Nairobi in 1949. However, The Nairobi office had some information and basic plans of the site but they were very poor and there was no reliable map coverage at all. We contacted the Kenyan white contractor, two brothers whose parents and their parents had been coffee growers for over 100 years. Now they were planning to get out before it was too late and getting some of their money out by contracting outside of Kenya. We went too their office in Nairobi, these two brothers who were born in Kenya and their grandfather had owned and farmed coffee plantations in the White Highlands. (They were not named White Highlands because most of it was farmed by white settlers in the 18th Century, the mountains appeared white from a distance and that was the origin of the name for them) It was established by propaganda that the name came from white-men taking over tribal lands – any land could be called tribal land. Unfortunately, as time went on and the Mau-Mau (Terrorists), Kikuyu Tribe, began to establish themselves in 1952 by gruesome killings of lonely farmers in their homes including women and children, decapitating them and mounting their heads on the gate posts to the farm land. Some of these atrocities carried out by the servants of the owners of the properties. (Whether you agree or not, at that time they were the legitimate owners of the land) As soon as these magnificent developed farmlands were turned over to the locals the great forests where we used to hear the Colobus monkey's screaming were all chopped down and the terrain became desert, so bad the new occupants had to move back down below again to survive, they had been told and expected that these farms would produce mysteriously and the produce now become theirs. We struck up an instant good relationship with these two brothers who were very dignified English in their ways having finished schooling at Oxford in England, I looked forward to working with them as we had the same sense of humor. Towards the end of that project in Somalia when Louise and I sometimes would fly out to Nairobi in one of their small planes we would stay at the home farm outside of Nairobi and have a wonderful barbecue (braai) made with big Lobsters caught (picked up) in the shallow sea water off the coast of Somalia at Kismayo.

We had done all we could now in Nairobi, the last of our civilization for a time, and arranged to be picked up by Allison's pilot early next morning at the Hotel. We used the Nairobi Airport and not the main international one for these kinds of jobs. The contractor was not obliged to fly us around or to supply us with all the goodies he always brought in to Somalia almost weekly for his progress check on the work. He had been losing money, of course since the job came to a halt when our engineer running the project decided he wasn't going to use a slush fund, it was against his principles, he told me upon arrival there. He told me, he was only going to work right down the middle of the pages in the contract and they (the contractors and Somali's could take it or leave it). They shut down the airport, the docks and certain police actions. When we were flying in the pilot said to me, the airport is shut down and they will shoot at us but don't worry about it, we will come in high and then spiral down very quickly, they can't hit anyone. It was quite an experience, the country we were going into to build a big sugar plantation for them were trying to kill us as we came in. The police rudely crowded us when we landed and fast walked us into their office and went through everything we had. I told them I was coming to run the project and it would be to their benefit if they stopped harassing us and let us go through just give us a chance and then get tough so, they let us go. Allison said it had been hopeless, George, our engineer should never have been there in the first place, you can't change a philosphy holding a project like this to ransom and we MWA were becoming most unpopular over his methods. My instructions, from Peter's partner, Russell Wilson, was to get there, Somalia, he didn't know how one did that and resolve the issues, he didn't know what the issues were but we know you can do it and do it quickly. I had picked up slush funds in Nairobi and fortunately they were not discovered by the Somali police but I was good at hiding them. The pilot asked if I wanted him to stay until I discovered what the delay was. They knew the cause was George but were being careful until they had me figured out and which tack I was going to take. I told him no, go back and tell Allison all will be well and you and he come in next week as usual, I will see if I can get the anti aircraft gun shut down and he said, spoil sport, and that answer was what I needed.

I moved into a shack that the contractor gave me with a promise of something better if I could undo all the knots. I was to be the resident engineer and until the management team moved on site, I was also temporary project manager sounded familiar to me. It was around 3 pm when I eventually showed up at George's office and I suggested we had a talk right away. I was in a vulnerable position as far as not being able to stand on my own two feet, no arrangements had been made for me by George Keefe although he had several small houses which were occupied by his staff. They asked me if someone had to move out of their house but I told them no, stay where you are. They said, it's not good if the contactor is accommodating you. I asked how old do you think I am? They smiled and said okay. Then George and I sat down together with his assistant in attention but I objected for our first talk but George said, he is going to take notes. I replied, if you are smart George there will be no notes or you can write a report after the fact. He said, I know why you are here and I replied, of course you do. He said, don't expect me to be involved in any buy offs, pay offs, bribes or under the counter arrangements. I said, I don't otherwise I would not be here. He did ask me what Russell, his mentor, had said, what were my instructions? I told him I didn't have any he simply said, go up there Frank and get that work going. Did he tell you how to do it, I said, of course not, he doesn't know how to do it no more than you do. George said, don't expect anything from me just tell me what you want me to do. I said, we'll work that out eventually don't worry about it now just bring me up to speed on where we are before the stoppage and I'm not interested in why you are doing what you are doing so leave that out. And now bring in your man and take notes if you want.

The next day I went out to the airport with the pilot and waved good bye and good luck next time in. Then I went over to the police shack and threw a big wad of local currency on the table but as soon as they went to pick it up I said Uh-Uh stop the damned gun! and they said they would try but it didn't come under them but I said try anyway and tell them I will make it worth their while. Next, I want you to stop searching everyone as we come in, just ask questions and you will be on my weekly pay roll. Their eyes brightened up and they told me this is how it should be done and I said, then don't disappoint me and we were all smiles. Next day with some of the contractor's supervisor a big mouth happy Yorkshire man and some of his men we went to the docks and I had a meeting with the right people. I threw down the obligatory wad and told them that it was just a flavor, there will be more but first let my ships in now and they did, they were there in about 3 days alongside. This is what they had been waiting for. Next I met with some local policemen and said, I need protection on pay days and I will put you on the pay roll for helping me but you must let through all our vehicles from Kismayo with materials and equipment and everything began to roll. George told me, Frank, it is good to see it all moving in but I wont do that, I can't and I don't know how to, this has all been a big mistake, I had no idea this is how you work here or I wouldn't have come. Then, I said, you could only work in Southern Rhodesia, the only honest country on this continent, or South Africa but even in SA there is some pay offs as on most docks. I felt sorry for him and I looked at myself and asked, what have you become O'Hare? Here is one of the smartest design engineers a graduate of Edinburgh University and he doesn't know how and me, not so qualified, but in demand everywhere. Something is sadly wrong. When the contractor flew in next time, no shots fired and when they got to camp it was a hive of industry, Stuart said, for Gods sake Frank don't leave this place, whatever you want just ask and we'll bring it in we have been losing thousands with Georges lack of experience. Is he going to stay? I said, I think maybe only for a short while, he has lost too much face with the locals with me now paying every body off. Stuart said, if you want money or need for us to pay anyone let us know, Frank you are the best, one week, a world of difference. I told them to contact Russell at MWA in Jersey, they knew him, of course, and tell him we are on the move, that's all he needs to know. Stuart & Co were laundering money out of Kenya by this contracting and time was running out on them. I didn't know at first but when they saw me put everything on the line, my life included, they shared all and we were the best of friends thereafter and I remained in their camp the whole time I was in Somalia. Russell's guys who came out once told me that it was not a good idea and I said, but it's my idea do you want this job to go back to George? And I got silence. Peter told Russell to tell his guys to shut their damned mouths and maybe keep away from Somalia.

On one occasion Russell and his senior design engineer and two others came out to look at the site. I don't know what Russell did wrong but his back was all eaten to bits with mosquitoes during the night and he was all swollen allergic to it and feeling unwell. We had arranged for the contractors big 8-seater plane to come in for them in three days time. We had no way of contacting them in Nairobi to come in sooner and Russell just had to live with it. I had given him a mosquito net but he must not have set it up right, most of us didn't use one but being unused to this kind of life I felt it was better he had one. All we had was calamine lotion and someone slathered that on his back. He told me not to expect anyone again and to proceed with all of his authority and wrote me an affidavit to this effect and said he would make it more formal and typed after, and if, he ever got back home. He said I just don't know how you guys live like this but I appreciate that you do. One of these other two guys who came along returned after a few weeks, he was not on Russell's payroll of employees but did various jobs for him and wanted to come back here on some pretext or other that I didn't figure out until later.

Most of the contractor's work force other than his basic employees and specialists that he brought out from England with him were locals. We were obliged to employ a percentage in all aspects of the job so, a lot of it was not useable but we had to do it. The laborers were mostly women as men didn't do that kind of work like digging, carrying head pan loads of concrete and all the usual unskilled and semi skilled positions. They were always dressed in their light weight cotton flowery sari type robes and it really was a sight. These, many, lovely girls with these robes all hitched up high on their legs working in all that humid heat. We had about five of them in our office, a comparatively nice clean job. Supposedly typists, filing clerks and so forth. We kind of spoiled them because the guys had selected pretty ones regardless of the job that they were supposed to do but we liked them and liked them around. It was amazing, they all spoke English and Italian – Italian Somali Land prior to WWII and the nuns taught English in the schools. The only thing we had been able to teach them was to make tea for us. One young girl, our favorite, busied herself with it all day long and smilingly brought it around. One of George's team, mine now I suppose, had fallen in love with her, it was no secret and we warned him not to do this but he wasn't listening. One day I noticed she was looking unwell and maybe losing weight and a day or so later she was too thin. Her guy came to me and said, there is a spell on her and she is sick. This did not surprise me I knew all about that, I told him he must find out what the spell was for and if possible who did it. He was gone from the job for about three days but got all the information. There were two types of people in that area, the Arabic type, superior, which she was and the more Negroid kind down on the river area. One character, son of a chief, wanted our tea girl as his wife and she kind of *looked down at him* which infuriated him and he put a spell on her and let her know it was done. Our guy said, what do I do now Frank? I told him to find a witch doctor away from the river where they mostly are but he got one and we upped the ante on the chickens to kill, we used four chickens to his three. We made sure she was there when the counter spell was performed and cast and, I kid you not, In three days she was her lovely self again handing out the tea and cookies. It is a delicate life that these poor people lead in that most poverty stricken country in the whole of Africa. These girls that worked in the office for us thought they had already died and gone to heaven.

I discovered that these girls were the reason Russell's man came back for another visit. He had lived in South Africa for a few years and was more accustomed to the life rather than Russell so our conditions in Somalia did not deter him for another visit although, in those days, South Africa was an advanced nation of the world. While they were here for those few days he had come with me on a trip down to Kismayo about 70 miles down to the coast and I had 3 of the girls along with me. They were lovely and exciting and I always got through the many police army and police barriers without delay when the were exchanging greetings or whatever with the police or soldiers, it worked like magic and I told them why I brought them along which created lovely smiles and laughter, they were easy to fall for. This guy, another one and a married man as well could not get these girls out of his head and came all the way back for that. I told him that I didn't give a damn but not to try it on with any of our girls and warned him that if he did then there would be trouble he may not want. He said there was one that liked him and I said that's crap now leave them alone it all works fine like this and I don't want any complications there are others around so try your luck elsewhere. These girls were lovely, happy and cheerful, and in my care and that is how it was going to be except for our one of Georges original team guy in love with the tea girl and that became a sad story.

Here is the tea girl story: He fell for her in reality, I could ramble on forever over the morals of situations like this, I should know, but I will leave that to you. I told George to tell him it was now time for him to return to England, he had a wife and three children in Yorkshire. Well, he refused to go and said you are only doing this because Frank is upset about it and my family affairs is not his business but George said, yes it is and he is in charge now. Anyway, his wife and eldest daughter age 16 were due to come out for a visit but I had tried to sidetrack it and get him home before they left because, I knew what he was going to do which was tell her he wanted a divorce. I thought if he went home it would all just become a sort of exotic memory, however, I was wrong. He came to me and said he was resigning his job and would remain out here in Somalia. I told him, I can't let him do that because you guys, all of you, not just you Derek, are my responsibility and I take it seriously. If it wasn't for the big group we have here God alone knows what may happen to any one of us. Of course, he said, he didn't care he wanted to be with his girl. It was a hell of a situation and I wasn't sure how I was going to handle it but I told him he could stay until his wife had been. I suggested he fly out to Nairobi, meet her there at our expense (mine – slush fund) and then see what he wanted to do but he said no, let her come in. I guessed what that meant, he was going to tell her he was divorcing her for this girl, I was really upset about it for his wife and daughter's sake. He told me that his marriage was a failure and had been for some years, he had thought it over and over numerous times and he wanted a happy life with this lovely girl. I told him, with the risk of insulting him that in this country he cannot have a happy life with this girl or any other Somali girl, what is wrong with you. He replied, then I will take her out to Nairobi and I told him they will never let you do it. So, I shut up because he wasn't all there in his head until this situation was resolved one way or another. He was a great guy and so talented and capable but now with this situation he was losing it. Somehow Russell got to know about it and I got a message, via Stuart the contractor, to get him out of there as quickly as possible. I told Stuart, short of chloroform I can't get him to go so, we waited for his wife to come. I will finish up here with this story. I thought she would freak out but, as usual, I misjudged women again. She was a lovely woman in every sense of the word and she told me she knew something was wrong because she had not heard from him for months. She asked me if I knew what was wrong and I said he must tell you first then you can talk to me if you want. She came right out with, has he got a girl? I was on the hot seat and stuck, she said, I thought so Frank, I want him back home and then he can do what he likes. She said, I will not embarrass you by hanging around and will leave with Stuart when he comes in again. I told her, I don't know what to do and he will not leave. She said, I'll get him to leave. She was in the office the next day and we all made a nice fuss of her but I knew that was simply papering over a huge problem. She told him, I know you have a girl and if it is a divorce you want then okay but you come home first and we settle up everything – smart girl, and to cut the long story short he headed out and I told MWA no return tickets to be issued and I knew he couldn't get a visa without our sending him out there so he was stuck. George told me later that Russell didn't fire him but he was working only in England and was not the same guy we knew out here. George also hung out in England for a while with MWA but finally resigned and went to work for a Saudi Sheik, how about that? That will teach him how to fix the books. I came across him in the Nairobi airport he was headed back to Jebba. He said he owed me an apology and he felt like a a damned fool and he added, you were so rational about it and just went forward, and got all the wheels greased and turning and everyone believed you were a hero and you are, you put your neck right out there many times and I was unable to do it. I felt embarrassed but let him get it out of his system. He too was divorced now and had an Arab girl he was living with in Nairobi. How the desert turns and changes, he also had two children and she started up a nursery school in Edinburgh. They were both graduates of Edinburgh University, what a waste of talent and a happy family.

There was much work to be done regardless of all the family intrigue with the Somali girls. We had a huge layout of townships and roads and big irrigation schemes because it was desert and all growth would have to be constantly irrigated so planning was underway for that. The sugar estate managers, a Canadian group, were partially on site although they were not scheduled to be there yet, and making it difficult by poking there nose into everything and complaining or objecting on this and that and telling me how this phase should be done, they didn't need a construction consultant on-site manager. I had decided, before they wore me down, that I wasn't going to allow this job to become me as I had done at Dwangwa, Malawi but there is only so much one can allow or put up with and one day I went over to the manager's huge comparatively palatial office, bureaucracy in the making, meanwhile I had tables made from packing case timber and did some work out of my house to avoid interference. I greeted him civilly and told him we had to talk and he needed to understand and accept that I was the construction manager on behalf of Muir Wilson and the client. He said he had been expecting me particularly in regard to the discussion we were obviously now going to have. He said he had had to go beyond his early designation because of George's somewhat light approach to the job in general. Then he said, that he and George were great friends and he hoped that we would get along in a similar vein. I said, well, if you keep on as you are now we are not going to be very friendly but I intend to do my job and get this construction work caught up and completed on schedule. You may go where you wish on site but don't interfere in the work unless you talk to me first, are you alright with that and he said, yes, and took the wind right out of my sails. In fact, he said, I am very pleased you are here and somehow seem to know how to work with the Somali people, how do you do that?, how do you get them to do what George couldn't. He said he needed to know for his future here as well. I said, oh it's just technique, he was a sanctimonious type and I wasn't disclosing anything of how I got it going. I suspect he knew, but wanted me to tell him which I was not likely to get around to. I didn't like the guy so that made it easier for me to keep my own council on this tricky matter. He did say, you seem to be very tight with the contractor and I had hoped that, informally, you and I could have sort of teamed up. He was right in that sense but I wasn't going to leave Stuart to the wiles of Somalia and the big mouth Yorkshire contracts manager was also a kind of Buddy now. I was not devoted to this project like I had been to Dwangwa and I just wanted to get my part done and get out of there.

We got on with the construction work and I confined myself solely to that, our interests crossed occasionally and I was most civilized and accommodating when it did cross. He went back to Canada after a little while and said he would be back soon and would inform me somehow which, of course, he didn't he simply showed up again a few months later. It is virtually impossible to send any mail direct into Somalia. We worked through the contractor's office in Nairobi. The Canadian guys all complained about the contractor but they all used him for in and out flights from Nairobi to the project. Before he left he decided to exercise his assumed authority once again and told us to shut down the swimming pool at the contractor's site, it was open to them too but he said it was not safe health wise and should not be located there he had a future plan to have one at the main compound. The contractor told him we would not be shutting it down and it was very safe. However, he became difficult over it and was compiling a complaint to the authority board. "Yorkie" said, leave him Frank I'll fix it. The drinking water supply was also routed through the contractor's compound because it was closer to the river and the management compound was not built when the water filtration chemical plant was installed. The following morning the manager came to the contractor's office to complain that they had no water at their compound housing and all. Dave said he would look in to it. Next day still no water and the manager was furious and drove in again in a cloud of dust. When he stopped yelling Dave said, I guess your water must be tied in to the swimming pool pipes and we had to shut them down. The manager said, I get the message Dave use your pool and that night he had water, I almost collapsed laughing. Dave got in all kinds of exotic booze and a lot of our American liquors which he kept me supplied with and he had many good parties going on. George evidently didn't mind getting booze from the contractor which he insisted on paying for and he too gave a few good parties which I attended and stayed too long because of my alcoholic condition and it took me too many days to recover. I had started in AA back in Empangeni, Zululand when we were building the Aluminum Smelter Plant for Alusaf and had made a good start but once being away from meetings I drifted back in to too much drinking again.

However, I was busy with a huge workload as usual, I have been accused of being the instigator of my own workloads and that may be so but it seemed to me if we were going to get it done I had to keep pushing and make sure we had enough workers of all requirements. Dave and his crew had gotten used to a George type routine but mine had an end and was much tighter I insisted on the contractor producing a schedule designed to my end date. Dave Scott (Yorkie) gave it to Stuart who did draw up a helpful schedule. Nevertheless, I worked with Dave and was able to bring him more up to what would be expected in construction progress. A lot of my time was spent in resolving issues with every one particularly the Somalis, even those that were not working for us came to get judgments for one thing or another and I gave them as much time as I could spare as their judge. They were likeable people but the country was ruled by tyrants and war lords with no end in sight and it only got worse.

A few weeks later I was holding a small meeting in my house which was small and made of shipping packing case timber meanwhile George and the Canadians lived in proper built houses. I was promised one as well but it never materialized so I let it go I wasn't all that bothered except for my wife's sake but she also said, if he, the Canadian, doesn't have the decency to give us one we will manage here. Dave was very good and helped us in many ways to ease the pain. While this meeting was in progress my house girl, Norte, was sitting in the entrance doorway which was unusual for her, a cute thing she normally held court at the back by the kitchen entrance and kept an eye on what was happening in our compound. I looked at her a few times but she sat there looking determined and I guessed she was waiting for me for some reason. One guy spoke to her saying, what's going on? And she said, her sister was picked up by the evil police two weeks ago and Mr. Frank (me) was doing nothing about it although he holds court over by the site and my sister is dying in jail. I somehow heard her for the first time and I jumped up and told everyone to leave. Somali money was virtually useless except for buying Ghat, a mild drug one has to chew for three hours to get any affect from it but they all used it and Norte had a stock in the kitchen area somewhere and doled it out to her friends. This money we kept in loose piles in the drawers and when needed for some purpose the girls just counted it out and that was it. I loved Norte and her sister Khadija they were like my own. She asked me, how much? and I told her about $10,000 worth and she whistled through her teeth. I also took about $10,000 real Dollars and off we went along a real bad trail to the District Police HQ the Chief was a bad man, evil personified and we needed to be very careful. I had no protection of any kind in that country and my standing as a white man would mean nothing to him, he would shoot me or cut my throat and Norte's and that would be the end of us. She knew that too but was very brave as most of the Somalis are, she sat chewing her Ghat stoically as we rattled along on this 70 mile trip. She asked me if I maybe would like some Ghat but I told her I couldn't chew it with my false teeth, she offered to break it down for me in her mouth first but I declined and told her she would get all of my juice to which she laughed beautifully, what a little doll she was.

We eventually arrived and I told her to be careful, no crying or screaming or killing no matter what we find. They searched me then took us through to the chiefs office and he looked up at us as evil as one can be without being a spiritual demon. He asked what do you want white guy with a sneer. I said we had come for Khadija and want to bail her out for money. He said, how much and I said Somali 5,000 he shook his head, I said Somali 10,000 and I knew I was close then I threw US$2,000 on top and he said more I put another 1,000 and he still wanted more so I took Somali 5,000 back and put down another US$2,000 and that did the trick. Before he could pick it up I did and said, where's the girl? He motioned to his gang to bring her out, they had to carry her she was naked and half dead burned to pieces with cigarettes, he didn't care. I said, put her in my jeep and you go hold her Norma but she wouldn't leave me. I gave him the money and he said, I have all control over you I just looked at him and said we are leaving and I could see him wondering whether or not to put me in jail but we left got in our jeep and headed back with a big sigh of relief from Norte and me, Khadija had no idea what was happening and I feared for her life. She was in jail because of the accusation of two Germans working for Dave, they were electricians and very good ones but, said Khadija had been stealing money out of their drawer which was a lie first, she would never have done that and secondly, had she, Norte would have known because Norte even had to give her Ghat, I let Norte buy her Ghat with drawer money I didn't give a damn about it. I told Norma to make a bed for her in our small kitchen; they sleep on the floor of course. We cleaned her up, made her comfortable and I went and got Dave's big medical safety box. I told him what was going on and where I picked up Khadija. I told him to chase those Germans off the site or I would shoot them both dead, they flew out in there old rattle trap plane the next day. Then I sent a note to the German doctor in Kismayo and told him to get out here urgent and he had to do some delicate stitching and burns to attend. He arrived 4 days later, he owed me, and inspected Khadija and I told him to stitch up her vagina but leave her like a normal western girl. He was suddenly terrified and said he can't do that they will also kill him, he has to leave her half closed, stitched up. I told him DO IT or you will be in jail, do it now and I will help you. So, we fixed Khadija real nice and took care of her other burns and bruises. I also told him, on his next visit he had to clean up Norte and leave her also like a real Western girl, he was worse than terrified. I was paying him good US Dollars to do it. Norte had some lingering infection from the old hags stitching her up, I had cleaned and treated her several times myself but she needed the doctor. If I said, are you okay down there she would jump on the bed and say, you look Mr. Frank and I did and patted her fanny, she loved that. Later, when I was getting close to leaving I inspected all the office girls and had all of them fixed properly by the doctor, I took them to his office in Kismayo, he refused to come and do it in my little house. After the last one he left the country, he said the word would get out and the few higher up girls would come from far and wide and wouldn't be long before he was dead. I can assure you I wasn't in the business of looking up the Sari's of these lovely girls, I just wanted them to have a fair and reasonable chance to live better. Not one of them objected to me looking at them *down there* and until I left, as far as I know, they kept their mouths shut which was surprising when it was a group of them that were re-fixed. Had they not, some old hag would have had them held down and sewn them up again and I probably wouldn't have made it out of there alive or dead. Even Dave said to me, I don't even know you Frank; I don't want any girls done from my outfit. I told him he should hire a doctor and get them all done like mine but he didn't want to know or talk about it. He told Stuart and he said you are a brave man Frank but you should leave soon all is going well here now, who will take over if you go. I told him I doubt any one from (MWA) Muir Wilson so I will hang on until you feel all your stuff is here. We were compatriots with a history of building up and living in a country, Kenya, East Africa that was unraveling very fast now. Stuart and his brother had been and bought a big property in the Isle of Man in the Irish Sea and had it all set up for a safe get away but they were still laundering their money while they could and had to complete their contract with the Somali Sugar Group mostly funded by the Arab group in Riyadh, Saudi Arabia.

I used to have to fly in to Riyadh periodically to get funds from the Arabs. I had to sign for work done against the last draw and approve a new amount to be used No one is allowed in there without a visa and that could take up to 3 weeks. The money had to be deposited in a bank in Nairobi, putting it in a bank in Somalia was worse than throwing it down a rat hole. I took the Saudi airlines to Riyadh and then got the agreement, no money, but waited until the transfer was executed, what a job that was! I had friends there and they worked for a sheik who had a guest house there like a palace and I was always able to get put up there. We even had booze as the American pilots for the sheik flew it in and, of course, no beer or liquor allowed and no swinging girls in Saudi. I was tired of Somalia now and I didn't want to be there in the first place but Russell wanted me to salvage it and Peter said, go and do it Frank, but I don't know you until you are out of there, you work for Russell. Neither Russell or any of his guys ever visited again, it was too hot, humid and stinking like the country. It was right on the equator with temperatures in the mid 40C's and maximum humidity, we didn't have any air conditioning, not even a fan but the Canadians weren't coming seriously until the new big generators were up and running. The generators were on the high seas now and the Germans were supposed to install them and so far neither Stuart nor Dave could find anyone to do the work. The Germans were down in Kismayo, for some reason there was a community of Germans there. I told Dave to get them back but house them well away from me and he brought them in again, I had both Khadija and Norte now but I didn't want her to go looking for a job until she felt safe again. Norte and Khadija shivered but they weren't too upset since the police chief was dead. I came home one day several weeks after Khadija was put in Jail and she was now almost recovered, she and Norte were rolling on the floor in glee. I said, what's going on and they demonstrated someone lying with a broken neck, the chief's Land Rover had rolled over and he had been killed. Did I love to hear that, he had told the cops on my payroll that he was going to get me and my two girls, one way or another; he also said I had cheated him out of thousands of Dollars and he was going to get that. Wonderful news!

The Canadian Sugar Estate Manager's finally moved on site and life began to change. I warned them about the terrorists who were responsible to no one but the manager told me they would take care of that with the government in power – there was no government. His answers to most helpful advice or information was not to worry he would take care of it. They never really became settled in before he sent his wife back to Canada within the year and he himself moved out in the second year. He should have employed his own security force as I did successfully only I used the police who were not being paid.

We wound up our part in the project; the contractor was now doing only finishing and maintenance work so it was time to move on for Louise and me. One morning in our packing case timber cabin I awakened and looked at Louise and said, what are we doing here? She said I have been waiting for you to ask me that question. Let's go home to the USA the time has come. However, we first had to go to Durban and finish up with Peter Muir. He strongly wanted me to stay on and go and prepare another feasibility study for another project in Ethiopia. I have to admit it was tempting – it was my life and the other future was completely unknown to me but I kept quiet. Peter sent us to Jersey in the UK Channel Islands to wait for him there at MWA Headquarters. We were given the keys to a beautiful private furnished home on Guernsey a neighboring island in the group. We were left alone for three weeks but it didn't work, we were headed for the US and a new life in Los Angeles, I didn't dare think about it.

We had experienced a great life in Africa but for us, Louise and I that Africa was changing fast and we weren't ready for it. We had lived through numerous changes and it was no longer our life, the time had come to leave and so we did closing the book on 27 years in Africa.